Working for Justice

WORKING
FOR A Handbook of Prison
Education and Activism
JUSTICE

By members of
The Prison Communication, Activism,
Research, and Education Collective
(PCARE)

Edited by
Stephen John Hartnett
Eleanor Novek
Jennifer K. Wood

University of Illinois Press
Urbana, Chicago, and Springfield

⊗ This book is printed on acid-free paper.

Library of Congress Cataloging-in-Publication Data
Working for justice: a handbook of prison
education and activism / by members of The Prison
Communication, Activism, Research, and Education
Collective (PCARE) ; edited by Stephen John
Hartnett, Eleanor Novek, Jennifer K. Wood.
pages cm
Includes bibliographical references and index.
ISBN 978-0-252-03770-2 (cloth : alk. paper)
ISBN 978-0-252-07922-1 (pbk. : alk. paper)
ISBN 978-0-252-09496-5 (ebook)
1. Prisoners—Education—United States.
2. Prisoners—Political activity—United States.
3. Prisoners—Civil rights—United States.
4. Corrections—United States.
I. Hartnett, Stephen J. II. Novek, Eleanor. III. Wood,
Jennifer K. IV. Prison Communication, Activism,
Research, and Education Collective.
HV8883.3.U5W67   2013
365'.6660973—dc23   2012046953

PUBLICATION OF THIS BOOK
IS SUPPORTED BY A GRANT FROM
FIGURE FOUNDATION

Contents

Acknowledgments

The Prison Communication, Activism, Research, and Education Collective (PCARE) is a national group of scholars, teachers, artists, and activists dedicated to ending America's addiction to mass incarceration and the failed social policies that have made the United States the world's biggest jailer. What began in 2002 as a small gathering of communication professors and graduate students hoping to share their work and interest in prisons has flourished into a vibrant community that connects prison educators, activists, and researchers across the country. Collectively and individually, PCARE members have authored dozens of journal articles and have organized mini-conferences and hosted panels embedded in other academic and political venues, including Critical Resistance, the Eastern Communication Association, the National Communication Association, the Rhetoric Society of America, and the Western States Communication Association. For more information about PCARE, readers are encouraged to visit our website (http://priscare.blogspot.com), which contains news postings from around the nation, commentary by PCARE members, sample syllabi, links to our essays, and other useful materials.

As founding members of PCARE, the editors of *Working for Justice* are deeply grateful for the long-standing and ongoing efforts of our colleagues and allies. We send our thanks to Kristin Valentine, whose more than forty years of advocacy on behalf of incarcerated women serves as an inspiration to PCARE's members. Bryan McCann has served as PCARE's president and webmaster; for his work as both a contributor to this book and a PCARE stalwart, we are indebted to Bryan for his high energy, uncommon courage, and goodwill. Emily Plec has worked alongside PCARE from the beginning, always modeling a form of activism that is relentless and kind, committed and gentle; Emily was our link to Sister Helen Prejean, who has graced the jacket of this book with her kind words and inspired many of us with her leadership. The editors also thank each of our contributors for their enthusiasm, their insightful contributions to this project, their generosity of spirit in the midst of our numerous editing exchanges, and their ongoing commitment to working for justice. It is always an honor to get to publish work that is strong and empowering, but to have the opportunity to publish the writings of friends and colleagues whom we hold high as role models and mentors is especially sweet. To the University of Illinois Press, the editors send great thanks to Laurie Matheson, our editor, who has been a tireless advocate for this project. Dawn Durante helped to keep the project on schedule, Jennifer Clark was a tireless and encouraging liaison during the final stages, and expert copyediting was provided by Angela Arcese. The book benefitted enormously from the detailed commentary of the press's anonymous reviewers, to whom we send our collegial thanks. Joseph Peeples worked with us on marketing, and Dustin Hubbart and his team created the beautiful cover, which features a photograph of a sculpture, carved out of a bar of Ivory soap by Arthur Keigney. To see more of Keigney's work, readers can go to Phyllis Kornfeld's wonderful website (http://www.cellblockvisions.com), which contains hundreds of images of art made by prisoners and links to Phyllis's moving essays.

We know that university presses do not produce best-sellers and that the publishing business is changing rapidly, which makes us even more grateful to the University of Illinois Press for fighting to keep alive the infrastructure needed to support intellectual inquiry and progressive social transformation.

Research assistance was provided by Nicole Palidwor, who, in addition to working on this book, has become a powerhouse teacher in her own right, serving as a collaborator with and advocate for prisoners in the United States and Canada. The index was prepared by Lauren Archer, who is well on her way to a stellar career as an intellectual, teacher, and activist. Design and content support for the PCARE website was handled in the summer of 2012 by Benjamin Swales, a tech-savvy activist with a deep commitment to social justice. Our work on this project was funded, in part, by a generous Dissemination Grant made possible by Daniel J. Howard, dean of the College of Liberal Arts and Sciences at the University of Colorado Denver—thank you, Dean Dan, for your ongoing support for civic engagement.

On personal notes, Stephen thanks his hiking buddy, traveling companion, and soul mate, Lisa Keranen, for easing the transition from prison work back into family life by always having a scotch and a smile waiting on those long nights after his teaching in prison. Stephen also thanks his co-editors, Jennifer Wood and Eleanor Novek, for their grace and patience, as they worked diligently on this book even while teaching their on-campus classes, tending to their families, and doing their remarkable community activism. To have the opportunity to work with the members of PCARE is an honor and, like all of the projects detailed herein, a labor of love.

Eleanor is grateful to her partner, Chad Dell, for his patience and good-natured enthusiasm for her prison activism, and she cheers his own emergent connection to the Alternatives to Violence Project. She thanks her co-facilitators in AVP-NJ, Sharon Brown and Charley Flint, for their deep, lifelong commitment to the healing of African American communities. And she owes an enormous debt of gratitude to her co-editors, Stephen J. Hartnett and Jennifer K. Wood, for their grace under pressure and good humor, their almost magical ability to make the impossible happen, and their fundamental commitment to the work of social justice.

Jennifer is indebted to her parents, Roselind D. Wood and the Rev. Rodgers T. Wood, who, through the examples of their lives, inspire her commitment to work for justice. For twenty-five years, every week without fail, her father ran a group for men incarcerated for life at a maximum-security prison in Pittsburgh. His devotion to that ministry fostered her interest in prison education and activism. For filling her life with love and laughter she extends a heartfelt thanks to Robert G. Steffes. Jennifer also thanks her co-editors, Stephen J. Hartnett and Eleanor Novek, for making the work on this project joyful—and challenging, in the very best sense of that word.

Most important, the editors wish to acknowledge the people we have known in prisons, both those who still live behind bars and those who have begun new lives on the outside. When they come into our classrooms and workshops, willing to share, to change, and to grow, they inspire and humble us with the courage of their struggle and the tenacity of their hope. Finally, we are deeply grateful to those men and women who labor for justice and reconciliation in our communities, in the understanding that we are all connected to, and responsible for, one another.

Introduction

Working for Justice in the Age of Mass Incarceration

STEPHEN JOHN HARTNETT,

ELEANOR NOVEK, AND JENNIFER K. WOOD

America's prison population has exploded: we now imprison over 2.3 million of our neighbors while keeping another 5 million former prisoners on probation, on parole, and under house arrest (Glaze & Parks, 2012). Some estimates place the cost of maintaining this vast prison-industrial complex at over $228 billion per year. In response to our becoming what critics are calling an "incarceration nation" and a "punishing democracy," a group of scholars, teachers, artists, and activists came together in 2005 to form PCARE, the Prison Communication, Activism, Research, and Education Collective (see our website at http://priscare.blogspot.com). *Working for Justice* gathers our best efforts into an anthology that demonstrates how to put democracy into practice by merging prison education and activism. While dozens of studies have described what is wrong with America's prison-industrial complex—its embedded racism and sexism, its perpetual violence, its skewed judicial and legislative aspects, its corresponding media spectacles, and so on and on—*Working for Justice* provides readers with real-world answers based on years of pragmatic activism and engaged teaching. In fact, the chapters that follow include testimonials from life-changing programs run in Arizona, Colorado, Illinois, Indiana, Massachusetts, Michigan, New Jersey, Ohio, Pennsylvania, Texas, Virginia, and Wisconsin. *Working for Justice* therefore provides a national snapshot of best practices, a sweeping inventory of how our neighbors are marshaling the arts, education, and activism to reduce crime and enhance citizenship.

There is no question that such work is necessary, for the evidence is stark, sobering, and sad: in the span of forty years, America has become the global leader in mass incarceration. According to a report from the Sentencing Project (Porter, 2011), the United States "maintains the highest rate of incarceration in the world, at 743 per 100,000 population" (p. 1). From 1972 to 2008, each year, every year, the number of people incarcerated in America's prisons and jails grew until, by 2008, 1 in every 100 adults was incarcerated (Pew Center on the States, 2010, p. 1). While 2009 marks the first year since 1972 that the overall prison population declined, as the Pew Center on the States (2009) reports, when Americans on probation and parole are factored into the equation, "a stunning 1 in 31 adults—or 3.2 percent—is under some form of correctional control" (p. 1). Moreover, while America's prison population declined in 2009, the number of people incarcerated in federal prisons continues to grow at a record rate, and some states recorded a rise in the number of people they imprison. For example, in 2009, Indiana, West Virginia, Vermont, and Pennsylvania all reported prison population increases of more than 4 percent (Pew Center on the States, 2010, pp. 1–2). These figures barely begin to document the sweeping effects of mass incarceration on America's progress and promise. As PCARE argued in 2007, America's mass-incarceration binge has turned our country into an "*incarceration nation*," threatening the heart and health of our democracy (PCARE, p. 404, emphasis in original; and see Hartnett, 2004).

Echoing this claim, Jonathan Simon (2007) asserts that "whether one values American democracy for its liberty or its equality-enhancing features, governing through crime has been bad." He adds: "The vast reorienting of fiscal and administrative resources toward the criminal justice system at both the federal and state level has resulted in a shift aptly described as a transformation from a 'welfare state' to a 'penal state.' The result has not been less government but a more authoritarian executive, a more passive legislature, and a more defensive judiciary than even the welfare state itself was accused of producing" (p. 6). The trends Simon identifies have had such a corrosive effect on the nation's political life that some scholars now refer to the United States as a "punishing democracy," as a land where a startling amount of resources are poured into the machinery of punishment and the narratives utilized to justify such choices (see Hartnett et al., 2011). Moreover, as Michelle Alexander (2010) contends, mass incarceration is the civil-rights issue of our day. "It is fair to say that we have witnessed an evolution in the United States from a racial caste system based entirely on exploitation (slavery), to one based largely on subordination (Jim Crow)," she argues, "to one defined by marginalization (mass incarceration)" (p. 207). Alexander stresses that "no task is more urgent for racial justice advocates than ensuring that America's current racial caste system is its last" (p. 245). The essays collected in *Working for Justice* meet at this crucial crossroads, where ending centuries of racism dovetails with reversing the trends of our punishing society.

Indeed, this collection speaks to an urgent need, for America must stem the tide of violence and mass incarceration. In the skateboarding community, youth talk about "burying the hatchet"; rappers ask their followers to "skip the beef"; prisoners committed to moving beyond lives of crime and desperation talk about the need to "squash the funk"—in each case, our neighbors ask us to use our words to solve problems, to seek restoration rather than retribution, to try to build community rather than rely on incarceration. *Working for*

Justice honors this call by offering ten essays that demonstrate how some of the nation's best teachers, scholars, and activists are working with prisoners, in prisons, and in our communities to try to reclaim justice from the prison-industrial complex.

■ ■ ■

To help readers think about the life conditions, incarceration patterns, and potential routes of redemption for the men and women housed in America's prisons, we include here an excerpt from a poem written by Erika Baro (2009), an imprisoned college student writing from the Denver Women's Correctional Facility, in Denver, Colorado. When she decided to run away from home, she wrote,

> I fled to the middle of nowhere holy,
> Tumbling through the abandoned streets
> Of the Mile High City,
> Losing bits of my soul along the way (p. 20).

We offer this fragment of Baro's poem as the living, breathing embodiment of much of what is wrong with the U.S. prison-industrial complex *and also* as an example of the potential to transform that system, one student at a time, by sharing the tools and skills of communication.

If we add up the number of Americans in prisons and jails, or on probation or parole, we get roughly 7.5 million of our neighbors incarcerated by the prison-industrial complex (BJS, 2008b). Based on this staggering number, criminologist Elliott Currie (1998) notes that incarceration has become "the most thoroughly implemented government social program in our time" (p. 13). In fact, a report from the Bureau of Justice Statistics (2008a) revealed that police forces in America cost us $99 billion per year; the courts involved in handling our prisoners cost another $47 billion; and the prisons used to incarcerate our neighbors cost us $69 billion: that is a total of $215 billion per year of what the report calls "direct" costs. If we add in the phone charges, commissary meals, clothes, visitation expenses, and other "indirect" costs involved in the prison-industrial complex, then it is easy to understand how incarceration has become one of the driving forces of our national economy. Once we comprehend how much money is involved in imprisoning Americans, then it becomes clear why the crime rate can remain stable but incarceration rates can soar: imprisonment has become a growth opportunity in an age of lagging capitalism (see Herivel & Wright, 2007; Hartnett, 2009; and Meiners, 2011).

Americans have been taught to turn a blind eye to the fact that the business of imprisonment now drives our crime and justice debates, but Europeans stand back and look at us in amazement. For example, an article in London's *Financial Times* (2010) suggested that activists trying to slow the march toward ever more mass incarceration "could be a problem" for prison-industry investors, yet "the size and power of the [prison] industry . . . [means that] it is unlikely to be dismantled any time soon" (p. 116). Because the tail of corporate profits wags the dog of legislative, policing, and judicial reasoning in the United States, we have come to the point where, in Colorado, we imprison one out of every thirty-three adults; in Georgia, the figure is a startling one in thirteen adults (Moreno, 2009; and see Pew Center on the States, 2008). Baro's misery in what she calls the land of "nowhere holy" needs to be understood, then, as a market-fueled opportunity for others: her alienation and disempowerment (and that of her fellow prisoners) appear to certain investors as a sure-fire way to make money.

Baro's journey points to another factor driving this absurd system, for her poem indicates how from as early as age thirteen, she was already involved in drug use. In our state prisons, roughly one in five prisoners is incarcerated because of drugs; in our federal prisons, the figure is more than one in two (56 percent) (BJS, 2009b, p. 22; and see Larson, 2011). We could choose—as the Europeans do—to treat those drug-using youngsters as neighbors in need of medical attention, family counseling, and educational tutoring, but instead we choose to lock them in cages (see Gray, 2001; Trebach, 2005). Baro kicked her habit and reinvented herself as a college student and poet, but most of America's addicted prisoners will leave jail or prison and return to lives of addiction, thus fueling the cycle of ruined lives and wasted tax dollars.

Baro's poem describes another common experience of those caught up in the prison-industrial complex: a troubled family life. Not everyone from an unhappy family ends up in prison, and not everyone in prison comes from a shattered home, but it is worth emphasizing that as we incarcerate more and more mothers and fathers, we are in turn sentencing more and more children to lives of misery. As of 2007, U.S. prisons and jails held roughly 800,000 parents who left behind them 1.7 million children (BJS, 2008c). Richard Coley and Paul Barton (2006) chronicle how, in California, over 850,000 children have at least one parent either locked up or on probation or parole (p. 24). Given the prevalence of poverty, crippling medical conditions, prior drug and alcohol use, patterns of homelessness, and histories of mental and sexual abuse among our prisoners and probationers, it is not difficult to imagine the hardships faced by the 1.7 million children left behind by their incarcerated parents (see Comfort, 2008). It is not a far reach to assume that a staggering number of those abandoned children will soon be housed in the prison-industrial complex, hence supporting Alexander's claim that prisons are leading toward a society wherein incarceration is a part of a generational inheritance, less a question of law and justice than of marginalization and disempowerment getting passed through family lines.

Baro's poem does not mention school, and this also is indicative of national patterns, where as many as 20 percent of all U.S. prisoners are completely illiterate, while another 20 percent are functionally illiterate, meaning they can read simple sentences at a fourth-grade level but cannot understand complicated texts, such as bills or court documents (see Prison Policy Initiative, 1997). This means that roughly four in every ten prisoners are functionally illiterate and hence excluded from the work routines and political functions that contribute to engaged citizenship. One of the driving forces behind the prison-industrial complex, then, is the ongoing collapse of our public school system. The situation has become so dire that many of us now refer to a "school-to-prison pipeline" that pushes poor students, especially poor students of color, out of lives of educational possibility and into the prison system (see Braz & Williams, 2011; Browne, 2003; and Lyons & Drew, 2006). The world Baro described as "nowhere holy" is a land where even basic education is scarce.

Like just about every man and woman we have ever worked with in prisons and jails all across the nation, Baro wrote that she felt lost, as if her soul was doomed, and that the world was "nowhere holy"—she had no safe space, let alone love, support, and comfort. The question of *alienation* is therefore crucial to understanding the prison-industrial complex, for the men and women who fall into the system almost universally feel abandoned, removed from the normal patterns of work and love that keep the rest of us focused and driven. To put this alienation in perspective, we turn to Jimmy Santiago Baca (2002), an award-winning poet who first learned to read and write in prison. In one of his autobiographical pieces about communication as empowerment, titled "Coming into Language," he notes that when he was younger, "I felt like a target in the crosshairs of a hunter's rifle. When strangers and outsiders questioned me, I felt the hang-rope tighten around my neck and the trapdoor creak beneath my feet" (p. 100). For Baca, as for Baro and for most of our imprisoned students, the world not only feels strange, foreign, and unwelcoming, but sometimes like an imminent death sentence.

Yet we know all this bad news only because Baro, Baca, and their imprisoned peers are trying to reclaim their lives through writing and public speaking. And that's the good news: while these imprisoned writers and speakers have every reason to give up on life, to quit trying, to retreat into a world of hurt and anger, they show up in our workshops and classes every week to share their writings and deliver their speeches. These imprisoned students and authors show us that with even the smallest amount of encouragement and guidance, they are capable of great things. We believe that these success stories demonstrate how we are wasting a generation of potential. Under different circumstances, most of the 2.3 million men and women held in America's jails and prisons could be working hard, paying taxes, raising healthy children, and even, in some cases, writing poems, plays, editorials, and other testimonials. The political fabric of our daily lives would certainly be more diverse and complex if these 2.3 million men and women were not incarcerated but living next to the rest of us. The essays collected in *Working for Justice* demonstrate how imprisoned students and our colleagues all across the nation are trying to make that potential a reality, how they are trying to make and support the long march from "nowhere holy" back to engaged citizenship.

The editors of and contributors to this volume recognize that the men and women we work with in prisons and jails have left behind them trails of wreckage. When pressed into gang life, or addicted to drugs or alcohol, many of our students and collaborators were threats to themselves, their families, and their communities. They harmed others and caused immeasurable pain. As victims of crime in our own lives, the editors and contributors can attest to how terrifying violence can be when it erupts into daily life, unsettling one's faith in humanity and leaving even the most banal interpersonal exchanges haunted by the threat of violation. Moreover, the victims of violent crime attest that their lives are forever altered, as they bear witness each day to the terrible consequences and costs of crime. We are fully aware of these facts. Indeed, like most Americans, we carry our own hard memories and simmering resentments generated by our brushes against or crashes into crime and violence. *Working for Justice* foregrounds these facts because we believe that the only way to end the cycle of violence is by moving past our anger and fear.

As Wood (2005) argues, "victim" and "offender" are not mutually exclusive categories. While the imprisoned men and women we work with caused great harm in their lives, they have also been the recipients of great harm. This explains why they tell us stories of unimaginable neglect and hardship, childhood abandonment and adolescent violence, educational failure and job-place difficulties. If we hope to end the cycle of violence, we must acknowledge their pain, as well; we must admit that our imprisoned students and collaborators fell through the cracks of a society that sees them as disposable and treats them as less than human. We therefore have a simple choice: we can continue to treat society's outcasts as monsters, in which case they will continue to treat the rest of us with contempt and sometimes violence, or we can attempt to work with them to help them shape new lives committed to new values. As Douglas "T" Tompkins says in *Jailbirds* (1998), a video documentary about prison education, "You can help educate me, so that I eventually play a contributing role in society, or you can keep me locked up in a cage. The one way, you have a citizen on your hands; the other way, when I get out, you got a monster." *Working for Justice* chooses the route of citizenship.

■ ■ ■

Working for Justice offers readers four perspectives for thinking about issues of crime and violence, incarceration and redemption, and education and activism. Part One, titled "Working on the Inside: The Transformative Potential of Prison Education," chronicles three efforts to work with prisoners to help envision a different America. Jonathan Shailor's chapter, "Kings, Warriors. Magicians, and Lovers: Prison Theater and Alternative Performances of Masculinity," demonstrates how he uses theater to help imprisoned men explore new modes of self-actualization. Recognizing that "bad masculinity" drives much of the violence in our culture, Shailor argues that imprisoned performers can draw upon Jungian archetypes, Buddhist meditation techniques, and collaborative theater to help craft new selves free from the habitual violence that lingers within typical male roles. In "Service-Learning in Prison Facilities: Interaction as a Source of Transformation," Shelly Schaefer Hinck, Edward A. Hinck, and Lesley Withers make a powerful case for the transformative potential of service-learning initiatives in prisons. As their chapter illustrates, undergraduate and graduate service-learning projects provide important learning opportunities to imprisoned students in Michigan and also transform the perspectives of the free students who participate in the projects. David Coogan's chapter, "Writing Your Way to Freedom: Autobiography as Inquiry in Prison Writing Workshops," chronicles his efforts in a Virginia prison, where he uses a biography-based writing workshop to help imprisoned authors think about their pasts, reframe their presents, and construct new possible futures. Touching upon theater projects in Wisconsin, service-learning courses in Michigan, and autobiographical-writing workshops in Virginia, this first section of *Working for Justice* demonstrates how some of our best teachers work within prisons to try to create spaces for self-reflection, experiential learning, and community building.

Part Two, "Working on the Outside: Building New Selves and Strong Communities," offers three chapters chronicling how those in free society partner with those in prison to try to work for justice, even while questioning the notion that imprisonment and freedom are stark binaries. "Courtesy Incarceration: Exploring Family Members' Experiences of Imprisonment," by Brittany L. Peterson, Beth M. Cohen, and Rachel A. Smith, examines the stigma experienced by family members of people who are incarcerated. Drawing from their studies and Peterson's experiences with her incarcerated brother, these authors examine how relatives and loved ones of people in prison try to build a sense of community and support. "Serving Time by Coming Home: Communicating Hope through a Reentry Court," by Jeralyn Faris, chronicles her long-running work with an alternative community court in Indiana. Faris demonstrates that a reentry court in West Lafayette enables former prisoners to build new lives and stay out of trouble by supporting them with a team of legal specialists, social workers, health and job counselors, and other staff. "Life After Incarceration: Exploring Identity in Reentry Programs for Women," by Nikki Nichols, draws upon in-depth interviews with formerly incarcerated women to examine the kinds of support they most appreciated, or would like to have received, while transitioning from prison back to free society. As Nichols's interviewees demonstrate, the notion of freedom is complicated, for even after incarceration the women's sense of self is impacted heavily by their experiences in prison. By exploring programs meant to empower prisoners, former prisoners, and the families of prisoners (in Ohio, Indiana, and Pennsylvania), this second section of the book frames the crisis of mass incarceration as a problem that individuals, families, and community groups can address in pragmatic yet transformative ways.

In Part Three, "Working on the Media: Representations of Prisons and Prison Activism," two chapters critique and explore images of prison and incarceration in popular culture. Bill Yousman argues in "Challenging the Media-Incarceration Complex through Media Education" that the United States faces *a crisis of representation*, for while crime rates remain stable, the TV and other corporate-controlled mass media bury viewers beneath an avalanche of fear-based spectacles in which crime and violence are portrayed as escalating, even life-threatening crises. Yousman accordingly outlines a new program of media education (based in Massachusetts) that enables consumers of mass media to form more informed and empowering views of the complexities of crime and violence. In a similar avenue of work, "'Prisoners Rise, Rise, Rise!': Hip Hop as a Ciceronian Approach to Prison Protest and Community Care," Craig Lee Engstrom and Derrick L. Williams offer a rhetorical analysis of "consciousness-raising hip hop." Merging personal stories with an encyclopedic knowledge of contemporary pop culture, Engstrom and Williams argue that a politically savvy subgenre of hip-hop artists are raising awareness about incarceration in the black community and producing effective strategies for community activism. Yousman's work in Massachusetts and Engstrom and Williams's work in Illinois and Montana demonstrate how media producers and consumers can play important roles in helping us to reconceptualize our responses to crime and violence while building new forms of community.

Finally, in Part Four, "Working on the Futures of Prison Activism," we turn to the challenges faced by those who advocate for political change. In "'A Fate Worse than Death': Reform, Abolition, and Life without Parole in Anti–Death Penalty Discourse," Bryan McCann argues that antiprison and anti–death penalty activists need to reexamine their rhetorical habits and political strategies if they hope to achieve any lasting change in the nation's prison system. McCann speaks as both an accomplished rhetorical critic and a longtime anti–death penalty activist who has worked with death-row prisoners in Texas. The book closes with "'People Like Us': A New Ethic of Prison Advocacy in Racialized America," in which Eleanor Novek tackles the question of how to move beyond our national addiction to racism. Novek argues that public attitudes can be changed from punitive to compassionate through closer knowledge of prisoners and their experiences. As evidence of this claim, she chronicles her personal experiences as a longtime New Jersey–based workshop leader for the Alternatives to Violence Project (AVP), a volunteer network that offers conflict-transformation workshops in prisons and communities. The chapters that constitute this fourth section of the book illustrate the many challenges faced by activists and former prisoners, in Texas and New Jersey, as they seek to reclaim their lives and transform the political landscape.

Considered as a whole, these ten chapters do more than document the devastating consequences of what can seem like an American addiction to mass incarceration: they identify proven and promising strategies that can help to wean America from its debilitating dependence on prisons. Our hope is that these essays will inspire readers to join us in the movement to reclaim democracy from the prison-industrial complex. To facilitate that process, *Working for Justice* includes an extensive bibliography at the end of the book, providing readers with easy reference to the best research available. Moreover, an activist-based "Resource List" is maintained by the PCARE collective and can be accessed on the PCARE website (http://priscare.blogspot.com). The PCARE website also contains links to the hip-hop tracks discussed in Chapter 8, sharing the empowering and propulsive songs that we hope will form a glorious backbeat as our readers, like us, continue to work for justice in an age of mass incarceration.

PART I

Working on the Inside

The Transformative Potential of Prison Education

We begin *Working for Justice* in the hands of experienced prison educators who detail their uses of theater and meditation, biography and narrative, and service-learning programs in the Wisconsin, Virginia, and Michigan prisons where they teach. As the three chapters in Part One demonstrate, working for justice inside the walls of prisons is challenging, rewarding, and potentially transformative for everyone who participates in such programs. As these three chapters describe in detail, the prison classroom can become a place for each participant to acknowledge and confront the past, to create physical and psychic sanctuaries for examining the present, and to imagine and co-create alternative futures.

CHAPTER 1

Kings, Warriors, Magicians, and Lovers

Prison Theater and Alternative Performances of Masculinity

JONATHAN SHAILOR

After thirty years of participating in, directing, and evaluating vio-lence-prevention programs, the noted psychotherapist James Gilligan came to the conclusion that "the basic psychological motive, or cause, of violent behav-ior is the wish to ward off or eliminate the feeling of shame and humiliation—a feeling that is painful, and can even be intolerable and overwhelming." One of the goals of interpersonal violence, then, is to "replace [shame] with its opposite, the feeling of pride" (Gilligan, 2001, p. 29). According to Gilligan, any social structure that systematically degrades a group or class of people increases the risk that individuals will act violently to redress their feelings of shame. Sources of shame include poverty and unemployment, lower caste status, racism, sexism, homophobia, and age discrimination. Each of these factors can contribute to feelings of isolation, powerlessness, and humiliation so intense that the need to eliminate them overrides considerations of right and wrong, empathy, and even personal survival. James Garbarino, author of *Lost Boys: Why Our Sons Turn Violent and How We Can Save Them* (2000), explains that "those who are shamed are vulnerable to committing violence and aggression because they know that acts of violence against self or others are a reliable method for reasserting existence when life experience has denied it" (p. 132). Throughout my own life, I have seen clearly how shame and humili-ation motivate aggression, both in my role as a man among other men, and in my work teaching men at a medium-security prison in Wisconsin. Not only in prisons, but also in schools, workplaces, places of worship, town halls, and private homes, men's identities and relationships are strongly conditioned by the norms of hegemonic masculinity.

In the United States (as in much of the world), hegemonic masculinity—"the most lauded, idealized, and valorized form of masculinity in a historical setting"—is characterized by "male dominance, heterosexism, whiteness, violence, and ruthless competition" (Sabo, Kupers, & London, 2001, p. 5). Hegemonic masculinity reproduces itself by creating structures of division and domination that evoke shame and violence; acts of violence become pretexts for strengthening structures of division and domination. Enter the prison-industrial complex, which is presented as a logical and necessary response to violence, but which functions as an oppressive regime that intensifies the performance of hegemonic masculinity. In a prison environment, men are subject to practices that degrade, humiliate, and shame through heightened performances of dominance, heterosexism, racism, and violence. The damaged human beings who enter the prison and suffer its inhumane culture generally leave it with a deep-seated sense of shame, and with their reliance on strategies of submission and aggression intact, if not augmented. Instead of focusing on the goal of rehabilitation, prisons function as boot camps for the cultivation of the worst kinds of immature, corrupt, and violent masculine identity.

Programs in the arts and humanities, offered within "a pedagogy of hope and empowerment," can be one of the most effective ways of subverting the prison-industrial complex's practices of hegemonic masculinity (Hartnett, 2011b, p. 8). I did not know this in 1995, when I began teaching theater classes at Racine Correctional Institution, a medium-security prison in Sturtevant, Wisconsin. All I knew then was that the men I taught, and myself as well, experienced in our classes and workshops a sense of exhilaration, freedom, and hope, a belief that we could recreate ourselves, and perhaps our world, by performing new lives together. Only later, through my meetings and correspondence with artists, educators, and activists, would I develop a clearer picture of what this all meant within a larger social context. For example, I met Buzz Alexander, co-founder and co-director of the University of Michigan's Prison Creative Arts Project, and learned about his program, which works with incarcerated youth and juveniles in Michigan prisons and juvenile facilities and is dedicated to exposing the injustice of mass incarceration (Alexander, 2010; PCAP, 1990); and I became involved with PCARE, the Prison Communication, Activism, and Research collective, "a group of scholars, activists, and teachers committed to challenging the continued growth of the prison-industrial complex in America" (PCARE, 2007). My growing connections with educators, scholars, artists, and activists have helped me to understand how important it is to write about this work, and to share it with others, so that we can learn from one another and inspire others, sharing our "roadmaps" for how to move from "a punishing democracy to one rooted in mutual respect, community-building, and redesigned arts and educational opportunities" (Hartnett, 2011b, p. 8). This chapter is one more contribution to that conversation.

My comments are based on almost two decades of teaching, scholarship, and activism, as I have spent the past sixteen years using storytelling, dialogue, writing, theater, and Buddhist meditation techniques to create environments that are sanctuaries apart from the normal performances of hegemonic masculinity; these spaces offer prisoners, the homeless, and at-risk youth opportunities to reimagine themselves and their places in the world. I have done some of this work with my students in the Certificate Program in Conflict Analysis and Resolution (CP-CARE) at the University of Wisconsin–Parkside. CP-CARE, which I established in 1996, is centered on a three-course sequence that culminates in a ten-week practicum where students facilitate dialogue, storytelling, and performance with marginalized groups (including youth and men or women in detention centers or prisons). From 2004 to 2008, I directed *The Shakespeare Prison Project* at Racine Correctional Institution. Each year, I worked with about twenty men over a period of eight to nine months to study, rehearse, and perform one of Shakespeare's plays. Most of the men had never acted in a play before. Through this program they had the opportunity to learn the craft of theater and to perform an ideal of masculinity defined by the values of creativity, discipline, teamwork, leadership, emotional intelligence, artistry, and moral imagination (see Shailor, 2008, 2011a, 2011b).

In this chapter, I focus on the *Theater of Empowerment*, a performance-based course emphasizing personal and social development. In particular, I discuss a version of the course entitled *Kings, Warriors, Magicians, Lovers*, which makes use of Buddhist meditation, Jungian archetypal imagery, creative writing, and experimental performance as methods to explore healthy, mature expressions of masculinity. The perspective offered in the course incorporates both the feminist critique of a sexist, patriarchal model of manhood, and the Jungian vision of a male identity that evolves toward wholeness, embracing both masculine and feminine characteristics. The objectives of the course are to show the destructiveness and futility of identity projects based on domination and violence and to investigate and practice meaningful and viable alternatives for masculine identity. For me, working for justice means marshaling the joy of performance to provide models, working spaces, and collaborative occasions for prisoners to explore new modes of creative, caring, and compassionate masculinity.

The Theater of Empowerment: Performing New Lives

My course in the Theater of Empowerment (TE) begins from the observation that we are all actors in the theater of everyday life. While our performances are always unique, they are also echoes of archetypal roles that human beings have been playing for thousands of years. According to Robert Moore, a Jungian psychoanalyst, and his colleague Douglas Gillette (1990), the four central archetypes for men and women are King/Queen, Warrior, Magician, and Lover. They offer a map for men to use in rediscovering these archetypes, so that we may progress from less mature levels of development to greater maturity. Based on these goals, participants in the course agree to form a learning community dedicated to the study of the archetypes, and to exploring their relevance to our lives through meditation, storytelling, dialogue, writing, and performance. In a safe environment where we agree to respect one another's dignity and privacy, we commit to a process of personal growth that is driven by the support and challenge we offer one another. Our goal is to more fully develop our capacities as human beings, with an emphasis on accountability, responsibility, and service to others.

I tell my students that the archetypal images help to make sense of the great and mysterious forces that permeate our lives: the sources of life and death, the nature of the cosmos, good and evil, emotional impulses, consciousness, and so on (see Jung, 1981, and Campbell, 1949, 1959, 1962, 1964, 1968, 1991). Moore and Gillette focus on the archetypal roles that humans have defined for themselves over the course of their existence, and with an emphasis on the masculine, they identify four: King, Warrior, Magician, and Lover. Although all men have access to each of these archetypes and, ideally, embody all of them to the fullest extent possible, our incarnation of the archetypes is a developmental process, and along the way, there are inevitably challenges.

From this Jungian perspective, archetypes are initially diffused patterns of energy that must be recognized, understood, and integrated into our personalities in order for us to be healthy, whole, and fully functioning human beings. When a constellation of energy such as the King (representing order, stability, centeredness, fertility, and blessing) is not fully recognized and integrated into one's consciousness, a person is said to be *possessed* by the *shadow* manifestation of the archetype. In the positive, active pole of possession, the person *identifies* with the archetype. (Jung uses *identification* to indicate an unhealthy *fusion* with unconscious material.) Through a process of fixation and ego inflation, the person comes to believe that they are (or must be) "the only King" (what Moore and Gillette refer to as the Tyrant). In the negative, passive pole of possession, the person inhabits the role of the Weakling and feels cut off from the qualities of the King, seeing (and often resenting) them only in others.

What I teach the men is that our development as human beings is a lifelong process of personal growth, where over time we integrate more and more of our human potential (represented by the archetypes) with our own unique histories, capacities, and circumstances. One way to achieve that integration is to study the archetypes, through specific persons (historical, literary, cultural) who illuminate and inspire. Another way to work toward such clarity is to recognize the shadow manifestations of the archetypes: in recurring conflicts, which can help us to see our particular brands of self-aggrandizement or self-deflation; in recurring patterns of emotional distress, which show us where we are "stuck"; and in our fixations on particular people or types of people, which can help us to locate the cut-off aspects of ourselves that we need more fully to appreciate and develop in order to be whole. (In addition to the previously cited works of Campbell, Jung, Moore, and Gillette, I recommend Edinger, 1972, Hollis, 1996, and Johnson, 1991, as essential readings on the subjects of archetypes, the shadow, and personal transformation.)

To put these theories into practice, my course in the Theater of Empowerment offers an invitation for imprisoned men to take responsibility for their own betterment through a conscious and intentional participation in their own archetypal journeys. The voyage involves mind, heart, and body, combining formal study of the Jungian archetypes with Buddhist meditation practice and theater. To illustrate for readers how I work with the Jungian archetypes, I offer in the following sections a commentary on each of the four major models of masculinity, explaining how I conduct the initial exploration of the archetypes with my students through film criticism, personal applications, and writing.

The King

The King archetype is the central male role, the father image, and it points to men's capacities to create, to make order, and to provide sustenance and blessings. These themes are exemplified in the stories of Jupiter and Zeus; of Aton, the Egyptian sun god; and of the Hebrew kings and princes. From the Jungian perspective, an important goal in human life is to find a way to access an essential archetypal energy, such as the King, in a balanced and integrated way. Too strong an identification with the King can result in the evolution of a Tyrant, someone who is insecure about his leadership abilities, and who defines himself solely in terms of his ability to control and dominate. When he sees others displaying the qualities of kingship, he feels elevated to the extent that they mirror him, and deflated to the extent that they are independent of him. In Jungian terms, this is the "active pole" of the King's shadow. Alternatively, too weak an identification with the King can result in the evolution of a Weakling, someone who cannot recognize or value his own abilities to create and make order. He sees others as possessing these qualities but cannot see them in himself. This is the "negative pole" of the King's shadow. The person who integrates the King's energy into his personality structure in a healthy way finds ways to appreciate his innate capacities, while at the same time developing means to embody leadership and creative force in appropriate ways. When a person has successfully integrated the King, he understands and respects the qualities of Kingship without needing to grasp them; the principles of creativity, order, sustenance, and blessing are served, not disowned or possessed (for more on the King archetype, see Jung, 1959; and Moore & Gillette, 1992a).

To examine these archetypal patterns as manifested in individual human lives, we explore a wide range of examples. I usually include one or two films for each archetype. For the King, I use John Sayles's film *City of Hope* (S. Green et al., 1991) and focus on Wynne, an African American city alderman. At the beginning of the film, Wynne is a highly principled, hard-working, and in many ways courageous leader, but his attachment to principle is overly professorial and somewhat detached from the everyday language and concerns of the black community. He undermines his own ability to lead (showing signs of the Weakling) by channeling the Innocent, Denying One (the passive shadow of the Magician—in this case, someone who does not want to engage in life fully, because that would entail the sacrifice of a perfect adherence to principle). As a consequence of his unwillingness to get his hands dirty, Wynne is disconnected from the working class and poor in his district, and even despised by some black activists. While in many ways he is a King (with a clear vision of social justice) and a Warrior (always fighting for what is right), Wynne's vision and courage are largely dissipated because they are not yet connected to his Lover (in particular, someone who feels connected to the black community), or the Magician in his fullness (in this case, someone who not only has high values, but also knows how to "play politics").

The turning point for Wynne comes when he seeks the advice of a wise elder: the former African American mayor of the city. The ex-mayor helps Wynne to see that it is possible (and necessary) to engage in political maneuvering, make calculated compromises, and fight for social justice. Wynne is inspired, and in a following scene, he accesses the energy of the King. At an African American community gathering addressing recent incidents of racial injustice in the city, Wynne calls for a spontaneous march on the mayor's banquet, which is going on at the same time, just a few blocks away. His constituents are energized and fully behind him. They march down the street and into the banquet hall, where the mayor is in the midst of addressing a gathering of the wealthy and powerful. As cameras flash and reporters scribble away, Wynne turns toward the podium: "Mr. Mayor, got a minute?" In this moment, Wynne has clearly arrived as the King.

I also use Bruce Beresford's *Black Robe* (Lantos et al., 1991), based on the historical novel by Brian Moore (1985). Father LaForgue, a seventeenth-century Jesuit in Quebec territory, is a Tyrant who (along with other French Catholic priests) imposes his vision of God's will on the Algonquin people in order to "save their souls." As we saw with Wynne in *City of Hope*, LaForgue's identity is interdependent with, and conditioned by, his orientation to all of the other archetypes. LaForgue's identity as a Tyrant (narrow-minded, controlling, punishing) is related to his inability to access the Lover (his own vulnerability, and his capacity for love and compassion). LaForgue's Impotent Lover conditions his orientation to the Warrior and the Magician as well. While his capacity as a Warrior can be seen in his unswerving commitment to his faith, he is often timid when confronting danger, and he clearly veers toward the Sadist and the Masochist when he literally flagellates himself in order to repress his sexual desires. LaForgue tries to impress the Algonquin with his Magician-like abilities, including his literacy, his musicianship, and his performance of sacramental rites. However, these displays lead the Algonquin to perceive him as more of an Evil Sorcerer, or Manipulator—someone who is trying to control them, rather than acting in their best interests.

In the central plot of the film, LaForgue is commissioned to join a Catholic mission in a Huron village some 1,500 miles from Quebec. A young French-man (Daniel) accompanies the priest, and so do a group of Algonquin, who serve as guides on this difficult and dangerous journey. While the youth is sympathetic to the Algonquin practices and beliefs, LaForgue is alternately aloof and argumentative. Over the course of the film, however, he begins to see the Native Americans with whom he has had contact as human beings who are worthy of love on their own terms. This transformation occurs gradually and incrementally, as LaForgue faces several trials. In one of these, LaForgue's Algonquin guides attempt to abandon him in the forest, where he must face his loneliness, his fear, and his mortality. When LaForgue is reunited with the Algonquin, his relief and joy are palpable. For the first time, he literally embraces them with real feeling and appreciation. In a second trial, LaForgue, Daniel, and the Algonquin are captured, imprisoned, and tortured by a group of Iroquois. It is the Algonquin who show LaForgue how to keep up his spirit under these desperate circumstances, and it is the Algonquin who help him to finally escape.

At the end of the film, LaForgue enters the Huron mission alone. He dis-covers that the natives in this settlement have been decimated by a smallpox epidemic, and in revenge, they have murdered all but one of the French inhabit-ants. The Huron, believing they can be saved by baptism, ask Father LaForgue to perform the rite. At first, LaForgue is reluctant, because it is clear to him that they are not looking for spiritual salvation. Then, a spokesperson for the Huron asks him, "Do you love us?" LaForgue recalls the faces of all the Indians he has met during his long journey, and his heart swells with compassion. In a voice thick with emotion, he answers: "Yes." The Huron man says, "Then baptize us." As a beautiful golden sun breaks over the horizon, the Huron gather, and LaForgue baptizes them. Through his long journey of shared experiences and suffering alongside the native people, LaForgue has developed from a Tryant, an institutional authority concerned mostly with enforcing doctrine, to a King, a compassionate leader who embodies the true spirit of his Christian faith.

The prisoners in the class suggest their own images of the King (examples have included Malcolm X, Prospero, King Arthur), the Tyrant (Adolf Hitler, Dick Cheney, Tony Montana in *Scarface*), and the Weakling (Fredo Corleone in *The Godfather*, Salieri in *Amadeus*, and Paulie in *Rocky*). They also write and speak about the men in their lives who have manifested these archetypes, especially their fathers. Jermaine, a student in the class, wrote of his father in this way:

> He couldn't read or write too well. He was a muscle man, 5'8," 200 pounds. He had muscles that stuck out of his shirt, and a voice that sounded like thunder. . . . All [nine] kids were scared of him. . . . My father worked construction so you can imagine how rough he was. He had these teeth that looked like a group of chain saws. When we ate dinner we could not throw away the bones—we had to put all the bones in the middle of the table on a plate. When everyone got through with their meat, he would still be chewing on the bones. It sounded like the walls were cracking . . . that alone let us know not to mess with the old man. He would probably chew us up and spit us out.[1]

As this passage suggests, this father was regarded by his young son as a kind of god—an awesome being with power over life and death. That power was balanced by a deep love, as the father showed when his son turned sixteen and his girlfriend became pregnant. The son wished to keep the baby, against the wishes of his girlfriend's parents, who wanted her to get an abortion. His father's first inclination was to say that his son and his girlfriend were too young to be parents. The son persisted:

> I said, "Daddy, who's to say when I'm ready? (Being really daring.) "Look, Daddy, I know that you didn't kill [abort] any of your kids and that you grew up during slavery [sic]. If it wasn't for you being the man you are, we wouldn't be here, so please help me. I'll do anything. I'll change my life for my baby. But don't let them kill my baby please." Then I cried real hard.
> Then out of nowhere my father said, "Son, don't worry. Daddy wants to say that I'm real proud of you for coming to us and telling us what was going on and for standing up like a man for your responsibility. That is what makes a man."

His father spoke to his girlfriend's family and persuaded them not to abort the child. The story abruptly concludes with an epilogue: "and now I have four grandkids—two by the first child, who I went through hell with, but I wouldn't change a thing."

As I respond to the men's stories (in writing and in discussion), I encourage them to reflect not only on the *content* of their narratives, but also on their *structure* (what elements are included and excluded, how the elements are arranged, and so on), and on the *function* these stories serve (to celebrate or critique others, to imply a set of values and a direction for their own lives). Hence, in my response to Jermaine's story, I commented on how he presents the image of his father as a powerful, sometimes intimidating, yet ultimately benevolent King who loves and supports his son in a time of crisis. In this narrative, however, it is not clear how (or if) his father fulfilled the responsibilities of offering Jermaine the structure, discipline, and challenge that would help him on his *own* journey to adulthood. In fact, it is the *son* in this story who does the challenging, by asking his father to live up to his own highest values. I asked Jermaine to consider his own values, and to reflect on how well he has lived up to them, especially in his role as a father. In this case, as in so many others, working for justice does not mean having answers, just asking tough questions.

As we have seen in these stories, and especially in the longer discussions of the film examples, the King archetype is very much interdependent with the other archetypes and can be fully realized and expressed only when the other archetypes are also properly accessed. In the following sections, we turn to the remaining archetypes: the Warrior, the Magician, and the Lover.

The Warrior

The Warrior archetype is characterized by aggressiveness: "a stance toward life that rouses, energizes and motivates. It pushes us to take the offensive and to move out of a defensive or 'holding' position about life's tasks and problems" (Moore & Gillette, 1990, p. 79). Other qualities associated with this archetype are vigilance, discernment, self-discipline, decisiveness, and loyalty to a cause greater than oneself. The Warrior's clarity and focus is in large part informed by his keen awareness of the imminence of death. There are many examples of warrior classes that have fought to extend and defend their civilizations, including the ancient Egyptian, Indian, and Spartan warriors. Too strong an identification with the Warrior creates a Sadist, someone who has become detached from relationships and who expresses his aggressive energy in cruel and destructive ways. Too weak an identification with the Warrior produces a Masochist, someone who fears his own aggressive potential and who finds meaning by submitting to others. Someone who has successfully integrated the Warrior has found a way to channel his aggressiveness so that it serves himself, his loved ones, and the larger society (for more on the Warrior archetype, see Moore & Gillette, 1992b).

Our study of the Warrior includes film examples like the story of Bull Meecham, a Marine fighter pilot who strives to be highly skilled, aggressive, and competitive (see Lewis John Carlino's film *The Great Santini* [Pratt, 1979] and the novel on which it is based [Conroy, 1976]). Bull puts an incredible amount of pressure on himself and others, in particular his family (consisting of a wife and four children). At home, he enforces strong discipline and tight schedules, and often, he is abusive. In many ways, Bull is the stereotypical Warrior, and the film offers an excellent depiction of the shadow side of that archetype, for he is fearful of intimacy, managing his needs to feel and to connect by getting drunk and playing practical jokes. Without a proper connection to his Lover (the self who is capable of love and compassion), Bull's Warrior tends toward the Sadist (cruel to others) and the Masochist (cruel to himself). Bull's raging alcoholism and his estranged relationship with his family reveal the costs of possession by the shadow poles of the Warrior. In class, we talk about the image of the Warrior for men in our culture, in particular as promoted by the military. We also talk about the costs of adhering to this image, and of alternative (more healthy) ways of demonstrating courage and strength.

Another film example of the Warrior is the story of Max Klein in Peter Weir's *Fearless* (Beasley & Forman, 1993). Max's life is thrown into tumult when he cheats death by surviving a plane crash. He comes away from the accident with an uncanny sense of personal power and moral clarity that is at first heroic and exhilarating but also, almost immediately, consuming and addictive. He is able to aid and comfort survivors at the accident scene, for example, while at the same time it never occurs to him (even a day after the crash) to contact his family in order to inform them that he is all right. His lifelong allergic reaction to strawberries is suddenly gone, which seems symbolic of his newfound vigor. However, whenever he is challenged by the threat of overwhelming anxiety or intimacy, Max seeks another exhilarating encounter with danger as a way of managing his emotions. He walks into traffic on one occasion; on another, he stands unprotected on the ledge of a skyscraper. Max becomes estranged from his family and cannot cope with much of the rest of life. He develops an obsessive relationship with a woman (Carla) who survived the crash and who is suffering from overwhelming guilt about the death of her infant, whom she was holding at the moment of impact. In a moment of inspired (and reckless) lunacy, he places Carla in the back seat of his car, gives her a baby-sized bundle to hold, and drives his car into a brick wall. His goal is for her to *experience* the fact that there is nothing she could have done to save her child. The experiment seems to work in provoking this realization, but the cost is high: both Max and Carla are hospitalized as a result of the accident. She ends their relationship, and Max returns to his family. While the plane crash seemed to have a narcotic effect, pulling Max into himself and away from other people, the car crash seems to have the opposite result, shocking him out of his addiction to near-death experiences and bringing him back into relationship with the living. His allergic reaction to strawberries returns, and he appears ready to reestablish his relationships with his wife and son.

I use this film as a jumping-off place for a discussion of Max's "Warrior addiction," his possession by the shadow side of the archetype. (The clinical diagnosis of this psychological state would be post-traumatic stress disorder.) Many of the men I work with have experienced severe traumas and have reacted to those traumas in a manner similar to Max: compulsively reenacting the trauma as a way to discharge their anxiety, without coming to terms with their feelings.

I also ask the men to describe their own images of "the Warrior in his fullness," based on their personal experiences. Mark, a heroin addict convicted of robbery and related offenses, chose to describe his social worker:

Here's a man that comes to work every day, battles a motley crew of extreme criminals, and tries, or I should say is determined, to make us understand and believe that we can be successful and responsible people, if we work hard, confront our issues honestly, remain strong in mental and physical capacities, respect others' opinions and perceptions, and most importantly be true to ourselves. He is a Warrior because he continues every day to fight for the right things in life.

When asked to describe a situation in which he accessed one or more of the Warrior's qualities, Mark wrote that he did so

> by remaining in treatment. I'm continuing to fight my addiction, addressing my issues with a fury. I'm determined to win this battle. I feel that I have the patience, understanding, willpower, and strength today to continue in my recovery! Today I'm spiritual, go to self-help groups, support groups, N.A. I orient newcomers to the Choice Program. I'm self-critical, receptive, and respect the rights of others. Today I challenge all my thoughts, and try to come to a decision that will not only benefit me, but also not hurt other people.

Mark's Warrior stories highlight the importance of fighting for the principles that one believes in. The image of the Warrior here is far from the common cultural images of the Terminator and Rambo. The Warrior Mark writes about is one who is able and willing to face his own frailties, to respect others, and to engage in whatever struggle is necessary in order to do the right thing.

Mark's language is elevated, and I have learned from my own experience (as well as from many conversations with other prison educators and social workers) that prisoners can become quite skilled at this kind of rhetoric, without necessarily demonstrating the values they speak of in their day-to-day actions. When I hear stories like Mark's, I challenge the narrator to describe (for example) a time when he was able to be "self-critical." We also test high-flown rhetoric when we move into theater mode and the men are challenged to *perform* values such as patience, receptivity, understanding, and respect. For example, for his Warrior, Ben chose Jackie Miller, a woman who was shot in the head by two youths who broke into her home:

> After months and months of therapy she was able to get most of her movement back. She had to learn to walk again and she still has trouble speaking.
>
> What I admire about her is after all she went through she was able to confront these two guys. When she came face to face with them, she didn't have any hatred towards them. She told them that she forgives them and even hugged them! And now she goes around to prisons and other places telling her story.
>
> I was inspired by Mrs. Miller to become a better person, after seeing how violence can affect a person's life. And to see someone able to forgive after having someone violate them like that, makes me want to be a better person.

In this fascinating story, Ben celebrates Mrs. Miller's fortitude in meeting her serious physical challenges and her courage in facing the men who attacked her. He is inspired by the example of a person who was at first victimized and humiliated, and who then sought strength not in bitterness, self-indulgence, or a desire for revenge, but in truth, forgiveness, and a desire for healing. Mrs. Miller offers the incarcerated (most who have been humiliated, and who see themselves as victims) an inspiring example of a different way to move forward.[2]

Ben also described a time when he was able to access the Warrior himself:

> One day we were having a family get-together and my grandfather had been drinking. He started yelling and cussing. Everyone was trying to calm him down, but he thought they were trying to get him in some way. So he pulled out a gun, pointed it at everybody, and threatened to shoot them. Everyone started to run, trying to get out of the line of fire. I was the only one left in the living room with my grandfather. Everyone was crying, telling me to get away from him. Instead, I stayed and tried to talk to him before the police came, because I know if the police came and he still had the gun, my grandfather would try to use the gun against the police, and I didn't want the police to kill my grandfather. I kept on talking to him and he eventually gave me the gun. When the police got there they took him to jail. By my doing this I gave everyone the opportunity to get out of the house safely.

Out of concern for his grandfather and his other family members, Ben willingly risked his own personal safety. I applauded Ben's heroism in this situation, and I also pointed out that it is important to recognize smaller moments of bravery and selflessness—how these come about, how we might cultivate them further—since our lives are mostly made up of these smaller moments. As seen in these examples, and contrary to the bad masculinity modeled by most Hollywood productions, the positive version of the Warrior archetype is not a soldier or a killer, but a forceful peacemaker, a strong community member willing to work for justice.

The Magician

The Magician archetype is the quintessential symbol of wisdom, insight, and mastery over the technologies of transformation. The Magician sees into the depths and can be found in a great variety of guises, including the shaman, inventor, scientist, doctor, and psychotherapist. Too close an identification with this energy results in the Detached Manipulator, the active shadow manifestation of the Magician. The Detached Manipulator is a confidence man, one who uses his power and knowledge to mislead and gain advantage over others. Too weak an identification with this archetype creates the Innocent, Denying One, someone who pretends to embody the qualities of the Magician, who enjoys the outward signs of status and respect that are given to him, but who is unwilling (or unable) to accept the responsibility, hard work, and commitment that the role actually requires. One of the keys to accessing the Magician properly is the ability to reflect upon one's emotional states, without repressing them or acting them out. This ability to self-reflect enables a person to manage his strong emotions, rather than be managed by them (for more on the Magician archetype, see Moore and Gillette, 1993a).

One of our film examples is David Mamet's *House of Games*, with a focus on the character of Mike, a professional con man (Hausman, 1987) who is the quintessential Detached Manipulator. With his associates, he creates an elaborate series of schemes that enable them to seduce and ensnare an unsuspecting psychologist (Margaret). One deception leads to another, until eventually Mike fools Margaret into believing that he loves her. He also convinces her that he will be killed if she does not give him $80,000 of her own money to pay off the mob. Mike's lies are exposed, however, and Margaret takes revenge by murdering him. This film is effective not only in showing the exhilaration and satisfaction experienced by the effective Manipulator, but also in showing the impact of his schemes on a victim (Margaret) and how "purposes mistook" can "fall on the inventors' heads" (Shakespeare, *Hamlet*, 5.2.368–369).

A second film example is Ramon Menéndez's *Stand and Deliver*, the fact-based story of Jaime Escalante, a teacher in East Los Angeles who inspires students to higher levels of achievement with his innovative teaching techniques (Musca, 1988). Over the course of the film, we see Esaclante overcome one obstacle after another: student apathy, teacher cynicism, parents' low expectations, and even the implicit racism of the Educational Testing Service, which initially questions the validity of the students' AP scores. This film works as a clear example of the Magician in his fullness and is especially good at showing how a true Magician is supported by the other archetypes, using his skills with the vision of a King, the courage of a Warrior, and the passion of a Lover.

Participants in the class offered a wide variety of examples of the Magician: the scholar and author Isaac Asimov; the fictional secret agent Angus MacGyver (because he always found a way to get out of a tight spot); an uncle who built racing cars from scratch and then raced them. One of the more interesting examples came from a participant named Trevor: Senators David Stetler and Carl Wherry (pseudonyms):

> Stetler has a certain classy style in his way of handling tough situations in life. I worked for Dave for a number of years on his estate in Madison as a groundskeeper. In this position I was aware of his daily moves and actions and life dealings. We had talked about my personal family problems. . . . I was not expecting anything special to happen. He moved to Washington, D.C., and I thought no more about it. My job changed and I began to work for Senator Carl Wherry on his estate. Later Dave Stetler sent Wherry a package. Inside the package was all the adoption papers, court adoption notes, my real birth name, family line. All the paper I ever wanted. I really did not

know how his power worked and never questioned his power, whether it be legal, political, or whatever.

Senator Carl Wherry is the same way, he does all he can to help me understand the way life was when he was a kid and who and what got him involved in politics. Now Senator Carl Wherry is my legal advisor, landlord, and employer . . . his family has sort of adopted me.

While the senators' actions clearly display some level of insight mastery, they owe much (if not most) of their efficacy to their class privilege. Once that is accounted for, their actions are not quite as wonderful and mysterious. Trevor's story painfully demonstrates the ways elite whites *appear* powerful to those without power.

Trevor is also able to see that his reliance on connections can sometimes be an expression of the Detached Manipulator:

Yes, I am/was a great person in manipulating some people . . . knowing and connecting with the right people to get what I needed and wanted. Now if I did not achieve what I was wanting . . . I pulled certain strings to get done what I wanted. There are some people who were scared of me because the people I knew who would pressure them . . .

Yet he also recognizes his ability to access the Magician in a more wholesome, integrated way:

I've been through a lot of counselors and therapists and I learned from them . . . how to act in ways to be accepted in a lot of circumstances. Being honest with a person in your relationships and not making them feel responsible for what happened in your life could also be an act of the Magician . . .

In my life I have learned that the only true person I could trust is my spiritual self and I now have learned that the person I hurt the most was myself in my actions and the way I shunned people who were doing their best to guide me on the correct path and teach me. . . . I can truthfully say that I am growing still.

As seen in Trevor's testimony, our exploration of the Magician archetype reveals that he is not a mere trickster or a confidence man; he is a character of vision, wisdom, skillful action, and courage who *serves others* with his knowledge and technical expertise. What Jung and many other scholars fail to address, and what I point out to my students, is that these categories (knowledge, experience, wisdom, and so on) are impacted by race- and class-based norms, meaning they are always political in nature.

The Lover

The Lover archetype is the primary energy of aliveness, vividness, and passion. A person accessing this archetype is sensitive, empathic, and compassionate, feeling deeply his connectedness with all things. The Lover also experiences the world in sensual terms and has a highly attuned aesthetic consciousness. Persons who have accessed this archetype strongly in one or more of its dimensions are great artists like Beethoven and El Greco, as well as spiritual leaders like Jesus and the Buddha. The active aspect of the Lover's shadow is the *Addicted Lover*, one who craves the oceanic, blissful feelings of oneness that can mark the high points of the Lover's experience but who is unable to integrate that longing into a balanced perspective on life and its demands. The Addicted Lover craves connection and good feeling and seeks them in compulsive and destructive ways. The passive aspect of the Lover's shadow is the *Impotent Lover*, one who has become alienated from feeling, connection, and aesthetic appreciation. The Impotent Lover is dull, depressed, and cut off from himself and others. As with the other archetypal energies, the active and passive poles of the shadow Lover are closely linked, representing an unstable and unintegrated relationship to the archetype. The Impotent Lover seeks more and more stimulation because he feels depressed and cut off from ordinary experience, and the Addicted Lover is someone who imagines and longs for (mostly unattainable) peak experiences (for more on the Lover archetype, see Moore & Gillette, 1993b).

Our exploration of film examples includes the film adaptation of Milan Kundera's novel set in Communist Czechoslovakia, *The Unbearable Lightness of Being* (Kundera, 1984, and Zaentz, 1988). The story is useful in showing how an Addicted Lover is finally able to face the destructive consequences of his behavior, evolving into a Lover in his fullness. The main character, Tomas, has two obsessions: his work (he is a highly successful brain surgeon) and women. His life becomes complicated when he meets Tereza, a waitress, during a visit to a small town outside of Prague. She follows him back to the city, and although Tomas accommodates her, he also continues to pursue his sexual liaisons. This is extremely painful for Tereza, who in response attempts her own tryst. She is consumed by guilt and fear and contemplates suicide. Through all of this, Tomas stays by her side and manages to comfort her, even as he continues to pursue his own bohemian lifestyle. Finally, the Soviet invasion of their country makes Prague unlivable for both of them, and they move to a farm where at last they can find peace. Tomas is no longer obsessed by his career or other women; he is finally able to devote himself completely to his marriage and to the simple pleasures of village life.

A second film that vividly depicts the Lover is Michael Cacoyannis's film adaptation of Nikos Kazantzkis's novel *Zorba the Greek* (1964). Zorba, brilliantly realized in an unforgettable performance by Anthony Quinn, is a poor laborer who passionately embraces life with a magnificent fullness of feeling. Film reviewer Bosley Crowther (1964) describes the character perfectly:

Love for all kindly fellow mortals surges in his breast. Hate and contempt for the mean ones flame in him like a roaring fire. Lust seizes him without resistance. Pathos moves him to tears. When the pressures pile up too much within him—either of joy or of sorrow—he must dance.

Zorba is an opportunist who quickly forms a relationship with an uptight British writer, Basil. Over the course of the film, in both their business dealings and personal adventures, Zorba invites Basil to participate in the dance of life. The film is an excellent jumping-off place for a discussion of what it means to live life fully and joyously.

Too many of the men I work with have been possessed by the shadow side of the Lover, through their addiction to drugs. Here Julian describes his relationship to heroin:

Heroin was the most important thing in my life. I loved it. I breathed it, I lived it, I thought about it every second of the day. The euphoria from it was hypnotizing. I loved the rituals of preparing the drug to ingesting it, to the final outcome ("the nod"). I loved it so much . . . I was infatuated with finding out everything about it, from where it came from, what climates it grew in, to what other drugs were derived from it! Everything else in my life became secondary, even my family.

The monomania of Julian's destructive love contrasts dramatically with the wide-ranging, wholesome love embodied by his ex-wife, Linda:

Linda possessed the Lover qualities in every aspect of her life. She was the kind of person who found good in everyone she met. She loved the day, the night, animals, nature, children. She was a very compassionate woman, who expressed her love openly, by possessing a special connectedness with everything in her life. She nurtured animals back to health, always talked to her plants, and took hundreds of pictures from the desert canyons and mountains, to the backyards of rundown neighborhoods, she was in touch with everything that lived. She was a sensual woman, from holding hands, to lovemaking . . . every moment meant something to her. She harmonized with all.

The idealistic nature of this description, along with Julian's note that this is his ex-wife, raises questions about how well he has integrated the Lover into his life. His description of a situation in which he was able to access the healthy Lover hearkens back to a singular, idyllic time:

I was able to access the Lover's qualities on a trip to California when we drove through six different states. All the scenery was beautiful to me. I was able to appreciate what life had to offer in that trip. I was able to feel respect for the creations that God had given us. I was able to recognize the beauty in dust, rock, and water. Everything seemed like it was illuminating, and as a result from this I was able to appreciate my family at that time in my life. It's something I wish I had paid more attention to!

The themes that run through Julian's positive narratives of the Lover in his fullness are the appreciation of beauty in even the smallest of things; a feeling of connection with people, animals, and the environment; and love for family. While these stories are told in the past tense, they can also serve as resources for Julian in the present and the future. Key for Julian is to understand that his pre-incarceration nostalgia is based upon gratitude for life itself. By recalling his gratitude (and longing) for the simple pleasures of family, travel, and nature, he can keep hope alive, looking forward to a life in which his mind, heart, and senses are cleansed and opened anew to the reality, and limitless value, of everyday existence and relationships.

In our work with the Lover archetype, then, we are able to clarify the differences between the Addicted Lover (one who is selfishly, and ultimately destructively, absorbed in the pursuit of pleasure), the Impotent Lover (one whose capacity to feel is frozen by fear and numbness), and the Lover in his fullness (one who neither represses nor indulges his emotional energies, but who lives *in relationship* to others, with a full and open heart).

Performance and Meditation

Our study of the archetypes and their shadow manifestations helps us to establish important reference points for the performance work that is central to the course. Through meditation, image theater, sociodrama, and forum theater, we work to integrate archetypal imagery and performance. I stress in my classes that we need to be aware of the useful tensions between a narrative approach and a performance approach to our explorations of the archetypes and their relevance to our lives. For example, the initial stories the men produce tend to be schematic, tidy, polarized (good/evil, credit/blame), and self-contained; they often come across as well-rehearsed justifications for a current view of self. While there is nothing inherently wrong with this, performance can amplify and open up these stories, as the men present themselves to each other, respond to one another as actors in their own stories, and improvise new ways of being in the world.

Indeed, in performance, the men reveal more of themselves. A statement like "I want to listen more carefully" is put to the test as the actor shows us (and himself) the embodiment of that objective. His fellow actors respond to his initiatives, and we all have the opportunity to observe and comment on the outcome. Our work is imbued with a sense of exploration, dialogue, relatedness, and hope. We *can* support one another and improvise new lives. By putting this acknowledgment into practice, performance helps us to understand some things about the archetypes that are more difficult to understand when we are restricted only to storytelling and dialogue (as valuable as those methods are). In performance, we cut through abstractions, reveal our shadows, and perceive interrelatedness and interdependence; we see, for example, how a Tyrant father cultivates the same qualities in his son, or how the Addicted Lover and the Impotent Lover give birth to one another.

While performance is outward-directed and meant to embody roles in ways that are visible to others (and usually audiences of others), meditation is an inward-directed practice meant to focus the practitioner's mind on her or his internal thought and bodily processes. Thus, in addition to the performance techniques described above, I also teach the men a basic form of meditation (*shamatha*, or "calm abiding") that helps them to rest and eventually stabilize their minds. We are usually subject to our habitual, cycling thoughts, and this produces a chronic undercurrent of anxiety, as well as a basic feeling of separateness and alienation from our moment-to-moment experience and from other people. Although we accept this state of affairs as "the way things are," it causes us tremendous pain and confusion. As we act from that state of consciousness, we create difficulties for ourselves and others.

Meditation is a useful practice for finding a reference point *outside* of our habitual spin of thoughts and emotions: by focusing on our posture and our breath, and by continually bringing our mind back to our breath and our body, we can more easily experience our thoughts *as* thoughts, and we can begin to loosen their grip on us. This begins to open up a space where we can relax with things *as they are*, without needing to label them, evaluate them, act upon them, or change them. Once we learn to relax in this way, we begin to sense a freedom of heart and mind. We develop a sense of our own personal dignity, our "basic goodness" (Trungpa, 2007, pp. 35–41). By slowing the cycling of anxiety, we sense that perhaps there is a more graceful way to work with ourselves, our emotions, and our world.

This is the practice I teach, following what I have learned and practiced over many years as a student in the Shambhala Buddhist tradition (Shambhala International, 2009): one sits (on a cushion or chair) in a relaxed, upright, and dignified manner, with a firm seat, a straight spine, and head and shoulders properly aligned. The hands are placed palm down on the thighs. The eyes and mouth are relaxed and slightly open, with the gaze directed outward and down toward the floor, about six feet in front of the body. The mind is focused on the breath and its natural movement in through the nostrils, down into the lungs, and back out through the mouth. On the out-breath, there is a sense of even greater relaxation and letting go. As thoughts and feelings naturally arise, one briefly takes note of this and returns one's attention to the breath. This practice is deceptively simple and, over time, very powerful. It helps us develop a sense of focus, clarity, and calm that is foundational to the rest of our work. It also introduces the men to a method for working with their own minds.[3]

This basic form of sitting meditation, while profoundly beneficial in and of itself, also functions to open up a space where new possibilities can be considered, visualized, and crystallized as intentions. In another traditional Buddhist form of meditation that I teach, the primary intentions we cultivate are love (wishing ourselves and others to be happy), compassion (wishing ourselves and others to be free from suffering), empathetic joy (rejoicing in others' happiness), and equanimity (extending our goodwill to others without bias). Within the Buddhist tradition, these four intentions are referred to as "the four immeasurables" (see Wallace, 1999).

To help inspire the men in their work with *shamatha* meditation and the four immeasurables, I help them to create a precise, disciplined, and uplifted environment within the prison. We begin every class session with ten to thirty minutes of sitting meditation, depending upon our other plans for that evening. Often we conclude the sessions with a brief reading or talk on the practice of meditation, and/or a group discussion about the challenges people are facing in their practice. I am always moved by the men's practice of meditation, because it involves a combination of self-discipline, awareness, openness, and gentleness that is not found elsewhere in the prison environment. I notice that one of the more common difficulties the men face is their tendency to slump on the cushions, even after repeated instruction in good posture, as if they can't quite believe that they are "capable of sitting like a king . . . on a throne" (Trungpa, 2007, p. 18).

In order for meditation to be an effective element in the class, it is important for the instructor to have practiced meditation him- or herself for some time before introducing it to others, in order to be already familiar with the practice and its challenges. It is also important for the instructor to be thoroughly grounded in a view or perspective that makes sense of meditation, in order to offer ongoing instruction and respond to questions about the practice.[4] On one occasion, when Marco (a member of the class) asked me specifically how meditation was supposed to benefit him, I offered this answer: "You'll see that a peaceful, aware mind that is able to hold emotions, that is able to feel anger without acting it out or letting it bury you, that you're able to have this straight spine and be dignified and awake while the anger's happening so that you can make a good choice, even with the anger." Marco's response:

> It's kind of hitting the spot—the way you explained. Especially the part, how you say, being able to deal with certain emotions, you know. Being able to be angry without lashing out to destroy whatever it is that made you angry. And when you first said it the first thing that came to my mind was, you know, there ain't nothing special about that, I do that on a *daily basis*. You

know, any time one of these officers look at me like a piece of shit, or run me raggedy doing something that I *don't* want to do, I'm angry all the time, you know, in my mind, "Boy, I'd like to fuck this motherfucker up," but instead, you keep this blank look on your face, and, "Yeah, okay," and do whatever it is that you've been asked to do. So it's like, I go through that every day. You know, maybe in class I'll learn how to do more than just *accept*. You know what I'm saying? I'll begin to not even get angry. A lesson in how I get angry or why I get angry. Maybe I'll get that out of this course.

What Marco experienced in my class was both the opportunity to experience and express his feelings (including his anger) without judgment or the need to repress. Meditation provided him with a tool to fully *feel* his anger without *acting it out* in an unreflective or reactive manner. Liberated from the struggle of the ego (self against others), anger can become a powerful source of clarity and energy. The action that flows from this kind of energy is precise and un-polluted by hatred or confusion. Irini Radel Rockwell provides a clear exposi-tion of this process of transformation in *The Five Wisdom Energies* (2002). As Rockwell shows, not only anger, but also greed, lust, anxiety, depression, and other conflicting emotions can be tamed and transmuted through an ongoing process of meditation, self-awareness, and systematic reflection.

My analysis of the relationship between Buddhist meditation and experi-mental performance is written here in two parts, to help explain to readers how each aspect of my teaching works, but I want to be clear that the two processes evolved hand in hand in the classroom—they are mutually reinforcing. While I was at first shy about bringing meditation into the classroom, I have been heartened by a growing body of theory and research that demonstrates the ways that mindfulness and meditation practices can work powerfully in conjunc-tion with more familiar teaching methods. (See, for example, the Association for Contemplative Mind in Higher Education [ACMHE], 2007; Hart, 2004; Haynes, 2005; Kahane, 2009, 2011; Kernochan et al., 2007; Zajonc, 2009.)

My own experience suggests that once one has achieved a certain stability of mind via meditation, it becomes easier to direct one's attention and thus to understand, imagine, and perform new versions of masculinity based upon creative integrations of the archetypes. And so, in addition to the *shamatha* meditation form described above, I introduce various forms of visualization practice related to the archetypes. I call one *The Council of the Archetypes*. I ask the men to imagine a huge round table in a vast chamber, where they take their seat among the King, the Warrior, the Magician, and the Lover. One by one, they seat the archetypes, beginning with the King. I ask the men to take their time and to visualize the King as he enters the room and takes his seat. What does the King look like? How does he move? I suggest that the students think of famous men in history, as well as contemporary cultural examples and men in their lives who have inspired them directly. Their images can be focused on one particularly powerful example, or they can be an amalgamation of several. When the men have difficulty thinking of examples, this is an opportunity for discussion and a sharing of cultural knowledge. We follow this process for each of the four archetypes.

The Council of the Archetypes can be extended into an exercise in active imagination, where the meditator brings a problem or a question to one or more of the archetypes and imagines their responses. On occasion, I have asked the men to write down these dialogues. Here is a condensation of one of them:

> I was just getting in from a night on the town when I staggered over to my recliner and relaxed. I thought I might rest for a few minutes before continuing my long journey on into my bedroom. As I became comfortable, I began to doze off into a world I had never experienced.
>
> I noticed the messenger bowed before all four archetypes, and therefore I did the same. The King gestured with his hand, and I was set at a very big round table in front of all that was present. I was told that I had been called forth to answer charges of . . . perpetrating a fraud upon the archetypes? In the lowest degree! I tried to explain to the High Court that there had to have been some type of mistake, for I had never committed such an act. But the King said, we have personally seen with our own eyes your atrocities, and your unrelenting disregard for the significant others that have shared your life. Then I heard the Lover say, "Do you *deny* the seriousness of the broken hearts you shattered and the fragile emotions that you simply disregarded as you left them in a state of pain and confusion?"
>
> I heard the King say, "How you plead to these charges?" Stunned by the things that I had heard spoken about me, I had to take a second or two before I asked the archetypes if I could answer to the charges when I honestly got in touch with my innermost self. That is when the Warrior told me that again, "This is not a time to act as a Weakling, a coward, and sissy myself out now, when all the other times you did whatever you wanted to—with boldness." But to my surprise, and to my defense, the Lawyer, the Lover spoke, and said: "Perhaps we could allow him time to search his heart, for he may be able to come up with an *honest answer* by reflecting upon his many transgressions and trespasses." At that point, I looked up towards the four sitting before me, and watched them curiously as they conferred among themselves. Finally, I heard the Magician say, "We have agreed that you can have one hour. Enter into this side room and you may have uninterrupted privacy."
>
> I soon felt ready to deal with the dilemma at hand. I called the guards and summoned the archetypes.
>
> *Showtime.*
>
> When all had gathered, the King said, "How say you? Guilty or not guilty to the charges at hand?" I humbly asked the court if I could speak my piece and explain my dilemma. The Magician said, "This should be most interesting—for even *I* don't have a trick for this one. " The Warrior shouted, "Fight, you weakened coward! Fight!"

The Lover said, "Please allow him to continue."

I said, "With all due respect to the archetypes, I must admit that I have been somewhat of a failure when it comes to emulating the characteristics of the archetypes. Perhaps I wanted to be more like one than the other, and I'm sure I used the tools of each *one* of your crafts to achieve my selfish objectives—and for that, I am indeed guilty."

Through curiosity, I seen eyebrows rise, and all the archetypes looked at one another and then again to me and said, "Explain"—in unison.

I said to the Magician: "Sir, indeed I have often used what we mortals call 'street sense' to manipulate and outsmart unsuspecting nobles to get over on, or to trick them out of whatever they have. Through lies and deceit, I have misused your craft to cover up my trail of unfaithfulness, and pulled off some pretty good acts, like only *you* could believe."

To the Warrior, I said, "Sir, it was always more easy for me to bully my way through pain and uncomfortable situations, rather than sit down and strategically come up with rational solutions. Many times I wanted to, but . . . I was *afraid* I would be seen as weak and vulnerable. Perhaps I was at war with the wrong things in my life. I should have been fighting my insecurities instead of the people I say I love and respect.

"And to you sir, O Great King—I acknowledge that as a father, a man, and a person in general, my conduct has been anything other than becoming. I also realize that at times I have allowed myself to fall short in experiencing my kingly qualities all in the facade of being a man. I assure you that after meditating I have begun to see the errors of my ways, and from this day forward, I shall institute new concepts in my thinking, and a new attitude towards my manhood.

"And last, but nonetheless, Sir Lover, I have lived under the assumption that I could never live in your fullness. Every heart, every emotion, every potential meaningful relationship has been almost nonexistent for me because of my addiction to, and love/lust for all that is curious to me. My desire for a love of my own has been forever elusive due to my unquenching desire to experience untold of and undiscovered riches that comes with every heart, every mind and soul, and even more so, *body* that is desirable to me. I apologize for bullying Cupid and taking his or her arrows and using them recklessly to spellbound unsuspecting hearts for play in my euphoric game of romance, knowing that a real relationship for me, was pretty much out of reach all the time.

"And with that, sirs, I must rest my case, and accept whatever punishment you all feel appropriate for my misconduct in becoming a human being who can't articulate an archetype in his fullness." I then went back to the round-table and took a seat to await the archetypes' decision. But before I had the opportunity to learn the result, I heard my girl calling and coming into the room.

"Honey—wake up! Wake up! Honey, we need to talk."

I looked at her and, remembering my dream, I told her that, "Yes, we need to talk."

I sat her down and told her of my dream and assured her that this time, I wanted to try something *new*. I told her that I had come to the conclusion that it is time I initiated a new perspective into my life's relationships—to being a better father, a better mate, lover, and person overall.

I paused, and thought about the archetypes, and what they may have thought of my new attitude. Right then I *knew* that the finding of the archetypes was that I was sentenced to allowing them to forever be my guides in helping me achieve my fullness. So from that day forward, I knew that the archetypes would be working for me, within.

This essay on the Council of the Archetypes gave the student an opportunity to synthesize and apply his learning in a way that was meaningful to him. The archetypes in this portrayal take on characteristics particular to the author's experience: specifically, his meeting with the council is at first framed as a courtroom drama, with the Warrior characterized as a punishing male figure and the Lover as his defense attorney. The author calls himself to account by naming the ways he has acted out the *shadow* manifestation of each archetype. He then allows himself to be "sentenced" to adopting the archetypes as permanent guides to a life lived in "fullness." I see this ingenious narrative as a vision of restorative justice, where a man who has committed offenses not only holds himself accountable, but also sets the stage for a meaningful path toward wholeness and reconciliation. The Council of the Archetypes, employed in various other creative ways by the participants in my classes, consistently leads to this kind of holistic, healing, and forward-looking vision.

Conclusion: From Cruelty to Compassion in the Performance of Masculine Identity

While prisons purport to rehabilitate inmates, they routinely function according to the principles of domination and violence, thereby reinforcing the worst kinds of masculinity. Practices of overt and covert aggression, shaming, and humiliation permeate the prison environment. The justifications most often offered for these practices—that they are necessary and effective—are invalidated by the evidence: "the prison, the reformatory and the jail have achieved only a shocking record of failure. There is overwhelming evidence that these institutions create crime rather than prevent it" (findings of the National Commission on Criminal Justice Standards and Goals, as quoted in M. Alexander, 2010, p. 8). The prison-industrial complex is in fact a vicious behemoth that feeds on the worst kinds of race-, class-, and gender-based discrimination (PCARE, 2007, pp. 405–7).

In the face of this cruelty and futility, my effort to offer prison classes in the Theater of Empowerment may seem quixotic to some. However, I know through my own experience how this work validates and nurtures the humanity of the incarcerated, as they allow themselves to be more vulnerable in one another's presence, and as their work is witnessed by their family members, by public audiences, and by the college students I bring in to work with them. Although I have not conducted my own study of recidivism rates, I know that the evidence in the United States over the past forty years is overwhelming: education in prison is always positively correlated with lower rates of recidivism (for example, see Correctional Association of New York, 2009; Harer, 1994; Steurer, 1996; Steurer et al., 2010). I also take heart in the fact that many other artists, activists, and educators are working in prisons to address the needs of this growing population (see, for example, the fourteen prison theater facilitators featured in Shailor, 2011b; the extraordinary prison educators who write in Hartnett, 2011; and the eloquent testimonies of these gifted artist-teacher-activists: B. Alexander, 2010; Lamb, 2003, 2007; Tannenbaum, 2000; and Tannenbaum & Jackson, 2010). In addition, I am heartened by the work of fellow travelers who have contributed to this volume. Shelly Schaefer Hinck, Edward A. Hinck, and Lesley Withers's studies of service learning in Michigan prisons demonstrate clearly that these experiences help college students to become more sympathetic to the humanity and the needs of prisoners. I am challenged by their work to continue and to expand student involvement in my own prison classes. Our efforts not only perform a direct service to the imprisoned men and women with whom we have contact, but they also shine a light on their humanity, while exposing the barbarism of the prison-industrial complex.

In this chapter, I have shown how the courses I teach in the Theater of Empowerment, and in particular my course on archetypal roles (King, Warrior, Magician, Lover), open up spaces for the exploration and enactment of more enlightened and compassionate forms of masculinity. David Coogan (Chapter Three, this volume), a teacher who also invites incarcerated men to engage in autobiographical reflection and reconstruction, espouses "the value of a critically reflexive but open-ended process of inquiry, as opposed to something more traditionally values-oriented like rehabilitation." I concur. The Jungian archetypes are not templates, but windows that invite us to explore our deepest potentials.[5] Our exploration of these potentials, which is conducted through Buddhist meditation practices, film criticism, storytelling, writing, and performance, helps us to discover the basic and positive potentials that exist within all men. We learn to recognize the shadow aspects of our identities—our inner Tyrants, Sadists, Detached Manipulators, Weaklings, and Addicted Lovers—and how these shadows are not to be feared or loathed, but understood as cut-off aspects of ourselves. The work of recognition and transformation is difficult but necessary, because "If we don't suffer ourselves, then we make others suffer for us" (attributed to C. G. Jung by Moran, 2003, p. 225). In well over a decade of work in prisons, I have seen how individual suffering is continuously projected and magnified, as prisoners and staff answer one another's fear, indifference, pain, and anger with their own. I have also seen how programming in the arts and humanities can interrupt this cycle, by creating opportunities for self-awareness, empathy, insight, and compassion.

I stress the word opportunities in the previous sentence because there are no guarantees in this work. Our meditation sessions are often compromised by distractions. The stories we tell are partial, fragmented, sometimes contradictory, and do not lead to neat moral conclusions. The connections we make are tenuous, and our insights are fleeting. Our performances are, invariably, improvisations that express both more and less than what we had hoped for. In other words, the work is difficult, messy, imperfect, and inherently incomplete. It is important for us to acknowledge, accept, and embrace this reality, because it is precisely within this acceptance that we find our tenderness, our vulnerability, our humility, our openness to one another, and our shared humanity. As Leonard Cohen puts it in his song "Anthem" (1992):

> Ring the bells that still can ring
> Forget your perfect offering
> There is a crack, a crack in everything
> That's how the light gets in.

In their work with the Theater of Empowerment, the prisoners are not asked to measure themselves against some standard of perfection. Performances are not perfect offerings, but they do ring the bells of mutual respect, produce heartfelt storytelling, and enable explorations of what it means to be a man. Through our study of archetypes of mature masculinity, our practice with Buddhist meditation, our experiments with enacting personal conflicts, and our ongoing support and challenge of one another, we do break open—and light streams out, in all directions.

Notes

1. All prisoners who are represented in this essay gave me explicit permission to quote them. I have used pseudonyms in all cases.

2. Along these lines, see also Rachel King's amazing collection of testimonies: *Don't Kill in Our Names: Families of Murder Victims Speak Out against the Death Penalty* (2003).

3. For an authoritative and extensive description of this form of meditation in the context of the Buddhist worldview, see the Sakyong Mipham's *Turning the Mind into an Ally* (2003).

4. In addition to Mipham (2003) and Trungpa (2007), there are many excellent introductions to meditation, including Chödrön (1991), Kabat-Zinn (1994), Kornfield (1993), Nhat Hanh (1975, 1976), and Suzuki (1970). For readers interested in further

reading on Buddhism and Buddhist meditation practice in prisons, there is a now-growing literature: Lozoff (1985), Malone (2008), Maull (2005), Masters (1997), Phillips (2008), and Whitney (2003).

5. There are also (not surprisingly) feminine archetypes, and the paths of investigation and performance that I outline in this chapter can be adapted to address these. For a beginning exploration of feminine archetypes, I recommend C. G. Jung's *Aspects of the Feminine* (1982), Jean Shinoda Bolen's *Goddesses in Everywoman* (1984), and Clarissa Pinkola Estés's *Women Who Run with the Wolves* (1992).

CHAPTER 2

Service-Learning
in Prison Facilities

Interaction as a Source
of Transformation

SHELLY SCHAEFER HINCK,

EDWARD A. HINCK, AND LESLEY A. WITHERS

Recently, state governments have turned to reducing prison populations in an attempt to cope with decreasing state revenues (Archibold, 2010; Schwartz, 2010; Steinhauer, 2009). While prison activists might greet these developments with some degree of satisfaction, such actions on the part of states leave the more fundamental issues facing incarceration policy unaddressed. Prison activists have argued against incarceration on far more complex grounds than simply wasting social resources, noting that prisons perpetuate racism, sexism, classism, and poverty (PCARE, 2007). Justifying a reduction in the U.S. prison population on the basis of a lack of resources rather than on the basis that prisons fail in achieving rehabilitation (Associated Press, 2009) implies that when economic times are brighter, we can—and should—incarcerate others to the fullest economic extent possible. This fiscal line of thinking distracts citizens from the more fundamental concerns that prisons fail in reducing recidivism rates and perpetuate the complex social problems facing society. Additionally, because the commitment to incarceration on the part of some states seems to be waning, concerns about rehabilitation programs for those who are currently serving time or who will be incarcerated in the future seem less than pressing. But for those who are deprived of rehabilitation opportunities, release offers little hope of improving their lots in life, and worse, might lead them back into re-offending. For these reasons, we are interested in the kinds of learning opportunities that hold the potential for changing the ways that college students think not only about the issues underlying incarceration as a response to crime, but also about the individuals who are incarcerated as a result of committing crimes.

We argue that prison activism, in conjunction with strong educational initiatives that foster deep understanding of how economics, race, and class interact to produce the prison-industrial complex (PIC), holds great promise for achieving long-term policy and institutional changes in our national, state, and local communities. Our claim is that activism, by itself, presumes the existence of an audience that is rational, compassionate, informed, and capable of developing an enlarged understanding of the systemic forces that produce and sustain the PIC. However, unless audiences are educated about the plight of the human beings who populate our prison facilities, they tend to reject prison-reform advocacy on the grounds of stereotypes about crime and criminality, compassionless frames of punishment for those caught up in the PIC, ignorance of the complexity of social forces that entrap individuals in the PIC, and ideologically driven justifications for ineffective social policy. The chapters in this section of the volume illustrate how engaged activism holds out the promise of rehabilitation for those seeking personal development through educational opportunities. As Coogan notes in Chapter Three of this volume, on autobiographical inquiry, "it is just as important that we need to find creative ways to show ordinary people living in society what they share in common with their counterparts in jail and in prison." Shailor's (Chapter One) premise for his program in teaching the Theater of Empowerment "begins from the observation that we are all actors in the theater of everyday life" and that studying the four archetypes of King/Queen, Warrior, Magician, and Lover shows how we all, whether incarcerated or free, struggle to develop maturity.

We believe that firsthand experience can become an important way to shape an audience's sensitivity for processing arguments calling for social change regarding the PIC; by countering mass-mediated stereotypes, such firsthand experiences can help to prepare the public for a critical examination of incarceration policy, thus giving the arguments of activists a chance to register with those who care about justice in our society. The chapters in this section offer persuasive firsthand observations of how activists' engagement in volunteering, teaching, and serving the incarcerated through programs designed to facilitate rehabilitation can hold out the possibility for positive change for prisoners. Similarly, our chapter presents a rationale for service-learning as a way to challenge stereotypes about the incarcerated and reports data from two research studies to substantiate the claim that service-learning projects in communication courses can play an important role in advancing a vision of a more just community. For the public to support such programs, citizens need stories demonstrating the possibility of prisoners pursuing personal development through guided communication programs in the arts (Coogan, Chapter Three; Shailor, Chapter One). The communication discipline should be at the heart of this struggle for justice by helping the public to develop ways of understanding how more inclusive, creative, and visionary communication processes can help to make a more just society possible.

Communication Education as a Practical Concern

Over the last decade, service-learning has been considered a particularly promising way to get students out of their college classrooms and into their communities for the development of citizenship and leadership skills (Astin, 1996: Astin, Sax, & Avalos, 1999; Astin, Vogelgesang, Ikeda, & Yee, 2000; Eyler, Giles, & Braxton, 1997; Fenzel & Peyrot, 2005). Barber (1992) has argued that colleges and universities can be understood as communities called together for the mission of facilitating conversations about shared norms and hopes. Applegate and Morreale (1999) note that the communication discipline is well positioned to take advantage of these trends in higher education. Writing in the preface to *Voices of Strong Democracy*, they state that

> As a matter of both ethics and survival, American higher education must be about the business of creating a new compact for the next millennium. That new compact could energize and reorganize the talent and power we possess for the common good and for maintaining the support of our constituencies. As the compact develops in research, the distracting opposition between applied and basic research will be replaced by a commitment to all research as praxis. Theory and practice will become inextricably intertwined as we discover the best ways to teach, to research, and to serve the greater good. The social impact of research will assume greater importance in assessing its quality. Community-based research will take on new status, and disciplinary narcissism will not be tolerated. (p. ix)

A community-based research program should be at once theoretically, pedagogically, and programmatically sound. An informed program of community-based research should be premised on understanding the roles and functions of field experiences in relation to classroom activities. Working back and forth between the concepts learned in the classroom and the way those concepts are illustrated in action, students' understanding of communication arises out of a reflexive relationship between theory and practice. According to Craig (1989), practical theory "takes shape in a dialectic of theory and practice, comprises a detailed technical account of practice, and fosters philosophical reflection revealing central principles, issues emergent in ongoing dialogue, and fundamental dilemmas" (pp. 116–17). Some communication professionals have initiated projects that reflect this vision of the discipline (Corey, 1996; Hartnett, 1998; Hinck & Hinck, 1998; Mettee, 1983; Warriner, 1998; see Droge & Murphy, 1999, for several examples). For the most part, however, understanding the proper balance of theory and practice and the full potential of service-learning projects in the communication discipline remains an ongoing concern.

This chapter reports the results of a service-learning partnership with two regional prison facilities in Michigan. Service-learning constitutes an educational philosophy that engages students, faculty, and communities in uncommon, unexpected, and unpredictable ways of talking to one another. In doing so, new possibilities for reflection, relationship development, and community building are actualized, even if only momentarily. Those moments hold the potential for changing social systems and structures in important, and perhaps enduring, ways. We argue that enabling students to engage in service-learning activities in prisons creates opportunities for them to confront the stigmatization of prisoners. Additionally, by helping students to understand how complex political, social, and economic forces account for crime and imprisonment, it was hoped that students would develop a greater appreciation of their possible roles as citizens.

Prison Facilities as a Context for Service

Historical studies of prison reform in the United States reveal that the meanings and purposes of incarceration evolve, to some degree, in response to political attitudes toward crime and criminals. Sullivan (1990) describes much of the first half of the twentieth century, from 1890 to 1950, as the "age of progressive reform," the period from 1950 to 1960 as a decade when prisons' function to provide "treatment" declined, the period from 1960 to the 1970s as a period of correctional transition, and then, in the 1980s, a decade culminating in "reaction and repression." Political attitudes toward crime and criminality coalesced around a conservative "get tough on crime" theme during the 1980s and 1990s (Blomberg & Lucken, 2010). Presently, the public views prisons as places to impose punishment upon those who have violated the law. For those citizens who do not know a relative, friend, neighbor, or acquaintance who has served time for criminal activity, it may be difficult to perceive prisoners as individuals worthy of remedial resources. Some members of society might perceive prisoners as individuals who have had their chance at education and social opportunity but, having failed to avail themselves of those opportunities, forfeited their claim to society's resources and concern. Embedded within this view is the idea that these individuals are morally degenerate and do not deserve help from taxpayers. Such a view of those who have been convicted of crimes seems to have taken hold since the 1990s. Writing about sentencing, Reitz (1998) observes:

> What remains clear is that the compassionate and optimistic attitudes of rehabilitation theory have dropped from their pre-1970s position. The public, and public officials, are now less likely to view criminals as disadvantaged, ill-treated members of society who can be changed for the better. This has had an interactive effect on viewpoints about other extant sentencing poli-

cies. Once the softening tendency of rehabilitation theory is removed, the other mainstream goals of punishment can be pressed toward visions of increased severity. If it seems that criminals cannot be changed, and have only themselves to blame for their behavior, then the most pivotal compunctions against harsh dispositions have been swept aside. (p. 545)

Recent studies have argued that these political attitudes explain, in part, the process by which mass incarceration creates a permanent underclass, first through the process of arrest conviction (M. Alexander, 2010), then through the process of ongoing stigma (Pager, 2007), making it difficult for those who have completed their sentences to reenter society and find employment (Pew Charitable Trusts, 2010).

Regardless of one's moral orientation to those convicted of crimes, unless prisons successfully rehabilitate the incarcerated, they fail to reduce crime, an important objective of the criminal justice system. Educating prisoners, either through vocational training or postsecondary classes, seems to have positive results in regards to rehabilitation. Research conducted in 1997 by the Illinois Department of Corrections compared the recidivism rates of Illinois prisoners enrolled in postsecondary education programming to those not enrolled in postsecondary education programming. The compelling results of the study indicate "that postsecondary education cut recidivism by two-thirds" (John Howard Association of Illinois). Further, this study found that if a prisoner, regardless of race, sex, age, or nature of offense, was able to receive academic or vocational postsecondary education, he/she was less likely to commit crimes when released. Despite this evidence, more and more states are cutting rehabilitative programs. In Illinois, fewer community colleges are willing to offer vocational and academic classes to prisoners because of the state's late and erratic payments. This is reflected in the current decline in prisoners (10 percent) enrolled in community college programs compared with the 14 percent of prisoners who were able to enroll in classes in 2002. Similarly, although the state's recidivism rate has actually increased, Colorado recently eliminated 3 million dollars in new vocational programs and 1.8 million dollars in wrap-around services due to budget constraints (Markus, 2010).

As a consequence of such cuts in programs all across the nation, more men and women who are incarcerated are being released without the benefit of appropriate rehabilitative programming. Kevin Johnson (2000) reports that "[m]ore people are leaving prison after completing their sentences than at any time in history: 520,200 in 1998, up 28% from 405,000 in 1990. The trend is expected to continue for at least the next two years, Justice Department officials say, as "more than 500,000 inmates leave each year" (p.14A). Citing statistics from Sabol and Couture (2008), Blomberg and Lucken (2010) report that since 2000, more than 600,000 individuals have been released each year, with over 700,000 released in 2007. Kevin Johnson (2000) warns, "In light of the sharp cuts in prison rehabilitation and education programs, and longer more punitive prison terms, officials are becoming increasingly concerned about what awaits communities that will have to absorb a disoriented and unprepared population of former inmates" (p. 14A). Jeremy Travis, director of the Justice Department's research arm, the National Institute of Justice, notes that "[u]nder current conditions . . . communities are assuming a big public safety risk as thousands of former prisoners stream back into society with little or no preparation" (K. Johnson, 2000, p. 14A). Currently, in an effort to address a statewide fiscal crisis and court rulings over prison overcrowding, California proposes to "reduce the number of [low-level] inmates in the state's 33 prisons next year by 6,500—more than the entire state prison population in 2009 of Nebraska, New Mexico, Utah or West Virginia" (Associated Press, 2009). Attention to rehabilitative programs that include drug treatment and job training, which help reduce recidivism, is limited. Since 2003, due to budgetary concerns, Michigan governor Jennifer Granholm closed a total of six prisons and reopened another (Hornbeck, 2009). Like many others states, Michigan has developed a reentry initiative seeking to address recidivism issues. However, Blomberg and Lucken (2010) note that "what we know about re-entry so far is limited and is based on programs that are very different in structure" (p. 252).

Because it is clear that budgetary pressures are forcing states to find ways to reduce the size of their prison populations, it is imperative to give attention to the rehabilitation needs of those being released. Programs must address how communication practices have shaped a person's self-concept and persona before, during, and after his/her incarceration. In this regard, the chapters in this section demonstrate how teachers and activities have developed creative and powerful ways for prisoners to reflect on their lives so that insight and personal transformation become possible. Whether the process involves "building an ethical code together from key moments in their lives" through a process of autobiographical inquiry (Coogan, Chapter Three this volume) or developing a performance-based course exploring the archetypal images of King, Warrior, Magician, and Lover "to show the destructiveness and futility of identity projects based on dominance and violence" (Shailor, Chapter One), these chapters reflect important ways of resisting the permanent degradation of humanity imposed both by incarceration and the flawed communication patterns that lead to imprisonment.

Goffman (1961) describes the process by which total institutions, such as prisons, strip previous conceptions of the self by subjecting prisoners to communication patterns that produce what he calls "mortification":

> The recruit comes into the establishment with a conception of himself [*sic*] made possible by certain stable social arrangements in his home world. Upon entrance, he is immediately stripped of the support provided by these arrangements. In the accurate language of some of our oldest institutions, he

begins a series of abasements, degradations, humiliations, and profanations of self. His self is systematically, if often unintentionally, mortified. (p. 14)

Incarceration can have the unintentional effect of internalizing a criminal self-concept through these "mortifying" communication processes. Payne (1973) argues that the language used to describe convicted criminals constitutes labels that create passageways to prison. Individuals convicted of crime begin to adopt the image of a criminal, since that is how others relate to them. The process of acquiring a criminal identity is intensified as a person is introduced to the social system of a prison setting. In a classic work, Wheeler (1961) tested Clemmer's (1958) thesis that a process of "prisonization" occurred where prisoners would take on, in greater or lesser degree, the folkways, mores, customs, and general culture of the prison. Assimilation into the prison culture, then, constituted a significant obstacle to rehabilitation, since prisoners identified with prison life and opposed correctional staff to maintain solidarity with fellow inmates. Wheeler found that the length of time served constituted a relevant variable in accounting for prisonization, but that for individuals classified as still in the early stages of their careers as criminals, a recovery process and a shedding of the prison culture occurred prior to parole.

Further, the linguistic forces contributing to one's identity as a criminal are difficult to oppose, even for the prisoner who desires to resist the process of internalizing a criminal self-concept. Because they are so powerful and ubiquitous, the communication practices that compose the social system of a penal institution can be observed in the language resources utilized by all participants in the prison social system. Both prisoners and those who supervise them remark upon the complex ways that the identities of those with and without power are based on the need to identify with each other's constituent group. For example, Wittenberg (1996) has detailed how group and self-defining argot, slang, acronyms, and private languages can serve as tools for building a sense of self and community, while also standing as barriers to cross-group communication in prison settings. Goffman (1961) argues that

> an "institutional lingo" develops through which inmates describe the events that are crucial in their particular world. The staff, especially its lower levels, will know this language, too, and use it when talking to inmates, reverting to more standardized speech when talking to superiors and outsiders. (p. 53)

Goffman further describes how individuals, forced to develop mutual support systems during incarceration, begin to adopt the identity of a criminal:

> Further, if the inmates are persons who are accused of having committed a crime of some kind against society, then the new inmate, even though sometimes in fact quite guiltless, may come to share both the guilty feelings of his fellows and their well-elaborated defenses against these feelings. (p. 57)

In addition, Juda (1983) explains how small-group-therapy programs, if not designed carefully to ensure alternative patterns of interaction apart from the normal prison environment, can

> provide the inmate with a repeat performance of his life experience that brought him to the prison in the first place. In fact, so used to this chaotic interpersonal mode of adaptation is the recidivist inmate that he will attempt—in any way he can—to preserve it inside the prison so that his adaptive/survival style of living will remain familiar and, therefore, be experienced as psychologically "safe." (p. 58)

For Goffman, Wittenberg, Juda, and those scholars and activists who have studied these processes, the conclusion is clear: prisons create and enforce communicative patterns that, when enabling, lead both to identification with and collaboration among prisoners, but that also, when disabling, lead to the exclusion of others and the retrenchment of the same damaging roles that led to incarceration in the first place. Moreover, this line of research demonstrates that even before individuals arrive at prison facilities, dominant communication practices within the judicial system begin to affect an individual's identity. Demonstrating that in the medico-legal context, the constitution of knowledge can be considered a master discourse, Arrigo (1997) shows through a Lacanian psychoanalytic analysis that clinicians, judges, and attorneys circulate and revalidate language practices of this master discourse, leading to linguistic hegemony. Defendants—considered "disordered" in relation to the hegemonic language practices of the system—become discursively marginalized and are often unable to resist the power exerted by the master discourse. Thus, even prior to incarceration, language practices constitute the roles of prisoners and guards, judges and lawyers, and compose communication systems capable of exercising power and inflicting punishment.

For teachers and social activists, the problem is how to deliver social resources to those who are capable of being rehabilitated while working within the political constraints of specific prisons and against the larger social forces that oppose the investment of taxpayer dollars in efforts at rehabilitation. For someone who has been convicted of a felony, the question is how to reconstitute his/her self-concept from that of criminal to that of a decriminalized, rehabilitated, punishment-served, debt-to-society-paid, law-abiding person—and to do so while residing within the walls of a facility that functions in just the opposite way. One side of the problem develops out of a pernicious communication system designed, consciously or not, to reinforce a criminalized self-concept; the other side of the problem denies prisoners the communication resources they need to resist the permanent criminalization of selfhood. Thus, communication processes constitute a large part of the forces that account for the failure or success of incarceration as a response to crime.

For someone who has been convicted of a crime, incarceration should not pose an insurmountable social barrier to reconstituting one's social standing in a community. Such a barrier turns the formerly incarcerated back toward crime and wastes both the taxpayer dollars used to incarcerate in the first instance and the further resources for incarcerating re-offenders. Given the wasted resources and failed policy, members of democratic communities should be moved to adopt a more effective response to crime. Of all the programs and approaches that have been tried, at least one finding is abundantly clear, and that has to do with the success of educational strategies. According to Vacca (2004), "Since 1990, the literature has shown that prisoners who attend educational programs while they are incarcerated are less likely to return to prison following their release. . . . Effective education programs are those that help prisoners with their social skills, artistic development and techniques and strategies to help them deal with their emotions (p. 297)."

However, observers have noted that little has been done to prepare hundreds of thousands of inmates to return to our communities across the nation over the next decade for more meaningful and law-abiding lives than when they began their sentence (Associated Press, 2009; K. Johnson, 2000). Given the social urgency of providing prisoners with the resources necessary to return to society, our goal was to develop students' awareness as citizens of the need for a more effective response to crime, a more humane way to secure offenders from the larger population they might threaten, and a more effective rehabilitative and educational experience for those whom we incarcerate. To do so, we turned to service-learning, a form of pedagogy that holds promise for activating awareness and thinking critically about social-justice issues.

Study One

The instructors of the service-learning experience have been working with the correctional facilities in mid-Michigan for approximately fifteen years. The activities directors at the correctional facilities, as a result of the interest of the prisoners in learning more about persuasive speaking and debate, contacted the instructors in regard to providing communication programming and activities for the men serving time at their facilities. It was hoped that the communication activities (Persuasive Speaking Club; Debate Club) and the communication programming (interpersonal communication skills, listening, persuasive-speaking workshops) would enhance the men's critical-thinking skills, their communication abilities, and their ability to present themselves appropriately to others with whom they would interact. Research study one focuses on the impact of the communication programming on the students who worked with the men incarcerated at the correctional facilities. Although steps are underway to incorporate prisoners' perceptions into this ongoing research project, the current study focuses on students' perceptions of the service-learning experience. Prison research has been significantly restricted in the last thirty years (Moser et al., 2004), since the Belmont Report (1979) recognized prisoners as a vulnerable population requiring additional protection from potential research abuses. While the protected-group designation is understandable and perhaps necessary, it nonetheless poses considerable challenges for researchers attempting to study this population.

The research utilized a longitudinal design of students' experiences in several service-learning projects with the men who were incarcerated. We worked closely with our partners in the correctional facilities to ensure that the instructional experiences we provided addressed the needs of the men within the constraints of the programs. Input was solicited from the prisoners regarding their hopes for the program, and adjustments were made accordingly. For example, in one project, the prisoners requested a specialized debate format that was then utilized; in another instance, the prisoners selected the subject matter for the debate. The men were also consulted concerning their interests in what topics might be addressed in the communication workshops. Thus the men were actively involved in various details of the design of the workshop. Finally, within the communication workshops, the students were careful to acknowledge the skills of the men who were incarcerated and adapted the exercises and discussions accordingly to reflect their interest in the subject matter.

Participants

Over the course of a two-year period, 133 undergraduate and graduate students in communication courses at a mid-sized university in the midwestern United States participated in the research. In order to meet prison requirements for LEIN (Law Enforcement Information Network) security clearance, background checks were performed on all participants. These checks required the submission of participants' names, Social Security numbers, weight, eye color, race, sex, and birthdates. All participants were over the age of eighteen. Some participants received extra credit for participation. In accordance with Institutional Review Board approval, participants were informed that they could cease participation at any time without fear of penalty.

Students interacted with prisoners in one of two similar conditions: through judging a debate/speech competition ($n = 108$) or through a public-speaking workshop ($n = 22$) with a prisoner (for three participants, it was not clear from their responses which service-learning condition they experienced). For the judging condition, participants sat in an audience composed of other judges and prisoners to observe and judge either a debate between a prisoner debate team and a university debate team, or a persuasive public-speaking competition. Each debate team consisted of two individuals. For the skills-training condition, participants were paired with a prisoner and conducted a public-speaking workshop. In both conditions, participants observed or interacted with prisoners for approximately one hour, under the close supervision of prison staff and university researchers. The assistant to the warden selected the twenty-two incarcerated men for participation in the workshops.

The following research questions were posed:

RQ 1: Does participation in a service-learning project positively affect perceptions of prisoners?

RQ 2: Does participation in a service-learning project regarding public-speaking concepts in a prison facility have a positive effect on students' perceptions of academic learning?

RQ 3: Does participation in a service-learning project have a positive effect on attitudes about allocating social resources to prisoners?

RQ 4: Does participation in a service-learning project have a positive effect on attitudes toward service?

Methods

After completing and signing informed-consent forms, participants received packets containing demographic items, pre-test (wave one) questionnaires, and post-test (wave two) questionnaires. Participants were instructed to write no identifying information on the questionnaires. For both the debate-participation condition and the public-speaking-workshop condition, students filled out a series of questionnaires before and after the events concluded. The instruments focused on perceptions of prisoners, commitment to service, the need for educational opportunities in prison facilities, and the value of service-learning experiences (see Appendix A). Students completed the questionnaires before entering the correctional facility. Once the service experience was completed, participants exited the prison and completed the questionnaires. Once all questionnaires were collected, student participants and faculty members had an opportunity to discuss their thoughts and feelings regarding the prison experience.

Results

Research question one asked whether participation in a service-learning project positively affected perceptions of prisoners. To address this question, a paired samples t-test compared participants' overall perceptions of prisoners at waves one (before entering the correctional facility) and two (after exiting the correctional facility) of the study. The t-test revealed that participants' overall perceptions of prisoners became significantly more positive (t (129) = −15.269, $p < .001$) from wave one ($M = 2.94$, $SD = 0.51$) to wave two ($M = 3.75$, $SD = .53$). At wave one, participants reported nearly neutral perceptions on the scale of 1 to 5 in which higher numbers indicate more positive perceptions of prisoners. However, at wave two, participants' perceptions were significantly more positive.

Research question two asked whether participation in a service-learning project regarding public-speaking concepts in a prison facility was relevant to perceptions of academic learning. To address this question, means were calculated for each of the student-learning-outcomes items. On a scale of 1 to 5, in which lower scores indicated more positive service-learning outcomes, participants agreed that participating in service-learning helped them to understand concepts discussed in their speech class (M = 1.93) and that participating increased their interest in the subject matter of their speech class (M = 2.1).

Research question three asked whether participation in a service-learning project was related to attitudes toward allocating social resources to prisoners. The service-learning outcomes means, on a scale of 1 to 5, in which lower scores indicated more positive service-learning outcomes, revealed that participants strongly agreed that enhancing prisoners' communication skills increased their chances of being productive citizens (M = 1.37), that prisoners deserve educational opportunities (M = 1.35), are capable of behavioral change (M = 1.76), and should have opportunities to improve themselves (M = 1.43). Additionally, a Pearson's Product-Moment correlation examined whether a relationship exists between the amount of change in perceptions of prisoners from wave one to wave two and the service-learning outcomes. The analysis revealed that change in perceptions of prisoners from wave one to wave two was significantly positively associated with participants' agreement that enhancing prisoners' skills increases prisoners' chances of being productive members of society after their sentence has been served (r = .201, p = .012).

Research question four asked whether participation in a service-learning project related to attitudes toward service. The service-learning outcomes means, on a scale of 1 to 5, in which lower scores indicated more positive service-learning outcomes, revealed participants' agreement (M = 1.77) that after participating in this study, they are more likely to volunteer for other service-learning projects. Additionally, a Pearson's Product-Moment correlation examined whether a relationship exists between the amount of change in perceptions of prisoners from wave one to wave two and the service-learning outcomes. The analysis revealed that change in perceptions of prisoners from wave one to wave two was significantly positively associated with participants' agreement that they are more likely to volunteer after the prison service-learning experience (r = .251, p < .001).

Finally, a post hoc independent-samples t-test analysis comparing participants who identified themselves as nonvolunteers (M = 2.19, SD = .71) and weekly volunteers (M = 3.00, SD = .82) revealed a significant difference in their belief that their participation in this service-learning project made a difference in a prisoner's life (t (47) = −2.75, p = .008). Nonvolunteers were significantly more likely to believe that their participation made a difference in a prisoner's life than were weekly volunteers.

Study Two

As a way to explore further how students experienced their interactions with the men who were incarcerated, reflections from two additional classes of graduate students enrolled in an advanced-interpersonal-communication seminar participated in service-learning experiences at a correctional facility in central Michigan. The assistant to the warden was interested in providing educational opportunities that addressed improving the communication skills of the men at the correctional facility and contacted one of the instructors about the correctional facility's needs. The content of the workshops was decided in consultation with the assistant to the warden at the correctional facility. The assistant to the warden talked with the men who were incarcerated concerning what topics would be of interest; additionally, the assistant to the warden talked with the educational-programming director about what she thought would be of interest to and use for the men.

Participants/Methods

Graduate students traveled to the correctional facility three times over the course of a semester, during classtime, and worked on either interpersonal communication skills (year 1) or public-speaking skills (year 2) for one hour with men who were incarcerated. In year one, fifteen graduate students worked with approximately twenty-two men and in year two, eighteen graduate students worked with approximately twenty-five men. After each hourlong lesson, graduate students were asked to reflect upon their experiences. Reflections were then sent electronically to the instructor of the class. After securing permission from the Institutional Research Board at our university and then from the students enrolled in the graduate seminar, the reflections were read and analyzed. The researchers were interested in the following research questions:

> RQ 1: How do the students' interactions with the men influence their expectations and perceptions of what it means to be an individual who is incarcerated?
>
> RQ 2: How do the students' interactions with the men influence their perceptions of the incarceration process?

Results

Analysis of the reflections from the graduate students who participated in the service-learning experience reveals themes that reinforce the results of study one. The first theme apparent in the reflections is that it appears that graduate students' perceptions of the men were initially stereotypically representative of what it means to be an individual who is incarcerated. However, after interacting with the men, these stereotypical images were positively changed. Of the twenty-seven reflections received after the first visit, twelve reflections discussed how media largely shaped their expectations of the men with whom they would interact (for more on the power of the mass media to influence thinking about crime and prisons, see Yousman, Chapter Seven of this volume). For example, one student shared that:

> For some reason I had the jailbird image in my head—the black and white striped outfits. To be honest, I don't know if any prisons still even have those kinds of clothes, but that is what I had pictured. The men I had pictured didn't really have faces, but they were all sort of rough looking. The men in my mind looked like people whose lives had gotten the best of them. Worn, weary, perhaps a bit dirty—these were the images in my head. I think that these images are influenced by the fact that I really like to watch *Law and Order*; in addition, I have recently seen the movie about Johnny Cash—*Walk the Line*—a few times and cannot seem to get the Folsom prison scene out of my head. In fact, I even found myself wondering if the Facility serves yellow water to their inmates. (year 1, subject 9).

Another student indicated that

> My expectations for the visit were very different from my actual experience. To begin, I expected the men we would be interacting with to be less well-spoken. Although I had never had a past experience with anyone that had been incarcerated, I thought that they would be young, Black men who spoke with poor grammar. My impression of them was partly formed from television shows about prison riots and movies. Needless to say, I figured they would be intimidating.

After students interacted with the men, these initial impressions changed. The student in the previous example also reflected that "the men I met were very well spoken and not intimidating in the least. The interactions my partner and I had with the men were very lively, and engaging" (year 2, subject 4). Other students offered similar conclusions:

> In fact everything that I have read, heard and seen both through the internet and television portrayed a very negative narrative about prisons and prisoners alike. I have to admit that what I expected and perceived was quite the opposite. My partner and I actually had a very lively conversation with the men who were incarcerated. The men were very eager to show us that they were interested. (year 2, subject 8)

The graduate-student comments reflected that after working with the men, the students concluded that the men wanted to learn, were bright, and were willing to address the subject matter being shared. Students found that the "guys were more interested than anticipated," "were courteous and seemed eager to learn," and were "more enthusiastic about the subject matter than the students at the university." Student reflections changed in the sense that references to the men as "prisoners" decreased, while references to the men through their first names became more prevalent. Examples were shared that connected the subject matter (listening or persuasive speaking) with the specific needs of the men as they utilized the communication concepts to improve their communicative abilities with their families. Clearly, the ability of the graduate students to interact with the imprisoned men enabled the students to see the men as more than their roles as prisoners; even the truncated forms of contact and interaction made possible by this service-learning project enabled the students to see their imprisoned learning partners as less monstrous and more fully human.

Second, it appears that after participating in the service-learning experience, graduate students believed that the workshops they designed and participated in generally yielded positive results. Twenty-five reflections were received after the third and final visit, and in these twenty of the students expressed that they found the experience beneficial for themselves, the men who were incarcerated, or both. Students noted the changes in themselves as they "smashed" the stereotypes surrounding individuals who are incarcerated and learned that the "prison system isn't at all what I thought it was going to be." Additionally, graduate students believed that the men's communication abilities improved. Graduate students claimed that during the workshops on listening, the men who were incarcerated seemed eager to share examples where they had put into action the listening skills that had been discussed in previous lessons. For example, one pair of graduate students wrote in their reflections that one of the men in their group offered a detailed example of how his inability to listen had hampered his relationship with his daughter and that in order to rectify the situation, he had written a lengthy letter to her outlining what he has now learned about listening (year 1, subjects 8 and 15). In the persuasive speaking workshops, graduate students noted that the men in the workshops were eager to work on their speeches, came prepared with drafts of their speeches, were ready to speak in front of others, and indicated an excitement about a possible competition (year 2, subject 18). Other graduate students shared similar comments concerning the willingness of the men to participate in the workshop and the improvement of their speaking skills.

However, the graduate students also recognized the limits of the communication workshops that they offered. As one graduate student noted, "Spending more time [than simply three hours] would allow the instructors to not feel so rushed to go through the material. It would also allow the men to bring their speeches and give time for feedback and further polishing" (year 2, subject 2). Recognizing the limits to what we could share fueled others to think about the types of rehabilitative experiences that are needed. One student reflected:

> I have learned that the system isn't working and we [society] are wasting lives and compounding a problem instead of solving one. You can't lock people up

and give them nothing to do and call that a rehabilitative program. . . . Nothing that I saw led me to believe that any of the men who were incarcerated had a way to learn skills that would help them toward a legal, legitimate path in life after leaving the prison, and conversations with my fellow students back up my observations. (year 1, subject 1)

Another student shared that

The men expressed a strong desire to be involved in any kind of educational programs that the administration would allow, they are eager to learn and really want to better themselves. I believe that if the State of Michigan really wanted to save money on prisons, they would focus on funding educational programs for inmates. By providing educational and social re-integration programs for inmates, it would enable them to find better jobs and better prepare them for reentry to society. Statistics show that by training and educating inmates, it cuts the recidivism rate in half, and the money put into educating and training them is far less costly than housing them. (year 1, subject 11)

Finally, some students did indicate that, as a result of noting the rehabilitation needs of the men, they [students] would like to work with the men in the future. One student stated that

I got so much out of this and my views on a lot of issues were challenged. The prison system isn't all that I thought it was going to be. While there were obviously some elements that were consistent with my preconceived ideas, the majority of them were smashed. This experience is something that I will never be able to forget, nor will I want to. I recognize a need now, and will hopefully volunteer again in the future. (year 2, subject 10)

Discussion

The results of the two studies indicate that service-learning holds the potential for addressing stigma associated with incarcerated persons. Regarding negative versus positive perceptions of prisoners, respondents in study one moved from a more neutral mean before interacting with prisoners, to a significantly more positive mean after interacting with prisoners. Similar conclusions were found in study two. These findings indicate that interacting with men in a prison facility, given appropriate supervision, potentially addresses stereotypes concerning those who have been incarcerated. Additionally, the experience has the potential to change how participants talk about those who have served time. For the participants, the media images, cultural stereotypes, and political messages that construct prisoners as social monsters can be countered with direct experience of prisoners as human beings. More important, the participants in both studies one and two made only one to three trips to a prison facility. For the time invested, we think this is a powerful change in the ways students view marginalized others in general, and individuals who are incarcerated specifically. Potentially, students with this service-learning experience will be more critical about messages concerning crime and criminals given their direct experience with those attempting to improve their lives.

Future research might explore more systematically the nature of the interaction between participants and prisoners to understand the degree to which specific elements of stereotypes were challenged in the project. Tying specific changes to specific aspects of the communication process would improve our understanding of how to develop future programs. Additionally, future research might determine the degree to which these perceptions endure, as well as their resilience as experiential resources in countering, or in some cases qualifying, media images of the incarcerated.

The research also provides evidence that service-learning is a way to advance academic goals of increasing student learning for the subject matter of a course. Respondents reported agreeing that the project helped them to understand concepts discussed in class and increased interest in the subject matter of the course material. Communication instructors in a wide range of courses might seek service-learning projects in the local community that draw attention to the needs of others related to economic, social, and political issues. Introductory communication courses, public-speaking courses, introduction to debate, and many other communication courses (e.g., interpersonal communication) offer instructors a rich set of experiences with which to engage students. Communication concepts regarding the formation of the self, the development of relationships, small-group interaction, advocacy, reasoning, evidence, and organization in presentations, among many others, come alive for students in the field. Students are confronted with situations that demand a more complex understanding and invite reflection on the course material and experiences. Future research might explore additional ways to generate reflection, especially since a substantial body of work indicates that reflection is the hallmark of a quality service-learning experience (Astin et al., 2000; Cooper, 1998; Correia & Bleicher, 2008; Eyler, 2002; Eyler & Giles, 1999; Eyler, Giles, & Schmiede, 1996; Hatcher & Bringle, 1997; Moffitt & Decker, 2000). Such reflection also would tie citizenship concerns more closely with the effects of policies on underprivileged, marginalized, alienated, and underresourced members of our communities.

The data also provided evidence that service-learning is important in developing positive attitudes toward allocating social resources to prisoners. These results provide strong support for the role of service-learning in developing citizenship concerns. Drawing on the observations of professionals in sociology and criminal justice, we have argued that correctional policies have neglected appropriate levels of support for rehabilitating those who have been incarcerated. This lack of support has been the effect of a political climate that views convicted felons as undeserving of resources for self-improvement. Although some politicians and programs might work to challenge this assumption, our findings indicate that service-learning is an effective way to change a collective group of perceptions that directly affect how participants view policies toward the underresourced group. Certainly, this finding is important for correctional policy, but the implication might be extended to other marginalized, alienated, and vulnerable groups in our communities. Taking students into the field enables them to confront the effects of policies on other human beings, possibly members of social groups with whom they might have little or no interaction had it not been for the service-learning program. More important, these results demonstrate the value of the investment in time and energy instructors make when they pursue service-learning as a teaching strategy. In short, service-learning holds the potential for transforming students' attitudes toward others and for engendering positive commitments for improving social policy.

The results concerning students' future service or commitment to serving others as an outcome of their participation in the project were interesting. We thought it might be the case that those who had little to no concern with prisoners and incarceration issues might have one of two responses to the experience: they might remain uninvolved after the project, or they might discover a sense of commitment to others if they had a positive experience. The graduate students who participated in the three communication lessons spoke of extending the time available for working with the men; some even suggested the construction of a class that would allow the students to continue to teach at the prison. The quantitative results seem to indicate that students felt that they might make a difference with their participation in a future service-learning project; at least, they found the experience valuable enough to want to participate in future service-learning projects. Combined with the post-hoc analysis, the more involved the participants, the greater the impact they seemed to believe that their actions could make. This finding is consistent with the positive effects on citizenship concerns we have noted in the discussion of the results above. This finding is also interesting in that it challenges the findings of other research indicating that, having participated in a service-learning project, students felt less satisfied and hopeful that complex social problems could be addressed through service (Miller, 1994). Future research should explore participants' perceptions of their capacity for influencing change in their communities. Presumably, instructors utilizing service-learning would want to know what design features led to more positive perceptions of participants' capacity for social change and, possibly, how to design service-learning projects to avoid perceptions of powerlessness in the face of complex social problems.

Although this chapter explores the kinds of learning opportunities that hold the potential for changing the ways that college students think about the issues underlying incarceration as a response to crime and the individuals who are incarcerated as a result of committing crimes, future research should also address how faculty experience service-learning opportunities. Limited research has addressed the effects of the service-learning experience on the faculty member in regards to social change and activism. In a preliminary study where the three authors of this chapter reflected upon their service-learning experiences involving prisoners (Withers, Hinck, & Hinck, 2007), we found that despite the tensions associated with service-learning, we became recommitted to our projects each time we brought students to the correctional facility. We saw the excitement of our students' newly developed understanding; observed students working through their firsthand encounters with stigma, advocacy, and stereotypes, among other communication phenomena the students had been studying over the course of the semester; and witnessed them engaging in many meaningful discussions of these issues with their peers. In these respects, future research might explore how service-learning strategies challenge instructors to manage the many tensions they must confront in the course of their teaching and renew their passion for addressing complex issues regarding social justice.

Conclusions

This research examined the effects of service-learning as a way to develop citizenship concerns for participants. The service-learning project directed communication skills in a variety of areas to incarcerated persons, a stigmatized and underresourced group for whom most students held neutral attitudes prior to participation. Results indicated that participants changed their perceptions of the men who were incarcerated from neutral to more positive, increased academic learning for the subject matter of the communication courses in which students were enrolled at the time, and developed positive attitudes toward allocating social resources to the incarcerated. For those who experienced the greatest amount of change in perceptions of prisoners, results also indicated that participants would be more likely to volunteer for future service-learning projects. The results indicate that service-learning offered a promising way to address stigma to affect attitudes toward social policy, and potentially to engage students in future service to their communities. On the basis of these results, we conclude that for the participants in this study, service-learning constituted a powerful instructional experience for the development of citizenship concerns as they relate to incarcerated persons, correctional policy, and future service.

So in our struggle for justice, we ask readers to imagine for a moment what kind of society might be possible if we had greater public support for systematic prison-education opportunities of the kind illustrated by the excellent programs described in this section by Coogan and Shailor. If following the work of Shailor, talented teachers developed programs that enabled the incarcerated to "perform new lives" in a Theatre of Empowerment, and if honoring Coogan's hope that we can "open minds where college students and residents of the jail can learn how to dialogue respectfully and imaginatively, supporting one another in shared inquiry about the many deeper causes of crime and the pathways out of it," we might move a little closer to the vision of a just society. As this study and the other chapters in this section indicate, communication programs create hope and understanding, affirm the humanity of the incarcerated, make personal transformation possible, and increase the possibility of developing the communication skills necessary to reentering society and reconnecting with friends and family.

Appendix A

Perceptions of Prisoners Scale

Instructions: Indicate what your perceptions are about prisoners by placing a single check along each scale. For example, on the first scale, if you feel that prisoners communicate very effectively, place a check at the extreme left side of the scale. If you feel that prisoners communicate very ineffectively, place a check at the extreme right side. If you feel somewhere in the middle of these two extremes, place a check at the appropriate place.

Prisoners:

communicate appropriately	___ ___ ___ ___ ___	*communicate* inappropriately
intelligent	___ ___ ___ ___ ___	unintelligent
articulate	___ ___ ___ ___ ___	inarticulate
respectful	___ ___ ___ ___ ___	disrespectful
hard working	___ ___ ___ ___ ___	lazy
caring	___ ___ ___ ___ ___	uncaring
socially competent	___ ___ ___ ___ ___	socially incompetent
honest	___ ___ ___ ___ ___	deceitful
aggressive	___ ___ ___ ___ ___	cooperative
responsible	___ ___ ___ ___ ___	irresponsible
appreciative	___ ___ ___ ___ ___	unappreciative
dependable	___ ___ ___ ___ ___	undependable
friendly	___ ___ ___ ___ ___	unfriendly
sensitive	___ ___ ___ ___ ___	insensitive

Service-Learning Outcomes Assessment

Using the scale identified below, please place the number that reflects your thoughts about the statement in the space provided.

1 Strongly agree
2 Agree

3 Neutral

4 Disagree

5 Strongly disagree

1. _____ Participating in this service-learning project helped me to understand the concepts talked about in my speech class.

2. _____ I found the experience of judging the debates to be beneficial.

3. _____ I enjoyed judging the debates.

4. _____ After watching the debates, I believe that prisoners deserve educational opportunities.

5. _____ Enhancing prisoners' skills increases their chances of being productive members of society after their sentence has been served.

6. _____ Individuals deserve opportunities to improve themselves while incarcerated.

7. _____ After watching the debates, I believe that prisoners are capable of behavioral change.

8. _____ My participation in this project has made a difference in an inmate's life.

9. _____ After participating in this study, I am more likely to volunteer for other service projects.

10. _____ Participating in this service-learning project has increased my interest in the subject matter of my speech class.

CHAPTER 3

Writing Your Way to Freedom

Autobiography as Inquiry in Prison Writing Workshops

DAVID COOGAN

I'm sitting in a circle with a few dozen men in a classroom sanctuary, a respite from the noise, violence, and negativity of a jail built to house 800 prisoners but that routinely houses more than 1,500. The walls of this sanctuary within the Richmond City Jail are covered with posters of Mother Teresa and Malcolm X, photos of prisoners doing their work, and photocopies of GED and Career Readiness Certificates. The room is full of books by poets and historians, computers, study guides, and plastic chairs filled with imprisoned men working on the craft of authoring new lives.

On this afternoon, I am reading "The Builder" from Pablo Neruda's (1967) poetry collection *Fully Empowered*. The poem begins with the speaker announcing that he "chose" his "own illusion" and let his "long mastery" of it "divide up" his "dreams." After dwelling a little in the experience of mastery, the narrator sees salvation in the shape of a ship. He even touches it. But "when it did not come back / the ship did not come back" and "everyone drowned in his own tears"; still, the speaker summons the strength to build a new ship. With an ax he enters the woods, concluding, "I have no recourse but to live" (p. 33).

The men before me also have no recourse but to live. Building from this key assumption, I make another: our "long mastery" of a "false illusion" can prevent us from truly living. It could even be one of the reasons that the men before me are incarcerated. There are other reasons, of course, as Michelle Alexander (2012), PCARE (2007), and many of the other contributors to this volume make clear, including unjust drug laws, rigid sentencing guidelines, a lack of jobs in the inner city, entrenched racism and poverty, and cultures of violence. We could multiply the external reasons, but we are writing about the *internal* reasons. And we're doing this not only for ourselves, but for one another. We're writing to try to learn hard lessons about the characters that we've been and to try to imagine our characters in new plots. We write to steer the drama away from crime and jail.

In this chapter, I explain how I have built autobiographical writing workshops in prisons. I share some scenes and writings from these workshops and probe the deeper communication issues that structure narratives of criminality and violence but that also, when addressed truthfully, enable imprisoned men to begin to author new lives. To give readers a broader understanding of these problems, I then contextualize the men's autobiographies within the larger field of prison writing since the 1970s, in particular, the emergent genre of prison autobiography. Though I have taught autobiography to women prisoners and read published autobiographies by women prisoners, I limit my discussion to work published by men primarily because the workshops I discuss here are filled with men. However, the process of crafting new selves via autobiographical writing is not inherently different for men and women any more than it is for black or white prisoners. What I am calling "writing your way to freedom" is a process of discovering and developing new characters amid the old plot lines that led to jail—it's also a process of writing new plot lines that lead out of jail.

Face to Face with Your Life Script

After reading Neruda's poem, I ask the men to stir things up by writing about a false illusion that they had chosen, an illusion that divided their dreams. "Did you have a ship that got away?" I ask. Some study my face. Others are already writing. "How will you rebuild?" When I call time after fifteen minutes of in-class drafting, Emanuel is already on his feet ready to go:

> The fortune, the fame, it's all in the game.
> Nice cars, big chains: crack to cocaine.
> Dope man serving dope man to whomever—rain sleet or snow man.
> My illusions came from dudes cruising with broads on Broad Street.
> Weekends popping, bodies dropping that's shhh.
> Money, power, respect is what I need to be that dude.
> My crooked teeth, Eddie Monster look and bow legged feet.
> Low self-esteem is what was causing my defeat.
> I had to cover these things up so people wouldn't pick on me no more.
> Then I could be the man.
> Then I got older and became the man.
> But I didn't realize that the game would bring so much pain.
> Police watching, homeboys plotting, dope-fiend wearing a wire.
> Boy, my block is on fire!
> Running, ducking, dodging, Mom crying
> Dad's dying from cancer.

My best friend's name is cancer man.
But this was my plan to be the Man.
Wow, this mess is insane.
All these false illusions
False power and perception because I wanted to be the Man
Now I realize that I suffer from low self-esteem.
Now I'm learning the difference between perception and what's real.

In this autobiographical poem, Emanuel presents himself as someone who chose the false illusion of selling drugs—the criminal lifestyle of a dealer—to deflect the teasing about his appearance. Glenn Walters (1998), a psychologist who works with offenders, explains that a criminal lifestyle forms when a person tries to eliminate existential fear or anxiety about one's purpose in life. Lifestyles are enacted through opportunity. Emanuel had the opportunity to eliminate his anxiety over his appearance by watching older drug dealers get positive attention. As Walters concludes: "One cannot develop a drug lifestyle in an environment where drugs are not available, just as one cannot establish a criminal lifestyle in the absence of salient criminal role models" (p. 14).

Emanuel creates his sense of agency by selling drugs, but the point of writing about it, at least as I invited him to write about it, is to judge it. Frederick Corey (1996), who taught juvenile offenders to perform their life stories in a communication course, describes judgment as a process of restructuring "relationships between discourse, identity, and self-determination" (p. 56). The discourse that Emanuel uses in the opening lines of his poem helps him to construct a secure and stable self: he has "dudes" and "broads" who give him "power" and "respect"; there are "weekends popping" and "bodies dropping." The way he uses the discourse of the drug game helps him construct his identity, but the look back at that identity draws another conclusion that is refracted through the discourse of therapy: it was "low self-esteem causing my defeat."

At this point, we might expect Emanuel to reject the former discourse for the latter. Certainly, that's what the genre of autobiography tends to promote, what Paul Eakin (1999) calls a "continuous" self in control of the past and projecting its own future. But a closer look at the genre, he argues, reveals a historical process of self-making. The tension in autobiography, then, is between our desire for a continuous self whose agency almost appears to be extratextual and a dialogic self struggling to contain that agency. As Eakin explains:

> Autobiographers are primed to recognize the constructed nature of the past, yet they need at the same time to believe that in writing about the past they are performing an act of recovery: narrative teleology models the trajectory of continuous identity, reporting the supreme fiction of memory as fact. "You" and "I" and "she" and "he" and "we"—the dialogic play of pronouns in these texts tracks the unfolding of relational identity in many registers,

in discourses with others and within ourselves. The lesson these identity narratives are teaching, again and again, is that the self is dynamic, changing, and plural. . . . Repetition of the past and self is always repetition with a difference. (p. 98)

If there is buried treasure in life writing, the glittering reward is not The Self but shards of self scattered about in what Eakin calls "discourses with others and within ourselves." Emanuel can no more bury The Man than he can bury the man of low self-esteem. Both are a part of his constructed past: feelings he associates with the mother crying for him at home, the father dying from cancer, the other kids teasing him, the power and prestige he sees in other drug dealers and then acquires for himself. That man and The Man both come from the environment that conditions him and presents him with choices.

The critics Robyn Warhol and Helena Michie (1996) make much the same conclusion about storytelling at Alcoholics Anonymous meetings, where the self, they argue, is a process:

If, in A.A., "self" is a process, not an entity, and if it exists in social interaction, not consciousness, then the A.A. master narrative does not merely shape or influence the identity of the recovering alcoholic. The acquisition and continual retelling of the story becomes the very process that constitutes the alcoholic's self. Paradoxically, the recovering alcoholic adopts a new identity, but the identity is a de-individualized or "anonymous" one: the "self" that exists in the world of social interaction within A.A. has no distinguishing appellation, no surname beyond the occasional initial: "I'm Bill W., and I'm an alcoholic." (p. 340)

Surrendering one's surname to the master storyline about alcoholics, a person may adopt a new identity, but only in the act of surrendering. This is why George Jenson (2000) finds the addiction autobiography troublesome. Jenson spent several years as an ethnographer at A.A. meetings, listening to speakers' digressions, contradictions, and constant reminders of their addict status. A.A. talk begins and ends in the middle, unlike traditional autobiographies that start at the start and end at the end. If the talk at A.A. is to be believed, Jenson concludes, nothing is ever truly solved for the addict: addiction is treatable but not curable. There is no transformation of self, only its management via humbling repetition.

Jenson's insight poses a compelling problem for any kind of autobiographical writing that tries to narrate a transformation of the self, a move from one discourse to another. As the critics Sidonie Smith and Julia Watson (1996) explain, the difficulty comes about when the writing ends and "we move about different locales in our lives where certain stories need to be told" (p. 13). Emanuel can find agency in more than one way, with more than one discourse, in more than one setting. To resist the conditions that led him to choose drugs and crime, he will have to enter back into the existential fear he once knew and develop a new response to it. While a writing workshop cannot fully enact these "locales in our lives," I believe it can simulate their gravitational pull.

After Emanuel finishes reading, I summarize what I hear and then try reentering the scene of his life through dialogue. I want to get closer to his reasoning.

"You say you felt bad because the other kids were teasing you, right?" He nods. "So you had to have the right car and jewelry to get their respect."

"Yeah." He splays his legs. He smiles, showing his gold tooth.

"Did the car respect you?"

"Huh?"

"Why did you think you could fix the internal with something external?" He creases his brow. I press on. "I got teased for my big nose like you got teased about your feet."

"All kids get teased, I guess," Emanuel offers.

"And I wanted a car when I was sixteen. And eventually I got one. But I didn't expect the car to get me a feeling of self-worth. I already had that from my parents."

"Whoa!" Ron interrupts. He'd been leaning deep into his chair. Now his feet hit the floor with a thud. "This is therapeutic! It's a lot more than *writing* you're teaching." The guy next to him is half listening to us and poking through the Diagnostic and Statistical Manual of Mental Disorders (DSM-MD). I notice the book.

"But you know what? Wait, can you hold up that book, Norm?" His tattooed arm rises like a totem pole. "Can you all see what he's reading?" They nod slowly. "That's what therapists use to slot your problem." More nodding as Norm lowers the book. I continue. "Honestly? I don't know how to do that. At the end of all this writing, I won't be able to tell you what your problem is or what you can do about it. Just so you know."

"Ahh!" Ron says. "That just makes me trust you all the more! You see, I've been around those kinds of people all my life to talk about my addiction. I *know* what they want from me. And I *know* how to give it to them. But *you!*" He folds his hands. "I don't *know* what you want, man!"

I nod toward the door, signaling the world beyond the sanctuary, then turn back to face him. "I want you to write your way out of all this. I want you to try. I don't know for sure if it will work. But I believe every man in here should try to help himself." Emanuel grins broadly.

"*Real* talk," Norm says under his breath. I lean in closer to hear. "I said that's real talk!" Then he shuts the book tight.

What makes our talk real is the emergence of agency, which Carolyn Miller (2007) defines as "a property of the rhetorical event or performance" (p. 153). To be clear, agency does not exist on its own in any one text or statement but in the inquiry of reading and sharing. If "agency is an attribution," not a substance, Miller continues,

> We should be less concerned about empowering subaltern subjects and more about enabling and encouraging attributions of agency to them by those with whom they interact—and accepting such attributions from them. We should examine the attributions we ourselves are willing to make and work to improve the attributions that (other) empowered groups are willing to make. (p. 153)

What we are attributing to each other are our *preferred* relations among discourse, identity, and self-determination.

In Emanuel's case, the process begins when he invites us to judge his old drug-dealing lifestyle as an attempt at lifting his low self-esteem. When I share my story of getting teased, I affirm a part of his story, or in Miller's language, I accept an attribution of agency from him. The process continues when we judge the limits of gaining respect through material possessions—the talk about getting cars. Then later when Ron and Norm join the conversation, we generalize a process of writing and self-determination that we distinguish from the process of psychiatric diagnosis: our lives are not filled with problems to label but contradictory and overlapping stories to sort out. We need to write so that we can learn the process of sorting out our stories and becoming self-directed, critically reflexive, and open-minded.

Robert Waxler and Jean Trounstine (2005) make much the same claim about Changing Lives Through Literature (CLTL), an alternative sentencing program that brings together offenders, a judge, a probation officer, and an English professor around a seminar table to discuss literature. One of the teachers in CLTL, Ben Stern, explains that success in CLTL "is about recognizing our vulnerabilities and doing what we can to heal our own and another's wounds. These may not be moments of salvation, certainly not moments of permanent conversion, but they allow us to transcend our isolated egos, and act instead through the community we help to create" (cited in Waxler and Trounstine, p. 35). Transcending "our isolated egos" is an important first step toward building community. Engaging in autobiographical writing is, then, one way to take that first step by finding the right words that best connect us with others for the right reasons.

Months later, after he was released, I talked with Emanuel on the phone and asked him to read a draft of this essay. He remembered vividly the moment of coming to see his false illusion. He was grateful he had that chance to write about it while incarcerated. I then asked if there are any other false illusions he has found since he's been released and what he's done about them.

Emanuel is currently working with the police academy, coaching men who are about to be released. He's a motivational speaker, too, who dedicates his time to speaking at high schools about the dangers of the streets. In these roles he hears echoes of his old self all the time. He hears both his old attitudes and the ways they are expressed by a new generation of hard young men. And so he has made a conscious choice to no longer call his people "niggers." The word was keeping the streets alive in his thinking. Since he wasn't pursuing the streets anymore but was trying to help others avoid it, why use the word?

I offer Emanuel's insight to highlight the value of a critically reflexive but open-ended process of inquiry. Workshop leaders cannot assume that their goal is to get each person, in Waxler and Trounstine's words, "to meet a prescribed standard of morality." That would be reductive and, perhaps more disturbing for the educator, it would rob the student of the chance to find the right words and really own them. As Waxler and Trounstine (2005) argue, the goal is "to create the conditions for everyone to give voice to their ideas, to convince everyone that they can be a part of civic life" (p. 34). Trying to create "civic life" by creating the conditions for more citizens to participate in public dialogue is, of course, complicated. Pamela Schultz (2005), a communication scholar who helps sex offenders create and then analyze their own stories of socialization by taping and then transcribing their speech, offers insight about why this work is so difficult. Schultz has shown how the thought process justifying crime emerges as a life "script" that, arguably, solves personal problems while further alienating the criminal from civic life. Scripts do not so much reveal a particular pathology but an adaptive, story-making sensibility that transforms the self into a "mythic persona" that is outside the law or commonsense morality. "These roles, and the scripts they enact as a result of environmental pressures, form the basis for determining sources of attribution, motivation, and accountability for their crimes" (pp. 189–90). Many of these pressures can be traced to childhood traumas of physical abuse, sexual abuse, abandonment, and other crises of psychological health.

Verbalizing the meaning of these traumas is the beginning of resolving the crisis of psychological health. Unfortunately, boys do not report sexual abuse as often as girls. The psychologist Richard Gartner (1999) speculates that boys suffer their abuse silently because they do not know how to identify the abuse *as* abuse, either because they are less disturbed by it than girls, or because they are better at denying it, or both. As a result, they may experience disassociation: an "unconscious severing of connections between one set of mental contents and another often before they enter consciousness." These are traumatic experiences, Gartner emphasizes, that "have never been encoded into language" (p. 31).

Everyone disassociates to some extent, Gartner concedes, but those who are sexually abused use disassociation as a defense mechanism, which often triggers other symptoms, including "severe interpersonal isolation, complex relational difficulties, a crisis about sexual identity, and post-traumatic stress disorder" which includes "hyper-arousal, intrusive thoughts, flashbacks, interpersonal detachment, and helplessness" (p. 15). Sexually abused boys can develop trust problems, control issues, emotional numbness, self-soothing behaviors including drugs, overeating, workaholism, over-spending, over-exercising, gambling, and sexual compulsion, behaviors that amount to "a repetitive attempt at mastery over the original victimization" and that are attractive to such actors because they provide "an emotional high that proves they are not totally deadened to feeling" (p. 31).

It is compelling to see writers learning how to verbalize the meaning of their trauma, because they can judge behaviors that once led to crime. Tim does that in the following excerpt from his autobiography, also written in the workshop at the jail. The scene begins with a flashback of his father, a violent alcoholic who used to beat Tim and his mother. He then walks to the train tracks to write poetry and meets a beautiful woman on her way to work. All seems well until the blooming relationship has to compete with what Gartner would call "self-soothing toward emotional numbness":

> I got home about an hour later and started searching for my mother's stash of Percocet, BINGO, under her pillow. She never knew there was any miss-ing because she pretty much stayed lit. I took three and washed them down with a swallow of Wild Irish when I heard the knock at the door. I walked to the window and peered out and what I saw stole my breath. It was an old Cutlass that my uncle drove. I looked at my trembling hands because I didn't understand how, at my age, I was still afraid of him.

At this point, the intrusive flashbacks take over. He remembers playing baseball at a family cookout, where Uncle Andy treated him "more like a son" than Tim's own father ever had. "That day built trust in me for the man that would later scar me for life." It's a scar that he feels more acutely when Andy walks through the door.

> He looked depressed, and borderline suicidal as he toted his luggage with both hands and under both eyes he carried a different type of bag. Sleep deprivation would be considered a fallacy in reference to his image, for he didn't appear that usual smooth character that I had once associated with him. He made eye contact with me, and it gave me the heebie-jeebies as the hands of discomfort ran their ice-cold phalanges along the contours of my spine.

Unable to reconcile the formerly smooth character/substitute dad with the "borderline suicidal" man sending out "heebie-jeebie" vibes, Tim hits him "with a straight right jab to the nose."

> He stumbled back and swung wildly in a sense of desperation but missing me by a good six inches. *You like that little Tim, you love your Uncle Andy?* "Yeah, I fucking love you!" I screamed through clenched teeth. I volleyed with a plethora of combos easily decimating this lifelong foe. Each punch relieved 10 years of built up rage and sorrow, and looking at his bloody carcass lying there, a sense of happiness flooded within me like the levees of bliss had burst wide open in my soul. Like I said, through every dark night, a brighter

day always seems to follow. I may never be able to change the circumstances
of my situation but I damn sure can find the satisfaction in that moment.

What satisfies him is the mastery over the terms of his sexual victimization,
presented dramatically as the silencing of the molester's voice. Or as Schultz
(2005) would put it, this is the moment in Tim's recollection when the mythic
persona became unassailable: because of the environmental pressures he experienced with his uncle and parents, Tim was justified in becoming violent
in this scene and justified in becoming a thief and an addict in the other
scenes. Writing about that self does not make it go away. But it does give him
other ways of relating to it, as he explains in the cover letter he attached to
the autobiography:

> Through my life I have experienced great pains battling with addiction, de-
> pression, suicide attempts and many other "false" gratifiers that I used in
> order to ease my heartache. However, where misery lies, there is always hope.
> Hope for me is what pulls me through. It gives me strength when I feel weak
> providing me with that lifeline that I sometimes need to stay afloat as I wade
> through the raging waters of tribulation. Although I'm incarcerated, I feel
> I have learned a great deal about living and how to cope with the intense
> pressures that my circumstances had inflicted upon me.

Tim struggles not only to understand how he has fortified his mythic persona
with "false gratifiers," but also how he can relieve the "intense pressures" he
still feels. He's reaching for a "lifeline" in this writing, with an emphasis on
"reaching": he is not done yet. As Smith and Watson (1996) warn: "Individuals may experience a sense of exhilaration and empowerment in telling their
new personal histories, in speaking the unspeakable; but exhilaration and
empowerment are neither guaranteed by the telling of their life stories nor
necessarily and reliably liberating. . . . The negotiation of everyday narratives
is an ongoing process rather than a certain achievement" (p. 16). What may
feel liberating as a process—writing and sharing difficult moments in one's
life—may not last beyond the writing workshop. Tim may not want to throw
a punch or use drugs again or attempt suicide, but will knowing that help him
resist the mythic persona that tells him he has every right to do so? Emanuel
may not want to turn toward "the streets" again to figure out his self-worth,
but will this insight into his feelings be enough to help him face anew the
existential fear that led him to the streets in the first place?

Maybe. As Smith and Watson (1996) might say, there are no guarantees.
Nonetheless, I am compelled to try to cultivate this self-reflexive quality in
prisoners who have not had people in their lives to help them develop it in
writing. And though I have worked with women writers at the jail, as a man,
I am driven to cultivate this quality in men. Critically reflexive men are the

ones who have begun to question, in Jonathan Shailor's (Chapter One, this volume) terms, the "destructiveness and futility of identity projects based on domination and violence." These projects—fueled by "shame" and uncritical enactment of "the ideology of hegemonic masculinity," to be "The Man" in Emanuel's terms—block out what Shailor describes as "healthy, mature expressions of masculinity" characterized by "creativity, discipline, teamwork, leadership, emotional intelligence, artistry, and moral imagination." It is possible for men to imagine other ways of being men—to write their way into that. Change is possible, however limited.

Yet for too long in America, we have been shuffling people like Emanuel and Tim through the system to do their time without caring if they develop their moral imagination or the capacity to think much of anything. We imagine, instead, that they're incapable of developing or that we already know what they think. If we trend toward the liberal perspective, we tend to think prisoners are victims of an unjust society. If we trend the other way, we tend to see them as lacking morals. Prisoners have just made bad choices, period. The problem with these stances is that they sacrifice the complexity of both choice and social conditioning and create along the way a frustrating stasis. While we busy ourselves battling one another with principles in public discourse, we neglect to ask prisoners themselves about their principles. Understanding how prison writers have articulated their own principles within and against the changing American political backdrop may help us better articulate our own principles for engaging people we incarcerate. Understanding where the larger rhetorical stasis has come from and how it has evolved may help us all to imagine new ways of working for justice in our jails and prisons.

Changing Selves, Changing Times: Prison Writing in Context

What we might refer to as the liberal side of the stasis began in the 1960s with what George Jackson calls the "racism that is stamped unalterably into the present nature of Amerikan sociopolitical and economic life" (Jackson 1998, p. 158). In this book, *Soledad Brother*, Jackson does not dwell on his life before prison, which, as Cummins (1994) documents, included quite a bit of stealing and violence beginning on the south side of Chicago. My sense is that this omission is by design, because in the larger system that Jackson is theorizing, "criminals and crime arise from material, economic, sociopolitical" injustice, not personal choice (1998, p. 158). The life in prison that he describes only deepens the groove of that injustice. Jackson is at pains at all times to connect that brutality on the inside to a "long chain of corruption and mismanagement that starts with people like Reagan" and ends with guards, "most of them" the

"KKK types" and the rest who are "so stupid they shouldn't be allowed to run their own baths" (p. 163). Only a revolution in prison *and* in society, Jackson argues, will bring about justice for all.

To be this leader in the prison movement and in his writing, of course, Jackson cannot self-characterize as a criminal. Not many from this era do. "Responsibility?" asks Jack Henry Abbott (1998), a white prisoner, in a letter to Norman Mailer in the 1970s. "I am not responsible for what the government—its system of justice, its prisons—has done to me" (p. 197). Isolated and brutalized for years in solitary, Abbott—like Jackson before him—doubts he will survive the system and remain normal. When he is released through the intervention of Mailer and publishes *In the Belly of the Beast*, however, he enjoys great book sales and celebrity. Things seem better than normal until Abbott stabs and kills a waiter, flees the scene, and is captured and imprisoned again. "I did not do this to myself" (1998, p. 197), he reminds us posthumously. Jackson's fate is similar for similar reasons: He dies in the act of trying to escape—shot by prison guards—after shooting other guards and prisoners. From the grave he explains, "I know that they will not be satisfied until they've pushed me out of this existence altogether" (p. 166). In these searing testimonies from the radical prison era, our protagonists fight Injustice, a beast that hungers for their humanity. Some readers may cheer their struggles for liberation because they know the odds are stacked against these imprisoned radicals, who have been socially conditioned toward criminality and violence.

Resistance to the idea of social conditioning of criminals is often tied to the Reagan revolution of the 1980s and to conservative criminologists such as Samuel Yochelson and Stanton Samenow, who wrote *The Criminal Personality, Volume I: A Profile for Change* (1976). They argue that crime is a choice. Cognitive behaviorists like Walters, cited earlier, could be considered pragmatists in this "choice" tradition. But prison writers also played a crucial role in the shift in public consensus. For example, Dannie "Red Hog" Martin (1993), a prisoner who wrote a popular op-ed column for the *San Francisco Chronicle* during the 1980s and early 1990s, spares no criticism of the inhumanity in the prison system. He is especially eloquent when he writes against interminably long and pointless prison sentences, the unchecked spread of AIDS in prison, and the indiscriminate use of psychotropic drugs to quiet down unruly inmates. And yet Martin refuses to blame society for his becoming a criminal. He accepts prison life because he opposes himself to the "law-abiding society, the work ethic, and Judeo-Christian values. My values are outlaw values" (p. 59). Martin does not claim that all criminals have made this conscious choice. Rather, he distinguishes the criminal or "self-respecting convict" from the one who doesn't "know this concept or the value system attendant to it. Their crimes were crimes of passion, crimes of mental illness, total unawareness of sanctions or sheer stupidity. I don't view these types of people as criminals because they never made the conscious choice. I either distrust or pity them. They don't belong in prison and they can't live in society. They are homeless in the world" (p. 59).

Convicts belong in prison, Martin argues, because they know the consequences of their choices and know how to do their own time. They don't ask other convicts about their lives or their crimes. They don't ask society to abolish prisons. All they ask for is mercy, a fair shake, and common decency. In this way, Martin asks less than Jackson and Abbott. He admits his own faults and the faults of the system. He won't promise to stop robbing banks. But that doesn't mean his fellow drug users in prison should have to risk getting AIDS from an unclean needle or from the advances of sexual predators without condoms. What Martin stakes out, in other words, is that middle ground between conditioning and choice.

Evans Hopkins's (2005) prison memoir is likewise instructive, maybe even more so than Martin's collected columns, perhaps because of the more complicated lessons shared with readers in Hopkins's memoir. Raised middle-class in the segregated southern town of Danville, Virginia, where Jefferson Davis, the president of the Confederacy, fled when it became clear the South would lose the war, Hopkins has no criminal street credentials like George Jackson. His idol is tennis star Arthur Ashe. But he's read all about George Jackson and his younger brother, Jonathan, who was shot dead by police trying to free his brother's prison associates in the midst of their trial (Jackson, 1998, p. 155). As an adolescent reading about this, Hopkins is enthralled. He wants to be a soldier in the cause. He joins a local chapter of the Panthers, eventually moves to Oakland to work for the party as a journalist, but becomes disillusioned over the years as the party drifts away from its roots in community empowerment toward drugs and thug hustles that exclude the more rank-and-file members like Hopkins. He returns to Danville defeated and prideful, self-soothing with marijuana and alcohol and self-loathing about his inability to support his family. That's when he gets the idea to rob a bank. In court he faces the racism the Panthers had been fighting. In prison with a life sentence, he wrestles as a Panther but also with his inner Panther. He becomes a journalist writing against the racism he experiences, but also against the brutality white prisoners face. Though it takes many years, he also comes to show remorse for his crimes and to find a universal love for humanity.

At issue in Hopkins's memoir, then, is not just the prison system, but the person struggling to make it through a range of social systems. This is a journey that many of the best prison memoirs describe and one that does not admit easily to generalization. Consider, for example, the way Jimmy Santiago Baca (2002) and Joe Loya (2005) contend with their Mexican American identities in their prison memoirs. Both Baca and Loya write, in part, to uncover the core reasons they ended up in prison. And both discover their ethnicity in that

core. But they discover different things, too. For example, Baca is abandoned
by his Spanish mother, who can pass for white and who leaves Jimmy's father,
an illiterate and alcoholic Mexican, for a rich white man. Baca learns to hide
his cultural alienation and low self-esteem by fighting other boys and hiding
the truth: that he's living in a detention center and doesn't know when or if
his parents will come for him. His white football coach offers to adopt him.
But Baca can't reconcile the coach's generosity with the notion that accepting
it would mean denying his parents and his heritage. To not have to make that
choice, Baca drifts instead into parties and jail, much like his father before him.
He then gets serious and starts selling marijuana, then cocaine, and quickly
gets in over his head. What propels Baca along the way is his search for what
he calls a place to stand, which is also the title of the book.

Joe Loya is propelled in much the same way and treads much of the same
ground, but in his own stride. His parents are young evangelicals who school
the boy at white churches and, in other ways, pave his way into an assimilated
life of classical music and quite a few books, though they were poor, too. Already domineering and an intellectual bully, Joe's father becomes even more
so when his wife dies. Alone with his boys, he begins bullying more and more
with his fists, at one point nearly drowning Joe's brother. A younger white wife
soon emerges, agitating an ethnic identity crisis that had been fomenting for
some time. Young Joe soon aligns himself with his white Republican preppy
friends, seeking capital at all costs, stealing clothes from the store he works at,
and stealing other things from friends, including white girlfriends. He learns to
manipulate. Then he gets tired of all the work that takes, gets his act together,
and starts robbing banks.

Like Baca, Loya finds the courage to face himself in prison. Both have to un-
tangle their Mexican American identities from their conflicted feelings about
their white mothers and, more generally, white America. Both are alienated
from a white and middle-class America, though they enter into that alienation
from different vantage points. And both base their mythic personas—their
criminal "scripts"—on this tangle of alienation in the midst of unprocessed
childhood traumas of abuse and abandonment. Baca writes about his own
culture in prison: the tattoos on the body of his Chicano mentor, Chelo, became
his first real cultural text, followed by the voices of Chilean and Spanish poets,
Neruda and Lorca, respectively. But Loya, in correspondence with the Mexican American writer Richard Rodriguez (1982), himself famously jaundiced
about his American assimilation, returns to the Western cannon of Marcus
Aurelieus, Pythagoras, Nietzsche, and, of course, the Bible, which he rejected
as a young man.

It may not matter which way a man turns—what books he reads, what
relation he takes to his culture and the world—in that hour of desperation, in
prison. My concern is *that* he turns away from the self-destructive and socially

destructive, to embrace the self-generating, the truly kind. I am concerned because not all prisoners are as talented or as motivated as Hopkins, Baca, and Loya to write their own memoirs, let alone publish them. That's why we teachers and activists and artists working for justice are needed in our jails and prisons.

The Jail Is in the Community:
The Community Is in the Jail

While criminologists and conservative social critics tend to ask about the means of "rehabilitating" prisoners, I argue that we need to find creative ways to help both prisoners and ordinary people living in society to imagine freedom. Shelly Schaefer Hinck, Edward A. Hinck, and Lesley Withers (Chapter Two, this volume) argue along similar lines when they ask us to teach service-learning courses in jails and prisons in order to "prepare a public" to create a more just society. The free and the incarcerated need each other not only to stem the demand for jails and prisons in America, but to stem the story-making sensibility that enables criminal lifestyles. Richmond City Sheriff C. T. Woody speaks to this point more generally when he reminds us that the jail is in the community, and the community is in the jail. This is why he welcomes people like me from the community. He knows we won't grow as a community until we can come together as a community of the incarcerated and the free. Let me conclude, then, by sharing what I've done to build those bridges between our jail and our community in the hope of facilitating greater understanding of our shared society.

The first bridge I have created is publication. When I first got the idea to publish stories from the workshop, my ambition did not stretch beyond self-publishing with the nonprofit Offender Aid and Restoration, which had helped me gain access and start my workshop. I visualized something like a 'zine or a coursepack that could be circulated to churches, nonprofits, legislators, and other citizen groups with an interest in learning more about stemming crime. But the gravity with which the men took up my invitation to shape their life stories for publication amazed me. They not only rose to the challenge of going beyond their first drafts, but they challenged me to write the same way that I taught: to tell my story of teaching them to write their stories. We have now produced a manuscript, "Strip Poker: Writing Your Way into New Life in Jail," and are seeking a publisher (for examples of such prison-based publications, see B. Alexander, 2005; Jacobi, 2008; Scaife, 2008; Wagenheim, 2009; Hartnett, 2012).

I didn't want to wait for publication to be able to share our work beyond the jail, however, so for my second bridge I created a special-topics course in prison writing that was recently made a permanent part of the English

Department's curriculum. (See Appendix B for the full syllabus.) The focus of the course, much like the focus of the workshop at the jail, is on the healing power of writing as told through stories like Hopkins's, Baca's and Loya's, especially those writings that bear witness not only to the brutality of prison, but to the brutality of the life before prison.

When I began the class, most of my co-authors were either still at the city jail or in some prison in Virginia, sending me handwritten drafts of their life stories. Often, I would read these aloud in class and connect them with whatever book we were studying at the time. I invited but never required students to help me type these and offer feedback to the guys. The assignment became quite popular, though. There is a hunger for involvement, to be a part of the solution, and helping an incarcerated writer by typing his words is exactly the right kind of involvement for some people. It enables them to dwell in the prisoner's choices—in writing and in life. It's a walk in their shoes (see Hartnett, Wood, & McCann, 2011).

Emboldened by my students' interest in getting involved, I developed a service-learning assignment to generate an inquiry about crime and prison, working with prisoners or the nonprofits that help them. (The full assignment is reproduced in Appendix B.) I see these inquiries not so much as outreach efforts but as intellectual and creative exchanges carried out by equals who are searching for common ground on issues that everyone has some connection to: family life, education, violence, addiction, racism, sexual violence, incarceration, and so on. We have found the space to work like this in creative-writing workshops at several of the local juvenile-detention centers, prisons, and nonprofits serving former prisoners in the city. And we have found the space to work as volunteers at those nonprofits teaching computer skills and taking part in fund-raising projects. Though I have not conducted research on service-learning classes in jails and prisons, as Hinck, Hinck, and Withers (Chapter Two) have done, I heartily agree with them that service-learning constitutes "a powerful instructional experience for the development of citizenship concerns as they relate to incarcerated persons, correctional policy, and future service." Students never seem to tire of telling me how the course—and the service-learning piece of it, in particular—moved them intellectually and ethically in ways they just had not expected. They found themselves in public spaces with something to say. It doesn't get much better than that for me.

Yet after running the Prison Writing course for years this way and paying close attention to the feedback, I realized there was room to expand that public. I would have to collapse the bridge. I would need to bring my college students to the jail. Then I would need to find a way to bring more faculty and students with me (along these lines, see Alexander 2011, and Pompa 2011).

Through a grant from Virginia Commonwealth University's Division of Community Engagement and the generous support of the Richmond City Sheriff's Office, we created a new program that brings college—and college students—to the jail. Class meets only there—three miles down the road from the university. We call the program Open Minds: Shared Inquiries, Shared Hope. In it, everyone learns how to dialogue respectfully and imaginatively, supporting one another in shared inquiry about the many deeper causes of crime and the pathways out of it; to write creatively and analytically; and to link course material to personal experience and ethical ways of living. Four professors (including myself) from four disciplines—English, women's studies, African American studies, and religious studies—and over a hundred students from the university and the jail are cultivating this space together. Here's how two students describe it:

> Once you walk through the jail, hear all the doors shut behind you, "stay in the yellow line," pass the doors with the tiny window that lets you take a peep into hell, and finally settle into the sanctuary, the feeling of being in jail wears off. For the next hour or so, you're just in class, like any other class. And as far as respect goes, there isn't much to say about it. We give it, they give it, we get it, and they get it; it's as simple as that.
>
> The dialogue is really good, and I feel like for a short moment of my day I'm actually in a class and not a jail. The students interact with us openly, and the discussions are always enlightening. I've learned so much about religions that in the past I just made many speculations about. I'm grateful to have been a part of learning at such a high level. The assignments are very challenging and require a lot of reading and research. I appreciate being held to the same standards as university students and not being categorized because of the situation I'm in. None of us deserves to be categorized. In jail or free, white or black, male or female—no matter the category—we deserve the same challenges, standards, and respect. We deserve the same chance to open our minds together. We need each other to get that work done.

Appendix A

Autobiography Workshop Topics and Overview

The purpose of this class is to write your way into a new life. This is an artistic process, not a confession. You get to choose what you write about, to teach us readers how to see. The challenge is to make sure your words convey meaning; that the people you write about, including yourself, become believable; that your scenes are vivid and engrossing; that your message comes through, primarily through the action and description; that the plot keeps us moving, wanting to learn; and that we are learning not only about your life but about Life.

The Past

- Describe the people from your childhood who really made a difference in your life, who really affected you somehow.
- What do you remember most about your neighborhood, your home, your room?
- What did you do with your friends?
- What about school—what was that like?
- What were your dreams for yourself at this time?
- What were your parents' dreams for you?

The Problem

- When did you start to get in trouble?
- What sort of trouble was it?
- Did you think of it as trouble then?
- In your mind, how did you THINK about what you were doing?
- At some point, did you want to stop but couldn't?
- Describe some of the people you knew during this time and how they fit into your world.
- What was this world you had created for yourself? Define it. Describe it. What were the rules there? How did that world make you feel?
- What links this world to the childhood place you came from?

The Punishment

- What are the facts of your crime or crimes?
- How did you get caught?
- What happened to you after you got caught?
- What happened to you emotionally?
- Did you do anything wrong?
- Have you learned anything from the experience of being punished?

The Possibilities

- What sorts of things do you struggle with now?
- If you are trying to change, how are you *really* changing? From what to what?
- Describe something from your life that gives you hope that things COULD BE different.
- What's your ambition for the future, and how do you think you'll get there?
- What's your vision of yourself in relation to other people?
- What do you think you can offer others, and what would you like in return?

Appendix B

Prison Writing Syllabus (abridged)

Course Description

This course takes a critical look at the memoirs, stories, essays, and poems shaped by the prison experience in America, including the radical prison movement of the 1960s and 1970s, the subsequent rise of the prison-industrial complex in the 1980s and 1990s, and recent efforts to resist this politics of "warehousing" and despair through the art of writing. In addition to studying the work of published prison writers, students will study the work of offenders and ex-offenders who were once housed at the Richmond City Jail. In July of 2006, I began teaching a writing workshop on autobiography in our city jail. The main purpose was to help the prisoners write new "scripts" for their lives. A closely related purpose was to publish their autobiographies so that together we might create more understanding in public discourse about the challenges facing men who want to change. At the time of this writing, three of the twelve men are still incarcerated. And of the ones who have been released, six are in Richmond and will visit our class.

STUDENT LEARNING OBJECTIVES

After this course, students should be able to

1. Determine how race, ethnicity, class, and gender figure into literary explanations about crime and prison;
2. Develop personal convictions about the causes of crime, the problems with prison, and the challenges of reentry to society;
3. Understand the limits as well as the potential of writing and rehabilitation;
4. Take action to address the crime/prison problem in a way commensurate with your own values, abilities, and time commitment.

Books

H. Bruce Franklin	*Prison Writing in 20th Century America*	0140273050
Jimmy Baca	*A Place to Stand*	9780902139085
Joe Loya	*The Man Who Outgrew His Prison Cell*	0060508930
Wally Lamb	*Couldn't Keep It to Myself*	006053429X
Mark Salzman	*True Notebooks*	0375727612
David Coogan	*The Prison Inside Me*	course reader*

Assignments

The following assignments are each worth one third of your grade. You are encouraged to meet with me, email, and share drafts as you go. And you may rewrite the first two papers for a better grade.

Prison Life Essay
Due: 10.6

Prison writers sometimes say that there's no difference between prison and society. Everything you have on the outside you have on the inside: an economy, vice and corruption, brutality, camaraderie, talent, etc. But prison writers also seem determined to show us how prison life differs from life on the outside; how the logic of prison changes the meaning of life (for the worse or for the better).

This assignment asks you to wrestle with this conundrum, realizing from the outset that there is no solving it. (I hope you'll agree that this is what makes it fun to write about.) It asks you to figure out how, why, under what circumstances prison merely extends (deepens, intensifies) the course of someone's life and how, why, under what circumstances, for which reasons, it changes their life.

There are many variables to consider here—many ways in which prison, argu-ably, changes or simply cuts a deeper groove in the pattern of life: the survival instinct, substance abuse, ethnic identity, racism, sexuality, materialism, spiritual-ity, power and authority, and so on. To focus your discussion, pick a few themes like these that seem related and compare the ways in which they play out in the lives we've studied so far.

The essay should be 7–9 pages, double-spaced. It should have a title and page numbers in the lower right-hand corner and follow MLA, APA, or Chicago Manual of Style, whichever you know best. It should discuss at least two of the three titles: *Prison Writing in 20th Century America*, *A Place to Stand*, or *The Man Who Outgrew His Prison Cell*. If you choose *Prison Writing in 20th Century America*, you need to discuss at least three different writers.

Activity Essay
Proposal Due: 9.3
Due: Essay Due 11.10 (negotiable)
Before I got the idea to teach Prison Writing at VCU, I was teaching writing at the city jail. It was my involvement—my activity—that led me to this subject and helped me form a point of view on it. In this assignment, I'd like you to play a variation on this theme; to take an idea or a conviction that you develop about crime and prison in this course and generate an inquiry about it.

You need to propose an activity to me by September 3rd and outline steps you will take throughout the semester to enact it. This is very important, as almost all options will require some planning. The point of the proposal is not to lock you in, but to get the ball rolling. You can always modify/change plans if you feel like it.

The following list gives you an idea of what you might do, but really, these are just suggestions. The goal is to choose something that you are comfortable doing that fits your schedule and your values; something compelling enough that you could write an essay about. By essay, I mean a piece of writing that introduces you and your journey toward understanding, partly through your direct engagement with it, and partly through your reading of the course material.

The essay should be 7–9 pages, double-spaced. It should have a title and page numbers in the lower right-hand corner and follow MLA, APA, or Chicago Manual of Style, whichever you know best. It should discuss at least three writers from the course. It may be turned in earlier or (with permission) later than November 10th, depending on the nature of your proposed activity.

To be crystal clear: this is not a report on work done or a long journal entry. It's an essay. It should have a point. Because I am grading the essay, not the activity, it doesn't matter how *much* time you devote to your activity. But it matters a great deal how you make sense of it. The smallest experiences can become incredibly interesting in nonfiction writing. And so-called "big" events can come across badly if they are not written about creatively. So take some time here. Put readers in your shoes so they can see what you saw and know the reasons why, learn what you're learning, and be satisfied. It's your journey into the idea, the experience, the readings. Make us want to go with you.

1. *Raise awareness about prisoner reentry.* On Saturday, September 26, a local nonprofit, Boaz and Ruth, will sponsor the third annual Long Walk to Freedom here in Richmond. It starts at the city jail, moves through downtown, includes speeches and info tables, the whole nine yards. They need participants and help recruiting more participants. A representative from Boaz and Ruth, Robert Gordon, will make a presentation in class. For more information, check www.LongWalkToFreedom.org. (Boaz and Ruth was recently honored at the White House by President Obama, along with other nonprofits that have innovative, entrepreneurial ways of helping ex-offenders.)

2. *Teach offenders or ex-offenders.* Offender Aid and Restoration, the nonprofit that helped me organize my writing workshop at the city jail, offers life skills classes in the city jail, job prep in their office downtown, and in other Virginia jails. They've got the curricula. All you have to do is get trained and (if you teach in one of the jails) fingerprinted. You do need to be 21 for this option. They're also pretty open to whatever volunteer work you would be most comfortable doing in their office *and* they're close to campus. Students from VCU and other universities have volunteered here before, writing resumes. No matter what you did for OAR, you'd get a window into the lives of ex-offenders. http://www.oarric.org/programs.asp

3. *Mentor juvenile delinquents.* Last semester, students from this class volunteered at the James River detention center in Powhatan, teaching a poetry workshop for boys: http://www.hsmm.aecom.com/MarketsAndServices/56/65/index.jsp. This went very well. More recently, I met Barry Green, the director of Juvenile Justice for the Commonwealth, who asked me to propose a writing workshop at one of the facilities for girls. If you have any interest in helping juvenile offenders with a creative writing workshop, either for boys or girls, please see me and we'll work up a plan.

4. *Advocate.* At the same event where I met Barry Green—a reading by Dwayne Betts, another ex-offender who was tried as a youth and served nine years—I learned about Families and Allies of Virginia's Youth: http://www.favyouth.org/home. Their goal is to end the insanity of sending fourteen-year-olds to adult prisons in Virginia. Their website is chock full of links on this issue. One is for the Don't Throw Away the Key campaign. I'm not sure what getting involved here would entail. But if you feel strongly about advocating on behalf of minors, it'd be worth contacting them and seeing what you could do.

5. *Do something practical.* Another organization that'd be into "doing" projects (like driving families of the incarcerated to visiting days, assisting with book drives for prisoners, helping with legislative-activism campaigns) is Resources

and Information to Help the Disadvantaged (RIHD): http://www.rihd.org/. I saw a documentary about prisoner abuse at the Red Onion facility in southern Virginia at an RIHD event, and my sense was that the staff was pretty open to any kind of support that would help the cause.

6. *Fight prison with art.* Raise awareness about the prison problem with your own art, music, drama, dance, graphic design, comic book writing, speech-ifying, op-ed writing, multi-media making. (Did I miss one?) I'm imagining a range of projects here from original music, sculptures and poems, all of it coming together as a public event or series of events on campus.

7. *Mentor women writers at Fluvanna Correctional Center* (in Virginia) *and research the effectiveness of writing workshops on rehabilitation.* This project, which will be led by a former member of Prison Writing (now a counselor at Fluvanna), is in the planning stages right now. See me for details.

Telling Your Story

We've all heard the phrase "I'm just a product of my environment." Or the opposite: "I didn't let my environment rule me!" We may have even used these phrases to describe ourselves or people close to us. But when you stop and ask just what it means, it's not entirely clear.

An environment, like "society," is an abstraction. "It" has no inherent capacity to do anything, because it's not clear what "it" is. And yet, before this class, didn't it feel like your environment created in you certain convictions about crime and prison? Didn't it feel like you came from somewhere, and that place made you who you are, enabling you to get to college while the boys in Salzman's book, the women in Lamb's, and the men in mine all ended up in prison? What is it, then, about your world that differs from the worlds of these people?

That's right! This time it's personal. But seriously, you need not divulge anything too personal to do this assignment well. Explaining the difference between your life and the lives in these books could take more of an essayistic turn. Likewise, when you start writing this piece, you may sense you have more to say about a family member or friend whose life seems more like the lives we've studied in this class than your life. That's totally fine. The key thing is to find a meaningful point of comparison to write about; to show readers how your ideas about life emerged alongside the lives in these books. Good evidence in your piece (as it is in the books) will come in the form of stories where you show readers the evolution of your character.

The essay should be 7–9 pages, double-spaced. It should have a title and page numbers in the lower right-hand corner and follow MLA, APA, or Chicago Manual of Style, whichever you know best. It should discuss at least four writers/characters from: *True Notebooks, Couldn't Keep It to Myself,* and *The Prison Inside Me.*

PART II

Working on the Outside

Building New Selves
and Strong Communities

The members of PCARE believe that the U.S. prison-industrial complex is a massive, multilayered, complicated nesting of institutions, ideas, laws, habits, investments, and daily practices. Whereas the essays in Part One addressed how our members work inside prisons, attempting to use educational and artistic settings as opportunities for pursuing personal growth and political engagement, the essays in Part Two explain how our members work in the communities impacted by prisons. Chapter Four thus examines the many ways incarceration impacts the families of prisoners and how these families strive to survive in the face of losing a loved one to prison. Chapter Five addresses a creative partnership among the courts, social services, prisoners, and their supporters, who, in a town in the Midwest, are working for justice by trying to build a pipeline to success for former prisoners. Chapter Six portrays how prisoners, following their return to free society, negotiate the labyrinth of hardships and opportunities that await them. Thus looking at families, courts, social-service providers, and prisoners and ex-prisoners, these essays illustrate how ending America's addiction to mass incarceration requires careful attention not only to prisons and prisoners, but also to the communities impacted by imprisonment. More than just critiques of problems within different aspects of the prison-industrial complex, these chapters offer hard-won lessons from PCARE members working for justice at the grassroots level.

CHAPTER 4

"Courtesy Incarceration"

Exploring Family Members' Experiences of Imprisonment

BRITTANY L. PETERSON,

BETH M. COHEN, AND RACHEL A. SMITH

Prelude

BRITTANY L. PETERSON

On Christmas Eve 2003, I remember nervously walking from the parking lot toward the imposing locked door of the local county jail. As we walked up, the locks clicked and we were allowed to go inside. The visit was short, only one hour in length. We sat on the hard metal immobile stools and looked at each other through double-paned glass. It was difficult to hear, so we leaned down against the cold steel shelf and talked directly into the small audio area. I was incredibly uncomfortable in the cramped, dirty, and poorly-lit room. Sixty minutes later, it was time to leave. We placed our hands up against the dirty glass as if to give each other a hug through the panes. And with that, we turned and walked, each in our separate directions, to spend Christmas Eve in vastly different environments. It was the first, but certainly not the last, Christmas Eve that my brother would spend behind bars, nor the last time I would visit him in prison.

As a scholar-practitioner and the first author on this piece, I aim for transparency when it comes to research on incarceration. My personal experiences shape the questions and areas of inquiry that we pursue in this chapter. These experiences have the ability to raise important questions that enliven research and help to make it meaningful. However, for research to be sustained and credible, that personal experience must be tempered by method and rigor. While some may perceive an irreconcilable tension between the profoundly "subjective" stance that comes from personal experience and the "objective" goals of a researcher, we argue that this juxtaposition is both common and nonproblematic.

To begin, the tension between objectivity and subjectivity is common. Corbin and Strauss explain that "each investigator enters the field with some questions or areas for observation, or will soon generate them" (1990, p. 6). Thus they acknowledge the improbability of entering a site without *any* ideas or questions but subsequently emphasize the importance of the researcher being open and able to let initial questions subside if the data point to other questions and constructs. Moreover, Glaser and Strauss (1967) suggest that scholars should acknowledge their role in the process because "certain ideas . . . can come from sources other than the data" (p. 6). Accordingly, "subjective" inspiration and experience are common in scholarly work.

This chapter is based on a collaborative effort designed to preserve the integrity and credibility of the research while capitalizing on the unique strengths that come with personal experience. Each methodological choice helps to balance and alleviate the tension between objectivity and subjectivity in scholarship. The juxtaposition of my "subjective" relationship to the prison system and our "objective" research goals provides a holistic approach to exploring the experiences of those with incarcerated loved ones in an effort to uncover and understand the communicative strategies used in these complex situations.

Introduction

The U.S. Department of Justice reports that nearly 7.2 million individuals are currently under the supervision of the justice system (probation, parole, jail, and prison), and nearly 2.3 million of those individuals are behind bars (Glaze, 2010). In this chapter, we explore the experiences and communication strategies of those who have loved ones in prison. In doing so, we strive to achieve three main aims. First, we challenge scholars to consider the importance and credibility of these often silenced voices in the system by giving their experience a name: *courtesy incarceration*. Second, we seek to uncover the communicative coping mechanisms used by loved ones to manage the often undesirable effects of incarceration on family and friends. We hope that this chapter will provide scholars with a new frame through which to study incarceration, practitioners with an important and overlooked group of individuals with which to engage dialogue, and families with a renewed sense of credibility that their struggles are real and important.

In order to achieve these aims, we first provide a brief overview of previous research on family members of the incarcerated. Next, we introduce the concept of courtesy incarceration and argue that family and friends of the incarcerated may experience its burdens and, consequently, find ways to manage them. In order to examine this claim, we present data from interviews with individuals in prison waiting rooms about their communication strategies through modified labeling theory (MLT) (Link, 1987; Link, Cullen,

Struening, Shrout, & Dohrenwend, 1989). We continue by exploring a second case, which offers insight into one communication tool for family and friends of the incarcerated, Prison Talk Online (PTO). We conclude the chapter by critiquing the idea of courtesy incarceration and challenging scholars to think in new and unique ways about families connected to incarcerated individuals. Finally, we provide suggestions and considerations for future research.

The Paradoxical Effects of Incarceration on Incarcerated Individuals and Family Members

In reviewing the literature in the fields of sociology, criminology, family studies, and communication on the intersection of prisons, incarceration, and the family, two themes became predominantly clear. The first theme that dominates prison literature focuses on the positive effects that family involvement has on incarcerated individuals. Often, these studies explore what mechanisms need to be in place in order for an incarcerated individual to have a successful prison experience and/or societal reintegration. Research demonstrates the family's role in prison adjustment (Jiang & Winfree, 2006), rehabilitation (Homer, 1979), recidivism (Bales & Mears, 2008; Hairston, 1988, 1991), reintegration (Flavin & Rosenthal, 2003), and even marriage stability (Lopoo & Western, 2005; Segrin & Flora, 2001).

The second theme focuses on the "collateral consequences" of incarceration (see Hagan & Dinovitzer, 1999). That is, scholars talk about the negative effects, costs, or consequences of imprisonment for those who are close to incarcerated individuals. Separation is one of the more overarching effects noted (Brooks & Bahna, 1994; Dodge & Pogrebin, 2001; Genty, 2003). This physical separation of families is often paired with childcare complications (Brooks & Bahna, 1994), financial hardships (Brooks & Bahna, 1994; Lowenstein, 1984; Swisher & Waller, 2008), spousal psychological distress (Green, Ensiminger, Robertson, & Juon, 2006), and spousal stress and stigmatization (Lowenstein, 1984; Radelet, Vandiver, & Berardo, 1983). Additionally, frustration with the lack of information about the prison system (Brooks & Bahna, 1994) and procedures (Sturges & Al-Khattar, 2009) as well as child cognitive delays (Poehlmann, 2005) and adjustment problems for children of incarcerated individuals (Lowenstein, 1986) all plague loved ones of the incarcerated.

These two themes provide a paradoxical picture. From the family members' perspective, the negative effects of incarceration are plentiful and painful. In contrast, research from the vantage point of the incarcerated highlights the overwhelming benefits of family interactions for those behind the barbed-wire fences.

Both themes focus on the effects of interpersonal communication, but not on the communication itself and how it may generate these positive or negative effects. This omission, in part, may be due to a lack of attention from these disciplines. For example, we searched articles published since 1970 in seven highly rated family studies and family communication journals[1] using the following terms: prison, prisoner, inmate, incarcerated, felon, and convict. In total out of more than 19,000 articles, we found twenty-three that directly discussed the intersection of families and prisons. In other words, around 0.12 percent of the articles published in these journals since 1970 have discussed these issues. The absence of articles on these topics is surprising considering the rise of popular discourse on prisons and incarceration that occurred during the same time period (e.g., "war on drugs," rising incarceration rates, politicization of prisons, etc.). Not surprisingly, however, most of the articles focus either on (1) the negative effects the prison system has on the family unit and/or (2) the benefits that incarcerated individuals experience if they have contact with or social support from their families.

Very few articles even broach the topic of communication, and those that do only peripherally consider the family members' communication strategies. Two articles in the family and communication journals addressed conflict tactics among inmates (Jones, Ji, Beck, & Beck, 2002) and communication implications for physical separation in marriage (Segrin & Flora, 2001). In other words, none of the articles specifically explored the actual communication strategies and processes that family members of the incarcerated use in order to manage their situations. Indeed, Murray (2005) came to a similar conclusion that "prisoners' families have been little studied in their own right" (p. 442).

Courtesy Incarceration

One of the reasons for this gap in communication and family studies could be related to the stigma surrounding imprisonment, for those behind bars and, in particular for this chapter, their connected loved ones. Indeed, this stigma-by-association already has been studied for correctional officers in workforce research. "Dirty workers" are known for being employed in occupations that are morally, socially, or physically degrading (Ashforth & Kreiner, 1999; Hughes, 1951; Tracy & Scott, 2006). In the prison system, correctional officers are often seen as doing "dirty work" since their jobs are viewed in one of two ways: effeminate baby-sitting or "brutish, deviant sexuality" (Tracy & Scott, 2006, p. 6). Tracy and Scott (2006) argue that correctional officers qualify as dirty workers because their jobs are physically disgusting and because they work with a stigmatized population. Specifically, because correctional officers must interact or communicate with incarcerated individuals daily, their positions also become tainted.

Goffman (1963) calls this phenomenon a "courtesy stigma." Courtesy stigma can occur when individuals are associated with stigmatized others, and consequently may share in some of the effects of that stigmatization. As a result, these individuals are extended the "courtesy" of stigma by association (Goffman, 1963). According to Birenbaum (1970), courtesy stigma can be attached to "friends or relatives of those publicly identified as . . . criminals, or mental patients," among other individuals and groups (p. 196). Other research shows that when incarcerated individuals are released from prison, the reintegrative shaming filters down to the family and specifically the children. That is, "in the absence of efforts to encourage reacceptance and reabsorption [of the incarcerated individuals into society], the stigma of imprisonment risks not only making parents into outlaws, but their children as well" (Hagan & Dinovitzer, 1999, p. 127). Those connected to incarcerated persons may experience, then, a *courtesy incarceration*. In other words, community members extend the same stigmatization often directed at inmates to those who have close relationships with them.

The original term *courtesy stigma* and our extension of it to *courtesy incarceration* may be viewed as ironic expressions. The word *courtesy* is typically understood to be an extension of positive thoughts, emotions, and actions. Conversely, when used in this context, it highlights the undesired and often inescapable effects of being associated with a stigmatized individual. In order to understand the term *courtesy stigma*, we turn to Goffman's original use of the term. Goffman (1963) begins by explaining that there are two different types of people who experience courtesy stigma: (1) "the own," which are "those who share his stigma and by virtue of this are defined and define themselves as his own kind" (e.g., incarcerated individuals), and (2) "the wise," or individuals "who are normal but whose special situation has made them intimately privy to the secret life of the stigmatized individual and sympathetic with it, and who find themselves *accorded a measure of acceptance, a measure of courtesy membership* in the clan" (p. 28, emphasis added). Family members of the incarcerated could be classified as "the wise."

Goffman (1963) goes on to discuss how "the wise" are often treated in a similar manner to those who experience the stigma directly:

> Thus the loyal spouse of the mental patient, the daughter of the ex-con, the parent of the cripple, the friend of the blind, the family of the hangman, are all obliged to share some of the discredit of the stigmatized person to whom they are related. One response to this fate is to embrace it, and to live within the world of one's stigmatized connection. . . . The individual with a courtesy stigma may find that he must suffer many of the standard deprivations of his courtesy group and yet not be able to enjoy the self-elevation which is a common defense against such treatment. (pp. 28–31)

At first glance, this group membership may appear to be anything but courteous. Nevertheless, while these individuals experience the pains of *stigma* by association, their newfound membership can also provide them with something positive: community, group support, and/or voice. In other words, family members of the incarcerated can be extended the courtesy of receiving support from similar others. For example, following one wife as she visits her incarcerated husband, Girshick (1994) writes: "We as prisoners' wives lead a double life. Nowhere are we free, not within the prison walls with our husbands, not outside in the 'free' society. I can only shake my head in wonder as to how we survive it all—the emotional and financial burdens, stress on our marriages, and undermining of our self-esteem" (p. 97). The wife in this narrative articulates the confining nature of her situation. However, she also hints that she is a part of something, "we as prisoners' wives." In this excerpt, it appears as though her courtesy-group membership provides her with an outlet or a venue of self-expression. She talks about how she is not free inside the prison nor in society, yet she is able to open up and express these sentiments to a sympathetic other, another "wise" individual, a researcher. While her affiliation with an incarcerated individual leads her to express frustrations with her own confining situation, she also seems to experience the "courtesy" aspect of membership that accompanies her circumstances. She shares her story and uses her voice. In this circumstance, that voice is heard and acknowledged.

Clearly, we are only now beginning to understand some of these processes. As such, this study attempts to explore how communication can mitigate, alleviate, moderate, or facilitate support for those who experience the "collateral costs and consequences of imprisonment" or courtesy incarceration (Hagan & Dinovitzer, 1999, p. 121).

Managing Courtesy Incarceration

We conducted two studies that explored the experiences of family members of the incarcerated in an effort to further understand courtesy incarceration's existence, manageability, and outcomes. In the first study, we explored the experiences of visitors of incarcerated individuals to understand how they might be experiencing courtesy incarceration and how they might use communication strategies, such as education, secrecy, or even withdrawal from interpersonal communication, to manage its anticipated effects. In the second study, we investigated the online communication strategies of members of an online prison support group to uncover the topics discussed by family members and friends of incarcerated individuals.

Case One: Visiting the Visiting Rooms

Aims and theoretical underpinnings. In this first case, we explore the experiences of people who visit incarcerated individuals in prison. We posit that these visitors experience courtesy incarceration and, as a result, seek out ways to manage their situations.

Modified Labeling Theory (MLT) provides a framework for this section (Link, 1987; Link et al., 1989), because it focuses on how people cope with anticipated and experienced stigmatization. Link and colleagues argue that people are socialized to associate stigmatized groups with stereotypes, to devalue stigmatized people, and to discriminate against them through interpersonal communication and mass media. *Devaluation* is defined as a loss of status, whereas *discrimination* is defined as extensive social distancing (Link, 1987). Labeling occurs when people are seen with a characteristic or engaging in a behavior that places them within a stigmatized group. Past research shows labels have been invoked, for example, by receiving psychological treatment (Link et al., 1989) or involvement in formal criminal proceedings (Bernburg, Krohn, & Rivera, 2006). People want to avoid being targets of stigmatization (Herek, 2007). Those individuals who find themselves in a situation in which they have conditions that can categorize them as members of a stigmatized group (i.e., labeled) anticipate these judgments of responsibility, the categorization and labeling, as well as the potential for devaluation-discrimination (Link, 1987; Link et al., 1989). Consequently, potential targets engage in coping strategies aimed at preventing negative reactions (Herek, 1996; Link, 1987; Link et al., 1989, Miller & Major, 2000; Smith, 2007). In MLT, these coping strategies include withdrawal, secrecy, and education.

MLT draws from Goffman's (1963) work and defines *withdrawal* as action taken to selectively expose oneself to only those people who accept the conditions associated with the stigma label (Angermeyer, Link, & Majcher-Angermeyer, 1987). *Secrecy* is defined as any action taken to attempt to conceal the distinguishing marks that would categorize one in a stigmatized group (Goffman, 1963; Herek, 1996; Link, Mirotznik, & Cullen, 1991; Smith, 2007). *Educating* is defined as "preventative telling" (Link et al., 1991, p. 304) or providing information in the hope of generating acceptance and warding off social rejection (Link et al., 1991; Peterset al., 2005).

Each of these strategies to manage anticipated stigmatization resulting from courtesy incarceration can restrict a labeled person's social network. For instance, if a labeled employee educates an employer, then he/she will likely stay with the accepting company (Link, 1987). By not extending oneself to new relationships, social networks become constricted, which has been associated with lower income, more unemployment, and lower self-esteem (Link, 1987). This first study attempts to ascertain if visitors of incarcerated persons anticipate courtesy incarceration in the form of devaluation and discrimination for visiting, and if they engage in communication strategies such as secrecy, withdrawal, or education to manage potential stigmatization.

Method

There were two primary research sites in this initial case, both in the midwestern United States. We assigned each prison a pseudonym to protect prison and interviewee identities. Before beginning the study, we worked with the Institutional Review Board (IRB) to ensure that all of the proper documents were in place to conduct research using this protected population. Additionally, the second author worked collaboratively with the prison administrators to create an action plan for conducting the investigational study within their facilities.

Careful attention was given to ensuring proper informed-consent procedures. All of the surveys contained two copies of full consent forms. One copy was for the participants; the other copy was for the researchers. In all cases, the consent forms were separated from the surveys, so the surveys could remain anonymous. The informed-consent documents provided an explanation of the study and gave the participants the option to continue with the survey or decline participation after reading. Additionally, when the second author was present at the sites, she verbally emphasized the voluntary nature of both the survey and follow-up interview. Upon completion, the participants deposited each of the documents into a locked drop box. Subsequently, the participants who elected to share more stories with the second author did so completely spontaneously and voluntarily after turning in the surveys, which preserved confidentiality.

The first prison, Caltron Prison, is a small, privately owned facility that houses about 250 prisoners. Its 108 cells accommodate both male and female prisoners, as well as those on work release. Incarcerated individuals are allowed one visit per week and must give twenty-four hours' notice by putting the visitor's name on the inmate's visitor request form. Caltron Prison has a low visitation rate and over the course of three months the second author collected a total of nine surveys and logged five hours of observation in the facility. The second author left surveys in the visitation room, and volunteer participants completed the forms. On four occasions the second author stayed in the visiting room and interviewed participants personally.

The second prison, Blaton Prison, is a small, privately owned prison that currently houses 300 prisoners. The facility accommodates both male and female prisoners and those on work release. Incarcerated individuals at Blaton Prison are allowed three one-hour visits per week. Prisoners must put a visitor's name on their visitation list, which can take three to five days for approval. In this facility, the second author sat in the visitation room and handed out surveys and performed personal interviews. Over a two-month period, the second author interviewed twelve participants and logged an average of twelve hours of observation.

The participants ($N = 21$) included both female ($n = 16$) and male ($n = 5$) and ranged in age from eighteen years to sixty-two years. The participants were White ($n = 18$), Hispanic/Latino ($n = 1$), and Unidentified ($n = 8$). They had the following relationships to the incarcerated individuals: girlfriend ($n = 8$), mother ($n = 5$), father ($n = 2$), stepfather ($n = 1$), brother ($n = 1$), aunt

($n = 1$), uncle ($n = 1$), grandmother ($n = 1$), cousin ($n = 1$). Using the scales developed by Link and colleagues, we investigated how visitors experienced labeling and coped with it (see Link, 1987; Link et al., 1989 for full scales and psychometric indicators).

Results

Labeling and courtesy incarceration. On average, visitors slightly disagreed that family members of incarcerated persons are discriminated against and devalued (see Table 1). However, visitors who know another person who is incarcerated ($n = 6$, $M = 3.83$, $SD = 1.16$) believed that family members experienced more discrimination and devaluation than those who did not know another incarcerated person ($n = 9$, $M = 2.22$, $SD = 1.07$), $t(13) = 1.61$, $p < .05$). That is, when visitors were connected to more than one incarcerated individual, they were more likely to report the presence of discrimination and devaluation than when they knew only one person who was incarcerated. Courtesy incarceration, then, seems to be more prominent when individuals are connected to more incarcerated individuals.

The qualitative results also support the presence of courtesy incarceration. Several of the visitors mentioned that when they came to the prison, they felt they were treated like prisoners themselves. Participants also talked about the strict rules they had to follow in order to visit a prisoner. When discussing this topic, they would make comments like "Why should I have to go through all these procedures? I'm not the inmate! I did nothing wrong."

Disclosure. Many participants ($n = 21$) did not disclose their connection to an incarcerated individual to everyone in their social network (see Table 1). Visitors reported that they would not tell their work associates (37%), boss (33%), parents (14%), and children (14%). The qualitative results suggest one rationale for this nondisclosure decision: shielding or protection. One father stated that he would not tell his other two sons in an attempt to "protect" them. On the other hand, participants reported telling their best friends (86%), siblings (71%), and friends (64%). In the qualitative data, participants talked about the reactions that met their disclosure. The data suggests that not all disclosures were met with support. Many of these disclosees would show support but not "get involved." Some disclosees were saddened by the visitor's situation, whereas others would say, "I don't understand how you are able to forgive the inmate." Still other disclosees would show disapproval, advise the visitor to move on, and say that they personally would never visit a prisoner.

Coping strategies. In terms of coping strategies, visitors were more likely to report using education to cope with stigmatization than withdrawal or secrecy (see Table 1). Although visitors reported greater use of education, disclosures about their incarcerated loved ones were strategic. That is, they communicated cautiously and often with a specific purpose in mind. For instance, one interviewee said, "I'm careful about telling people about my son being incarcerated, because people have made comments about what type of individuals are inmates." The qualitative results also highlight some of the specific communication messages that visitors of incarcerated individuals would share with others in their social network. For example, one mother reasoned why secrecy might be an option in some cases: "If it were a crime like, rape, I would keep it a secret." Moreover, participants discussed the withdrawal strategy as well. One interviewee said, "There are only a few [that I tell] and they really are just family, and they are just glad he's being supported."

Education. Finally, the participants talked about their education strategies in a variety of the following ways. Some would counsel others, "Don't be affected by negative stereotypes of prisoners." One woman stressed the "need to educate the public on prisons: their rules, structures, personnel and how inmates really are, not what is shown in the media." Another interviewee explained the need to educate society: "People just forget about the prisoners. Society just locks them away and forgets about them. They have no idea what they are really like, or the difficulty of the procedures to visit the inmate. Everyone thinks inmates are criminals and that is not always true. They are not bad people."

Discussion

The results of this study shed new light on the experiences of people who visit prisons. This preliminary case suggests that visitors of incarcerated individuals did not necessarily report that they were devalued or discriminated against, though they were more likely to recognize these negative outcomes if they were connected to more than one individual in the prison system. Arguably, visitors who communicate with more than one incarcerated individual might be more aware of the discrimination, devaluation, and courtesy incarceration than their less connected counterparts. Of note, the greatest privacy was held out for work associates.

Many of the participants in this study reported and elaborated on the education strategies that they used during the disclosure process, while few visitors reported use of secrecy or withdrawal. One reason that visitors may report lower personal use of withdrawal and secrecy can be explained by the third-person effect (Davison, 1983). Third-person effect is a coping method where users deflect a problem onto someone else, by acknowledging that other people in one's situation experience the problem, but they do not. In fact, several of the participants in this study said things like, "It may affect other visitors, and they may keep their visits a secret or not support the inmate, but that's not me."

Moreover, the methodology of this study might have affected the participants' discussion of their preferred coping strategies. During the interviews, the second author perceived a small amount of hesitation from some of the interviewees when answering her questions. In other words, it is possible that the social-desirability bias (Press & Townsley, 1998) could have influenced the visitor responses. Social desirability occurs when study participants respond in a way that would be viewed favorably by the researcher(s). This bias often leads participants to share more information that reflects on them positively and less information that reflects on them negatively.

The second author collected the surveys, performed many personal interviews, and was physically present in the prison facilities with many of the visitors. As such, the visitors were aware that she already knew that they were in some way connected to an incarcerated individual. The visitors did not need to disclose their status, as it was already apparent. In this situation, the social-desirability effect could have led participants to dismiss or gloss over any coping strategies they saw as undesirable from a researcher's perspective (e.g., secrecy) and highlight those that would be viewed as positive (e.g., education). In case two, we tried to address the possibility of this bias and decrease the likelihood of its occurrence by examining existing online narratives of family members of the incarcerated. Moreover, we explored the potential positive side of courtesy incarceration: the opportunity for support and ability to have a voice.

Case Two: Prison Talk Online

In case one, we saw a preliminary example of how family members and friends of incarcerated individuals use strategies consistent with modified labeling theory to manage their situations. Accordingly, in case two we wanted to take a closer look at one particular communication avenue available to these individuals. This case was specifically designed to find out more about the online communication strategies and topics discussed by family members and friends of incarcerated individuals. One guiding research question informed our study: In what ways do Prison Talk Online (PTO) members use the website to communicate?

Method

A Google search for the exact phrase "prison support groups" yielded nearly 30,000 hits and twenty-five potentially pertinent websites. Each website was evaluated based on the following criteria: length of time established, authenticity, nature/purpose, and anonymity. Using these criteria, the Prison Talk website was the most appropriate location to serve the needs of this study. Not only was it the largest and oldest of the support sites surveyed, it was designed by a real "ex-con" for the purposes of supporting families on the outside. "Fed-Ex," a pseudonym for the site creator, outlines his vision for the site:

The Prison Talk Online web community was conceived in a prison cell, designed in a halfway house, and funded by donations from families of ex-offenders, to bring those with an interest in the prisoner support community a forum in which their issues and concerns may be addressed by others in similar circumstances and beliefs.... PTO's goal is to bridge the communication barrier that exists in and around the criminal "justice" system today and bring everyone in the prisoner support community closer together to effect change in policy, prisoner rights, sentencing and so much more. (PrisonTalk Online, 2011)

PTO's emphasis on "bridging communication barriers" and bringing members of the "prisoner support community closer together" makes it an especially relevant site to study communication strategies and topics discussed by those who have loved ones in prison.

Anonymity provided another justification for using the PrisonTalk Online website. PTO's policy forbids individuals to post personal information (e.g., phone number, email address) online, and moderators are in place to enforce the community rules. Posts reveal only members' pseudonyms and locations. PTO states that this policy is in place to protect members' safety.

In sum, the PTO website met the above criteria and therefore was the most appropriate location for this study. Data were collected over a two-week period (twenty-five hours' total collection time). This process resulted in 105 pages of single-spaced data, 60,273 words, and 198 unique narratives (from individual posters).

Analytical Framework

This study employed a grounded theoretical approach (Glaser & Strauss, 1967), where one of the goals of the study is to "make sense of" (Denzin & Lincoln, 2000, p. 3) and explore the online narratives of family members/friends of the incarcerated to understand how PTO functions as a site of social support. While grounded theorists may draw on prevailing literatures and theories, most fundamentally they produce an analysis that is rooted or grounded in the data itself (Charmaz, 2000). Accordingly, this study was devised to create a substantive theoretical interpretation of the online social support for those in socially stigmatized situations.

In order to meet these aims, the first author analyzed the data using the constant comparative method (Glaser & Strauss, 1967; see also Strauss & Corbin, 1990). She engaged in several rounds of open and axial coding, wrote theoretical memos, reviewed existing literature, and conducted analytical checks (Corbin & Strauss, 1990). The narratives were first analyzed using an open, emic coding process (Lindlof & Taylor, 2002). During this first step, each thought, idea, word(s), and sentence(s) was assigned a representative category. Each piece of data was placed in either existing categories or new categories until all of the data were coded and category saturation was reached (Bryant & Charmaz, 2007). This process yielded sixty initial categories (e.g., ties to family, inspirational stories, personal disclosure, judgment of others).

The first author also engaged in several rounds of axial coding to help draw links between categories, create new categories, and rename or collapse categories where the data deemed it appropriate (Strauss & Corbin, 1998). Data were compared within and across categories, examined within categories, and scrutinized for distinctions between created categories. The axial coding processes yielded fifteen broad categories, two of which were relevant to this case. Throughout the data-analysis process, the author employed the precepts of analytic rigor.[2]

Results

In this case we sought to explore the various ways that PTO members used the website to communicate. Two predominant themes emerged. First, the members used the website to express their experiences of courtesy incarceration to others who would likely understand their struggles. Second, the members used the website to create new relationships online perhaps to overcome and manage their courtesy incarceration. These relationships also begin to shed light on the positive effects of courtesy incarceration. That is, the narratives highlight the presence of support and opportunity for voice.

Express courtesy incarceration. The first prominent theme that emerged from the data was that PTO members communicated in this forum to talk about their courtesy incarceration and related feelings and emotions associated with managing potential devaluation and discrimination associated with their relationships. Members of PTO noted that their friends and family members on the outside were, at best, not helpful or unsupportive and, at worst, unapologetically critical and adamantly against the member's relationship with an incarcerated loved one.

Some PTO members simply stated in a factual tone that they didn't have anyone to support them, showing the restricted networks predicted by MLT. That is, PTO members found it challenging to identify friends or family members willing to talk about their stigmatizing situation for fear of judgment. For example, "Lady Dee" talks about how many family and friends are unsupportive of her relationship: "Most of my friends and family would not understand, let alone support, my decision to befriend someone in prison, especially someone that I didn't know on the outside." Similarly, "KyChika" shared her daily strife as she struggled to survive under the roof of an unsupportive mother:

> The man has made his way back inside the gates once again . . . He's doing really well this time. He's handling things great. This will be the longest stretch he's ever pulled, but he's keeping his head up. He's been attending church in

jail, and tells me that he wants to get married and "do things right" when he gets out. All I can do is pray for the best and support him while he's in there ... My son and I currently live with my mother, which is hard, because we rarely get along. She absolutely loathes Anthony, which has put a strain on our relationship, but we make it. We've been together 4 years now, and she's hated every day of it.

In the example above, the PTO member seemed caught between her relationship with her mother and her child's father. With no support system to sustain their relational needs, these individuals seemed to experience their own devaluation and discrimination because of their relationships. Moreover, society in general also reinforced the feelings of courtesy incarceration.

PTO members expressed their feelings of confinement, persecution, judgment, and rejection by people they hardly knew. One individual in particular, "Vidalouise," explained how she kept "everything inside to prevent a lecture," showing the strategy of withdrawal in MLT. The freedom to share her story was not a luxury she felt she could enjoy; the member was likely experiencing some of the constraints of courtesy incarceration.

In an evocative example, "Cjay5929" explained the pains associated with her own struggle with stigmatization:

I have no one in my corner. I love this man sooooo much and will support him through this until the day we can be together and go on with our life. I'm sure others can relate to the dirty looks from people and whispering behind your back at work when they find out your man is in PRISON!!! Everyone assumes your some pathetic loser that's the scum of the earth because you love someone who made a mistake. I was raised by wonderful parents that taught me not to be so judgmental.

The language "Cjay5929" used has undertones of judgment, courtesy incarceration, and discrimination. The narrative suggests that she felt like she was on the outskirts of society and experienced a world of incarceration all her own.

The members of PTO used the website to communicate their feelings about courtesy incarceration. They discussed their struggles and perceptions of judgment. In addition to sharing these feelings, the members talked about creating new relationships online.

Virtually created relationships. As part of the PTO community, members developed online or "virtually created" relationships, perhaps to meet their support needs and to cope with courtesy incarceration. Thus relationship creation, or development, emerged as the second prominent theme in this virtual community, suggesting that these relationships are an important support strategy for managing courtesy incarceration. The PTO members talked about other members as both friends and family.

Friends. Family members of the imprisoned often expressed their gratitude to have found a place where they could meet new friends who understood what they were going through. Frequently, PTO members talked of how they were excited, relieved, and beside themselves to finally have new friends who could relate to their experiences. The following excerpt by "G-Gal" clearly illustrates the excitement and joy connected with these virtually created friendships:

> This is my first time here at prisontalk. Let me say, I'm so happy 2 b here!! I'm looking forward 2 sharing the information i have learned, and also absorbing any u have 2 offer. I'm excited to meet friends that understand the situation we r living in and how difficult some days can b!! Make everyday count!! looking forward 2 meeting.

Another PTO member, "Moleta," showed her supportiveness as she invited other members into a relationship with her in order to experience true community and friendship:

> I love to get to know new people and I will be here for anyone anywhere who needs to laugh, cry, vent, or even scream! The way I see it, no matter who we are, or what our individual circumstances . . . we are all in this together . . .

The expression of emotions such as laughing, crying, venting, and screaming usually occurs when individuals are true friends. Most people do not share such emotions with mere acquaintances. The excerpt demonstrates how the members of PTO provided one another with emotional support (Cutrona, Suhr, & McFarlane, 1990). In sum, the members of the PTO community created virtual friendships, while perhaps attempting to free themselves from the bonds of courtesy incarceration.

Family. PTO members occasionally claimed to share an even stronger bond, that of family. The woman in the following example not only had a loved one behind bars, but worked within the prison system, as well. In the following example, she explained how she assists others in her situation in order to aid PTO family members in need. "His4ever" writes:

> So to my PTO family, if you want info on a specific loved one, without posting it feel free to send me a private message. Of course I will respond with information that would not jeopardize your loved one or my position. I am not looking for ANYTHING, just to help my pto family. If I can't help I will direct you to someone that can.

The PTO member in this example stated that she wanted nothing in return, only to help out her PTO family. The kind of selfless love that many individuals have for blood relatives came across clearly between members of the PTO community. Thus individuals in the PTO community expressed sentiments of courtesy incarceration, and they turned to the online community to cope by virtually creating new relationships.

Discussion

In case two, family members of the incarcerated constantly battled to understand the reality of their courtesy incarceration. Dealing with the judgment of society, friends, and family, these individuals used the PTO website to communicate their experiences. "Fed-Ex," creator of the PTO, put it best when he said, "We needed a forum where our families and those that care could *come together with a united voice*, one that the administration would hear better," and so it was that PTO became a virtual reality (PTO, 2010, emphasis added). The examples above demonstrate how the members of PTO were able to seek out relationships in an effort to experience the potential positive side of courtesy incarceration. That is, they were able to have a voice, and they were able to support one another.

The PTO website provides an important communication opportunity for family members and friends of incarcerated individuals to receive support and share their stories. It provides anonymity and decreases the costs of self-disclosure. First, the PTO website affords users the ability to be relatively anonymous, where *anonymity* is defined as "the condition of not being identifiable to the other person" (Derlega & Chaikin, 1977, p. 109). Bargh, McKenna, and Fitzsimons (2002) state that anonymity is key because it

> enables one to express oneself and behave in ways not available in one's usual social sphere, both because one is free of the expectations and constraints placed on us by those who know us, and because the costs and risks of social sanctions for what we say or do are greatly reduced. (p. 35)

PTO members expressed their inability to share their thoughts, feelings, and experiences with friends and family in their usual social circle due to courtesy incarceration. However, the members of PTO seemed perfectly able to express themselves online "free of the expectations and constraints" of the face-to-face world (Bargh et al., 2002, p. 35). One member explained her exasperation with her social circles and their expectations in the following example:

> I live in Oklahoma where a lot of the people here are very conservative and can't understand why a woman would want to be with a man that's incarcerated. They assume he's a monster although they don't know all the facts. Ignorance irritates the bejesus out of me.

This example highlights members' frustration with the constraints of courtesy incarceration and demonstrates why individuals might want the anonymity afforded online. Thus anonymity is one quality that makes PTO an especially useful communication tool.

Second, the Internet and websites like PTO decrease the perceived costs of self-disclosure. In face-to-face interactions, the cost of disclosing taboo information about oneself, even to friends and family, is high (Derlega, Metts, Petronio, & Margulis, 1993; Pennebaker, 1990). Interestingly, the costs lessen considerably when self-disclosure occurs outside of one's typical social circle (Derlega & Chaikin, 1977). PTO members' narratives appeared to affirm this assessment. Members articulated the lack of support they experienced from those they know, often juxtaposed with the overwhelming support offered on the site. "ShaadyGryl" explained it this way: "PTO is a major part of my support system due to the fact that my family is against my relationship with him." Accordingly, the physical separation that online support groups provide could potentially decrease the perceived costs of self-disclosure and courtesy incarceration associated with conversations in face-to-face settings.

In summary, the anonymity and the decreased costs of self-disclosure that the PTO website provides could be particularly useful for those individuals experiencing courtesy incarceration. The website and stories therein highlight the "courtesy" aspect of courtesy incarceration. That is, PTO members were able to experience support of the "wise," or those who would accept one's situation, while sharing their stories and using their voice (Goffman, 1963).

A Critical Examination of Courtesy Incarceration

Throughout this chapter we have used the term *courtesy incarceration* to name the stigma and labels that can be attached to loved ones of the incarcerated. However, this term, like any classification system or category, has both its weaknesses and strengths. *Courtesy incarceration* is a pithy yet also ironic term meant to evoke the circumstances and experiences of those whose friends and family members are in prison. These individuals suffer from their group membership but also receive support because of that affiliation. Yet using ironic terminology could hamper some people's ability to take the issue seriously. We then run the risk of trivializing an important issue, something we absolutely do not want to do.

Still, we argue that the term *courtesy incarceration* is the most appropriate name for this phenomenon, in that it most accurately describes what so many individuals experience: a feeling of being incarcerated right alongside their family members or loved ones. The results of case one seem to indicate that people experience this "courtesy" to an even greater extent when they know more than one incarcerated individual. In addition, the word *courtesy* highlights the inherent irony of the situation. That is, as society tries to punish those individuals who are convicted by the courts, they also extend that punishment to the family. Innocent family members are caught up in the web of the prison system against their will. By trying to protect law-abiding citizens from the "criminals," the system is unintentionally extending family members the "courtesy" of incarceration, or stigmatization and punishment, by association. The word *incarceration*, on the other hand, emphasizes the severity of the situation. The narratives cited in the second case offer evidence that the language of oppression is present in online conversations as family members of the incarcerated lament their current situations. These family members appear to be experiencing the ill, stigmatization, and often raw pains associated with incarceration. While their incarceration may not be physically binding, it is emotionally, mentally, and communicatively confining.

In the discussion above, the term *courtesy incarceration* functions most fundamentally as an ironic term. Yet membership in the courtesy group also includes a few positive, or "courteous," benefits. Membership in this group, albeit not always pleasant, allows individuals to have a voice and provides them with an outlet for self-expression and support. Many of the participants in this study talked about how they felt confined and unable to share the story of their son's, daughter's, or parent's incarceration with outside family members and friends. However, these same individuals opened up and shared their stories on the PTO website. Their courtesy membership in the stigmatized group provided them with a place where they could lift their voices, vent their frustrations, share their stories, and ultimately be heard and supported by similar others. Thus there is some small degree of actual courtesy involved in the experience of courtesy incarceration.

The fact remains that much of the scholarship to date does not acknowledge or discuss these issues beyond the negative effects of incarceration for the family. Naming this phenomenon may empower scholars to investigate these issues and the various communication strategies that might provide relief for family members and friends of incarcerated individuals. In fact, the term *courtesy incarceration* carries some distinct benefits. First, for those scholars familiar with Goffman's (1963) work on courtesy stigma, this jump to *courtesy incarceration* is an easy and discernable application. The use of this term could open up this interest area to scholars beyond those familiar with criminal-justice issues. It could allow those scholars with a specialization in stigma or family communication to enter the conversation. Moreover, adding other voices to the discussion could allow scholars to better equip those experiencing courtesy incarceration with useful communication strategies for success. Finally, once we begin talking about these issues openly, family members and friends of the incarcerated will be able to see that they are not alone.

Future Research Directions

Future research should consider how a phenomenon known as the *digital divide* threatens the effectiveness of reach for family members of the incarcerated. Digital-divide research suggests that minorities and individuals of lower socioeconomic status are less likely to have access to the Internet (Norris, 2000; Schiller, 1996; Strover, 2003). Yet these same individuals are incarcerated at higher rates than the rest of the population (West, 2010). Accordingly, future research should examine how PTO and other similar sites can be modified to reach a much broader audience.

Further, we need to consider what communication research can do to help families and inmates cope with the stigma of incarceration. Paradoxically, while incarcerated individuals clearly benefit from familial interaction, family members often suffer. The first step may simply be to recognize and provide forums in which to recognize and support family members' experiences as supporters. Support groups, both traditional and online, could offer one avenue for social support and communicative coping for those struggling to manage the stigma or courtesy stigma associated with their situations. Additionally, Nichols (Chapter Six) also suggests that formerly incarcerated individuals can combat the negative stereotypes by giving back to their communities.

Moreover, scholars and practitioners should consider the role recidivism plays in the lives of the family members. Families can also find themselves unexpectedly thrown back into the system as they struggle to follow the countless rules and regulations. Thus together we should explore possible communicative coping strategies to help families manage their readjusted realities. One strategy to ease the reintegration process and possibly avoid recidivism might be to expand the use of problem-solving courts. As Faris explains (Chapter Five), these courts aim to gradually reintroduce incarcerated individuals to their communities with oversight and support.

In this chapter, we have made the argument that courtesy incarceration is a real phenomenon, experienced by real people, who need real communicative support. While we believe we have achieved our aim to bring these topics into the light, collectively, we wonder if this chapter would be received differently if we had studied family members of individuals who struggle with cancer, eating disorders, or other more socially acceptable, less stigmatized conditions. We contemplate the reality that courtesy incarceration may not strike some individuals as the "real problem" that it truly is. Accordingly, we implore communication scholars to consider the silenced voices, less obvious conditions, and unseen situations as they very well may be the ones most in need of our attention and our help.

Postscript

In September of 2010, my brother was released from prison, and the courtesy incarceration held on strong. Mom and Dad continued to stay silent about his time behind bars. Moreover, they would not talk about the ten-year parole sentence and its influence on their lives. They explained that the incarceration of a loved one is something you just cannot escape—or, as my mom often says, "You can run, but you can't hide." Unfortunately, my family has found out that statement could not be truer.

On January 2, 2011, things changed dramatically. Through a series of circumstances, and a clear parole violation, my brother was back behind bars. After several months in jail, my brother was sentenced to an additional two and a half years in prison, where he still sits as I type these words. Each time this cycle of incarceration repeats, it is a gut-wrenching experience for our family.

While my parents have returned to the hard, metal, immobile stools of the jail visiting room once a week, my family members all metaphorically sit with him daily. Together we bear the cross of courtesy incarceration as we struggle to have our voices heard and, sometimes, strive to keep them silent. As such, the challenge to scholars and practitioners is to amplify and acknowledge voices like those of my family. Moreover, we need to equip those experiencing courtesy incarceration with communication strategies and tactics to manage the clearly documented negative effects from which they may try to run but ultimately cannot hide.

Table 1. Case One. Responses by Visitors in Prison Visiting Rooms: Descriptive Statistics and Correlations Among Variables

	M	SD	Range	1.	2.	3.	4.	5.	6.
1. Devaluation-discrimination	2.87	1.34	4.58	—					
2. Know others	.43	.51	1.00	.61	—				
3. Disclosure	1.07	1.33	4.00	.25	.31	—			
4. Education	5.12	0.64	2.00	.12	−.16	−.42	—		
5. Secrecy	1.62	0.85	2.50	.18	−.16	.51	−.07	—	
6. Withdrawl	2.87	1.32	4.60	.29	.21	.05	−.35	−.27	—
7. Age	40.93	14.86	44.00	−.23	−.17	.04	.12	.08	−.19

Notes

1. Journals surveyed included *Family Relations, Journal of Child and Family Studies, Journal of Family Communication, Journal of Family Issues, Journal of Family Psychology, Journal of Marriage and Family,* and *Journal of Social and Personal Relationships.*

2. Through the course of the data collection and analysis, the first author carefully employed the processes of reflexivity, negative case sampling, and memo writing (Altheide & Johnson, 1998, Glaser, 1978; Johnson, 1999; Strauss, 1987). Additionally, the first author acted solely as an observer during the data-collection process and took steps to ensure that the data guided the analysis.

CHAPTER 5

Serving Time by Coming Home

Communicating Hope
through a Reentry Court

JERALYN FARIS

Ben[1] had been a participant in a reentry Problem Solving Court (PSC) for a month when he stood at a podium in the courtroom for his weekly conversation with the judge. I listened, observed, and wrote field notes as Ben and the other nineteen participants took their turns interacting with the judge. Ben had served eleven years of a twenty-four-year sentence and volunteered to participate in the reentry-court program in order to be released from prison early. The judge opened the conversation with a positive tone: "I'm hearing good things about you. How do you feel you are doing?" Ben's response increased my sympathy for his situation: "I'm finally getting adjusted to being out from behind bars, but it's been the scariest time of my life. I'm thankful for this program. It gives transition. I have to tell you that when I'm out looking for a job, out in the community, I can't breathe until I step back into work release.[2] The positive things that I have to hold on to are my faith, my recovery, and my family." Two weeks later, after being placed in his own apartment,[3] Ben returned to the PSC and read an essay he had written:

> I have hoped and prayed for this day for many years. But I didn't realize the challenges or fear that would come with it. It's a new chapter in my life with new expectations and trials but with hope and optimism. After so many years of having no say-so about who I lived with, where I lived, or how I lived, it has been a big adjustment to make those choices and decisions. I am stepping up to a role of being responsible and accountable instead of being needy. I'm learning to live again—free, clean, and sober and somewhat independently. My first night in my apartment was filled with anticipation, excitement, and overwhelming joy. I opened every closet, every cabinet and every drawer repeatedly just to exercise that freedom to do so. I couldn't sleep in the bedroom. The space was overwhelming, so I took my sheets, blanket, and pillow and slept on the bathroom floor. It was more like the space of my prison cell

and I just needed that. I'm not ashamed of my vulnerability but will use it to help me to stay grounded and with humility. I'm grateful for God giving me this new perspective on life and the ability to live it.

Ben tells of the struggles he faced as one stripped of much of his autonomy while in prison, and of the post-incarceration challenges of transitioning to freedom and regaining his agency—this is a narrative of "learning to live again." As McCann (this volume, Chapter Nine) suggests, orienting the public toward anything remotely resembling a prison abolitionist politics will first require efforts to humanize the incarcerated. Indeed, because Ben wants to move beyond the numbness of incarceration, he confesses his fears and vulnerability while declaring his intention to rebuild his life by becoming "responsible and accountable instead of being needy." These reentry-court discourses afforded Ben a public forum, and I was proud of him for taking the first steps in mastering basic communication skills to reestablish his place as a citizen. As we shall see, Ben's lived experience in reentry court is rooted in what Foucault (1980/1993) calls the "art of governing," which utilizes a "subtle integration" of coercion and self-agency (p. 204).

Ben and his peers in the reentry court are among the approximately 730,000 individuals released annually from U.S. federal and state prisons. Over 67 percent of those people will be rearrested within three years (West, Sabol, & Greenman, 2011). A reentry PSC is a strategy designed by practitioners and social-reform scholars to release prisoners early and assist them with holistic rehabilitation as they return home. The court is labeled "problem solving" because it responds comprehensively to substance-abuse issues, employment and housing needs, mental and physical health care problems, educational opportunities, family traumas (including rebuilding responsibilities to dependents), and the myriad other daily needs and events that make transition from incarceration to freedom so complicated. These alternative courts operate at the intersection of social policy and criminal justice, with various agencies collaborating to provide services and assistance to court participants (Casey, 2004; Travis, 2007).

While reentry is a part of the criminal-justice system and "doing time," a reentry PSC is also an effort to reform the prison-industrial society. Working for justice as an engaged communication scholar, I offer a critical account of the communicative processes of one reentry PSC and experience the same tension recognized by Brittany Peterson and her colleagues in this volume—a tension between the "subjective" of personal experience and the "objective" of research goals. My fifteen years as a chaplain to women in a large county jail, four years of ethnographic study of a reentry court, participant observation, and direct involvement in the court's operation provide a nuanced view of the processes, relationships, and outcomes for prisoners reentering the community. I implicate myself in this project as I work alongside Ben and his cohorts, the judge, and other members of the reentry team. The reentry court is much more to me than a site of research, for I have a strong sense of calling to engage this stigmatized community, which is full of those whom Hartnett (2010) depicts as "literally doomed, a permanent caste of surplus bodies" (p. 69). During one of our PSC sessions, our county prosecutor cordially referred to me as the "bleeding heart" on the team, but I am much more than that, for I serve as co-coordinator of the reentry court and as the liaison with officials of the Indiana Judicial Center to ensure that we meet state requirements for certification and maintain eligibility for funds from the Indiana Housing Authority. I collect, type, and store the handwritten essays of the ex-prisoners, host biweekly dinners for them, and mentor some of the women in the program—like Ben, I am enmeshed in the PSC's layered modes of coercion, empowerment, and community building.

This chapter explores the deep power structures whereby the reentry court shapes ex-prisoners' experiences and navigation of court boundaries and surveillance as they become both disciplined and agentic in their (potential) path to becoming contributing citizens. My premise is that the PSC demonstrates Foucault's art of governing by creating a "subtle integration" of coercion and agency via its communicative organization. To pursue these claims, this chapter begins with a brief overview of PSC development in the United States' criminal-justice system and places particular emphasis on the emergence of reentry PSCs. Second, I describe a local reentry court, including a listing of its social actors and their various roles and relationships, and explain the types of discourse central to the process of the court's work. Third, I explain the co-production of power within the court's dealings. Fourth, I address Ben's nineteen-month journey through the reentry-court program and describe his performance of a subtle dance that mingles self-agency and coercion.

My research is rooted in the contention that engaged communication scholars can collaborate with those involved in efforts to reform the criminal-justice system, *both* those who are practitioners in the system and those who have experienced it from the inside of a prison. Therefore, as this chapter unfolds, I implore academics, criminal-justice practitioners, and prisoners to consider the salience of reentry in the prison-industrial social fabric. Throughout the chapter, I pursue one fundamental question: Is the reentry-court model a viable means of redeeming stigmatized men and women from the prison-industrial complex and, therefore, worthy of expansion? Or does the reentry court need to be exposed and dismantled as an extension of the power structure of that complex? I present this inquiry as part of what Hartnett (2008) refers to as "the radical project of exploring the edges of what is possible," a phrase borrowed from Salah-El, founder of the Coalition for the Abolition of Prisons. Hartnett argues that "working toward abolition means creating structures that reduce the demand and need for prisons" (p. 521). As I unravel the dynamic process of the reentry PSC, I explore the edges of what is possible and find that it is one way to weave a new design, one that overlays or perhaps replaces threads of coercion with threads of self-agency, thus helping to create a tapestry of hope with and for those who are coming home.

Reentry Problem-Solving Courts

Rehabilitation remained an ideal in the U.S. criminal-justice system until the late 1960s. A number of authors chronicle the decline of its popularity (Allen, 1981; Applegate, 2000; Bayer, 1981; Cullen & Gilbert, 1982) by describing the attacks that came from opposite ends of the political spectrum. Conservatives perceived a breakdown in the social order (e.g., civil rights and anti–Vietnam War riots), while liberals observed the same events as evidence of the abuse of government power. Conservatives asserted that rehabilitation had been a means of coddling criminals; liberals, on the other hand, posited that "correctional officials could not be trusted to act benevolently under the ideal of rehabilitation" (Applegate, 2000, p. 19). Thus both ends of the political spectrum joined in a strange marriage to reject rehabilitation and embrace a movement toward consistently tougher punishments for offenders (the conservative version) and less freedom of judicial discretion (the liberal response).

In 1974, sociologist Robert Martinson entered the mêlée, publishing an influential article that painted a bleak picture of rehabilitative programs, leaving the impression that "nothing works." He concluded that "with few and isolated exceptions, rehabilitative efforts that have been reported so far have no appreciable effect on recidivism" (1974, p. 25). For years, policy makers and citizens agreed with Martinson's analysis, and suspicion reigned with regard to any efforts at reform, but others have contested his analysis, and a heated debate has continued. Douglas Lipton (1995), director of the research that Martinson's article summarized, lamented that "the belief that 'nothing works' still enjoys widespread acceptance and is one of the main reasons drug treatment programs are given low priority despite high recidivism rates, especially among drug-abusing offenders" (p. 14). Other researchers (Andrews & Bonta, 2003; Andrews, Bonta, & Hoge, 1990; Cullen, Wright, Gendreau, & Andrews, 2003) were undeterred in developing models for prison interventions that have proven effective and so, over time, attempts to provide community-based alternatives to prison-based rehabilitation have developed. Indeed, the advent of drug courts in the 1990s was followed by the development of several other types of PSCs, including reentry PSCs. Perhaps most important, reentry courts emerged as social scientists and the judiciary worked together to understand theoretically and empirically that crime and drug- or substance-abuse problems are highly correlated with a host of additional social problems (Miller & Johnson, 2009; Travis, 2007) related to education, unemployment, poverty, homelessness, public health, and family (Barnett & Mencken, 2002; Freudenberg, 2001; Oh, 2005; Room, 2005; Wenzel, Longshore, Turner, & Ridgely, 2001). Because non-court reentry programs are often focused on a single dimension, such as unemployment, they cannot respond effectively to the multitude of issues faced by prisoners returning home; in contrast, PSCs offer more comprehensive and holistic routes to post-incarceration empowerment.

The Office of Justice Programs, a branch of the Department of Justice (DOJ), launched the Reentry Court Initiative in 2000, when nine states (California, Colorado, Delaware, Florida, Iowa, Kentucky, New York, Ohio, and West Virginia) were chosen to host pilot sites (see Lindquist, Hardison, & Lattimore, 2003). Individualized strategies tested reentry courts in their communities while following a core set of components (e.g., assessment and planning, active oversight, management of supportive services, accountability to community, graduated and parsimonious sanctions, and rewards for success). The evaluation of the sites three years later (Lindquist et al., 2003) revealed great variation in the programs that had been adapted to "accommodate the unique legal, political, and community context in which they operate" (p. 56). These PSCs therefore embody a major shift in criminal-justice policy away from in-prison rehabilitation efforts and toward community-based responses meant to address the exceptionally high needs of reentering ex-prisoners and to enhance community safety (Travis, Solomon, & Waul, 2001).

Based on preliminary results, the state chief justices of the United States, professionally organized as the Conference of Chief Justices, unanimously endorsed the PSC model and formed a committee dedicated to the concept (Becker & Corrigan, 2002). However, in 2003, they passed a resolution (#13) calling for an evaluation of PSCs, noting that "there has been no national longitudinal impact evaluation of these courts" (Conference of Chief Justices, 2003). In response, a rigorous five-year study, the Multi-Site Adult Drug Court Evaluation (MADCE), is currently being conducted by the Urban Institute (UI), Research Triangle Institute (RTI) International, and the Center for Court Innovation (CCI) on behalf of the National Institute of Justice (NIJ), the research arm of the DOJ. The purpose of this study is "to analyze the effects of different drug court models on participant outcomes" (Lindquist, 2011). The hope is that MADCE will provide evidence as to whether or not PSCs reduce recidivism. While these large-scale research projects are designed to cull empirical evidence for the effectiveness (or not) of PSCs, my research focuses on the impact of the court's practices on individual participants' lives by scrutinizing Ben's case. As we shall see, Ben's journey through the PSC offers heartrending insights into how one former prisoner sought to rebuild his life while negotiating the court's "subtle integration" of coercion and agency.

The Tippecanoe County Reentry Problem-Solving Court

In 2005, a circuit court judge in Tippecanoe County initiated plans for a reentry PSC. From his bench he was well positioned to see who came into court over and over again over a period of years, and who was caught in the revolving door of the criminal-justice system. A sociology professor designed the program, and a team of people including the professor, judge, prosecutor, and other community stakeholders delineated its structure, procedures, and policies. This team of people took power into their own hands, so to speak, and in November 2005, the first participant was admitted into the program. At the time of this writing, the Tippecanoe County Reentry Court (TCRC) has been in existence a little over five years. During that time, there have been a total of eighty-two participants, with forty-two having graduated, twenty-three expelled, and seventeen currently participating. Of the forty-two graduates, six have been rearrested (TCRC case manager, personal correspondence, January 20, 2011). The recidivism rate for reentry-court graduates is therefore 14.3 percent, whereas a control group of Tippecanoe County ex-prisoners with similar criminal histories who were not in the program had a recidivism rate of 58.2 percent (Dr. J. Miller, personal correspondence, February 17, 2011). These numbers can be understood only in the context of the policies and procedures that dictate participants' experiences in the court, yet they suggest that this particular PSC is working: the more holistic model of reentry offered here is indeed reducing recidivism and providing former prisoners a successful pathway to renewed citizenship.

The design of the program is based on three principles of evidence-based practices (Friedmann, Taxman, & Henderson, 2007; Henderson, Taxman, & Young, 2008). First, the participants must be at high risk of recidivism or repeated crime, with preference given to those incarcerated for serious drug abuse or with symptoms of a serious mental illness. Second, intervention programs utilized by the reentry court must have research-based proof of effectiveness. Third, the reentry program and the participants must undergo continual evaluation to ensure program effectiveness and efficiency. The process begins while a prisoner is incarcerated, highlighting the reality that a reentry-court program is part of "doing time." Persons interested in voluntary participation in reentry court can petition for a sentence modification and must have at least two years left to serve of their original sentence at the time of the application. The county prosecutor has the discretionary power to reject the modification request and to prevent a prisoner from an early release from prison. The prosecutor voices his/her approval or rejection of a prisoner's request at the reentry-court team meeting, a biweekly meeting with the presiding judge that occurs an hour before the public court session with the participants. Team members include the reentry-court case manager, county and city police, a probation officer, the prosecutor and public defender, mental and physical health treatment providers, adult education and housing personnel, and a researcher. Team members discuss each ex-prisoner's case report and look to the case manager for direction when clarification is needed as to what happened in a particular situation. The team offers advice to the judge, but leadership in overall interpretation comes from the judge alone, who functions as the authoritative "face" of the team and maintains final say in matters of the court.

When participants are accepted into reentry court, they meet with a public defender who explains the participant agreement (PA) that delineates the control mechanisms of the program (e.g., signing of forms for drug and alcohol policies and waiver of consent to search, required drug screens and counseling sessions, housing and relational restrictions). The PA also lists the time frames of the four-phased program, with the specific restrictions of each phase (e.g., phase 1 curfew is 9:00, with daily check-ins required; phase 4 curfew is 11:00, with four check-ins per week), and overviews specific sanctions that can be expected if the person commits violations to the rules of the program. Once an ex-prisoner signs the PA, s/he is placed in the work-release facility for at least thirty days. Community corrections offices are located in this facility, which is about a mile from the county jail and provides dormitory-style housing for county prisoners who are on less restrictive confinement. Prisoners come and go for jobs and other appointments but are "locked up" and under surveillance when not working.

The first week after their release from prison, the reentry-court participants face many requirements: obtaining an identification card and a library card, initiating participation in required treatment programs, registering to vote, and applying for entitlement programs such as food stamps and Medicaid. Empirical studies show that involvement in the life of the community (e.g., voting and using library services) while receiving support services increases a person's social capital and thus his/her stake in society (Manza & Uggen, 2006; Wolff & Draine, 2004). Therefore, the program is designed to include aspects of community involvement at the very beginning of a participant's reentry. While these cultural factors are included in all PSC deliberations, the most important determinant of a person's readiness to leave the work-release facility is acquiring and maintaining employment for at least thirty days. The judge and team are acutely aware of the stigma of a felony conviction, and interventions are made with employers to strengthen employment opportunities (e.g., the judge has met with local factory CEOs to develop alliances; previous employers of ex-prisoners are asked to consider hiring new participants, etc.).

The participants engage in a cluster of programs, including cognitive behavioral therapy, substance-abuse treatment, education and employment assistance, and housing services. A participant's progress is monitored weekly by a case manager who is responsible only for reentry participants, and each individual in the program is initially required to check in daily with the case manager or office staff. The case manager manages the resources allocated for the ex-prisoners while keeping their routines and the safety of the community at the center of the judge's and team's decision making (e.g., providing unannounced drug and alcohol screens, reporting each participant's progress or setbacks to the reentry team). The case manager's reports become the focal point for decisions as to specific rewards and sanctions delivered to specific participants. The case manager is therefore sometimes friend and sometimes foe, illustrating the art of governing through the subtle integration of agency and coercion.

When the team meeting concludes, the judge and some members of the team enter a public courtroom where the current participants are waiting for a session that lasts ninety minutes. Each participant is called to a podium with a microphone in front of the judge's bench and engages in dialogue with the judge. During these public conversations, the judge queries participants about jobs, family relationships, future plans, and other topics. The judge also issues sanctions (e.g., four hours of work crew or writing an essay on an assigned topic) to those who have violated regulations during the previous week. These sanctions may be in response to a participant failing to check in with the case manager, being late to work, or missing a required meeting. If a person's offense is more serious (e.g., drug-abuse relapse or getting fired from a job for good reason), s/he may be cuffed by an officer in the courtroom and taken to the county jail. Tears are shed during these high-pressure moments in the court, but more often there is a celebratory atmosphere when successes are highlighted. When a participant is being lauded for a job well done or congratulated for graduating from the program, the courtroom erupts in applause, and laughter is often heard as humorous accounts of daily experiences are shared. All participants witness these court actions and interactions, and the court session is open to the public, with participants' supporters present for the courtroom sessions. The PSC therefore combines closed sessions with public forums, both bureaucratic deal brokering and performative presentations.

Indeed, the oral discourse that occurs in the public sessions is observable to everyone. The dialogues between the judge and participants provide ongoing commentaries on the everyday lived experiences of people who are in the process of navigating the terrain of the court's practices. The introduction of this chapter demonstrates how Ben read aloud one of his essays, performing for the judge, the team, his cohorts, and supporters who had come to hear his story and see it enacted on the stage of the courtroom. I use Goffman's (1959) dramaturgical metaphor to describe these social interactions of the reentry court as "performances" because Ben and the other ex-prisoners are working on self-presentation, but they know they must be authentic. Their performances must not be seen as "staged," yet they sense the tension of wanting to express humility and submission while at the same time increasing their sense of agency. Their performances are on a real-life stage for everyone to see—in real time, describing their lived actualities in the course of their work of reentering the community. The challenge is to understand Ben's reality as it is performed by him for others in the courtroom. As I demonstrate below, the actions and inter-actions during these sessions are important in the analysis of the power relations in the court, for they reveal the power exerted by those of us who govern and use court mechanisms for imposing behavior on reentry-court participants and by Ben and the other participants as they navigate those mechanisms.

The case manager's reports are prepared and distributed to team members by email a few days before the team meeting and are referenced during the court session. They contain extensive yet concise information about each individual (e.g., demographic data, criminal record, employment history and status, fam-ily relational status, dates of drug screens, record of sanctions while in the reentry-court program, etc.). Power is exerted by the judge, law enforcement officials, the case manager, and other members of the team in activating the texts in the reentry court. However, it is important to recall that participants voluntarily sign the agreement to join the program, knowingly passing from one system of governance in the prison to another system of governance in the reentry-court program. In the reentry court, the judge does not wear his robe, indicating a different relationship with the former offenders. The art of governing that the judge exerts here is often paternalistic in tone, with refer-ences to his own fatherhood usually in a kind, coaching way, but always with an understanding of his authority and power.

The participants shape meanings through their oral discourses and the reading of the essays they write. As they respond to the judge's queries about their daily lives, they navigate the power of the material texts, bantering with conclusions made by the judge and team, exercising personal agency as they engage with the judge and others in the courtroom. Ben's case study demon-strates such bantering and engagement with the judge, for although the judge is ever ready to control through language and text, s/he joins the participants in accommodating, reproducing, and sometimes transforming the interpretations and meanings of the court's everyday life. The judge, team, and ex-prisoners all create meanings week by week, and the ex-prisoners particularly are called to form new identities (see Nichols, Chapter Six, this volume; Baumeister, 1986; Schlenker, 2003).

Ben, for example, in the introductory vignette, references his "new per-spective on life," described in the context of a "scary" time of adjustment and transition. He expresses his thankfulness for the supporters in the courtroom and describes himself as "learning to live again." Ben therefore presents a new identity, one different from his criminal past, and places repeated emphasis on his newfound faith in God. He is now self-identified as "free, clean and sober" and "somewhat" independent. Ben thus places his limited independence—he is "somewhat" free—in the context of the court-imposed structure, with layers of meaning created by Ben and those of us who govern in the court. The PSC in general, and Ben's experiences with it, thus embody Mumby's (2001) notion of how complex organizations create a "constellation of intersubjective meanings" (p. 614).

The judge speaks forth the meanings created by various team members from their contacts with the participants during the week. For example, the mental-health therapist reports on observations from the counseling sessions, being careful not to violate confidences. Law-enforcement officials interview participants being considered for advancement to the program's next phase, a practice that has an interesting effect of establishing greater communication and trust among parties who have not trusted one another in the past (Miller & Johnson, 2009; Travis et al., 2001). The housing coordinator reports on those who volunteered on a cold winter morning to move homeless people into apartments. In open court, the judge is the spokesperson for the meanings created by the team about the ex-prisoners' lived experiences. These accounts of meaning are juxtaposed with the meanings created by the ex-prisoners themselves as they dialogue with the judge and with other team members during our weekly meetings. Thus the constellation of meanings made visible in the public court session is created by all reentry-court social actors.

The court's activities produce practical outcomes for participants. Offenders who would have been homeless when returned to the community with $75 and a bus ticket now have a place to live, and those who had little or no education have earned their GEDs and are pursuing higher degrees. A few, however, are expelled from the reentry-court program and returned to jail or prison for failure to comply with the demands of the court's rules and regulations (e.g., relapsing on drugs or alcohol, failing to attend required meetings). The court's outcomes are therefore pragmatic and reveal what I believe is good social policy enacted via the art of governing. Indeed, the court empowers but also shackles; it enables agency for the ex-prisoners while practicing necessary repression in its role as a guardian of public safety.

The events of the reentry PSC can thus be conceptualized as occurring at a time when people are pulled in multiple and often conflicting directions. Social actors in the scene—ex-prisoners, the judge, and members of the team—confront what they want and need to do while they search for structure and meaning. Because dialectical tensions (Baxter, 1990) are inherent in the court processes, I focus on "the complexity and disorder of social life, not with the goal of 'smoothing out' its rough edges, but with a goal of understanding its fundamental ongoing messiness" (Baxter & Montgomery, 1996, p. 3). Yes, contradictions exist and are, in a sense, embraced as people like Ben give voice to opposing tendencies as they relate to others. Yes, we, as members of the court team, are in the courtroom scene both to control Ben's actions and activities and to provide support to him as he regains the power inherent in self-agency. As evidenced in the introduction of this chapter, Ben knows he must give proper submission to reentry-court requirements, but he also exercises and communicates an increasing sense of self-sufficiency and agency as he engages in the process of reentering the community as a productive citizen. And so, while dialectical tensions cut across this scene, I contend that the tension between the development of Ben's self-agency and the coercion of the reentry court may not be an issue that can or should be "resolved." Rather, this tension is an ongoing issue that everyone in the courtroom scene faces; it is complex because we all exercise agency, volitionally affecting events of the court.

The Co-Production of Power in a Reentry Court

Power can be viewed as organized by the institutional governing processes, yet those processes can also support the sharing of power in everyday talk and actions (Belenky, Clinchy, Goldberger, & Tarule, 1986; Habermas, 1984). Sociologist and organizational theorist Max Weber (1978) defined *power* as "the probability that one actor within a social relationship will be in a position to carry out his own will despite resistance" (p. 53). His definition includes the realization that persons in positions of power and control encounter resistance. Accordingly, critical communication scholars have offered analyses of control and domination in organizations (Clegg & Dunkerley, 1980; Kondo, 1990; Tretheway, 1999) and of resistance to those control mechanisms (Collinson, 1994; Scott, 1990). Mumby (2005) discourages the privileging of one aspect of this dichotomy over the other and adopts a dialectical approach to control and resistance, contending that they are "mutually implicative and co-productive" (p. 21). For example, Fleming and Spicer (2008) suggest that "instead of having two diametrically opposed worlds of good and evil, organizations are more like a chiaroscuro of power and resistance whereby light and dark play off each other through mixture, contrast, and blurring" (p. 305). These authors prefer to conceptualize control and resistance as a "struggle," framing it as an interconnected and dynamic process. I contend that the PSC examined here features these control–resistance dynamics.

In *The Practice of Everyday Life*, de Certeau (1984) theorizes that elites use strategies to control people who are "walking in the city" at street level. But the people move in ways that are tactical, taking shortcuts and meandering in directions not determined by the strategies of the ruling powers. The human spirit cannot be underestimated: when situations of domination exist, individuals respond creatively, finding ways to implement interesting and diverse tactics (Scott, 1985, 1990), thus exerting some measure of agency. In regard to the reentry court, the judge and team members apply "strategies" in efforts to support reentering ex-prisoners to become productive, law-abiding citizens. These strategies include rules and structures deployed to manage participants' behavior, and surveillance to provide proof of conformity. Court sessions are the setting where sanctions are administered to punish persons who violate regulations and reward persons who engage in the court-defined transformative process of becoming a contributing citizen within society. De Certeau theorizes that the strategies of the powerful, though designed to control, produce an unintended outcome: the development of "tactics" by individuals who are the targets of control. For example, participants in the reentry court can develop tactics of accepting or complying with the strategies of the judge, case manager, and surveillance officer, or they can learn to evade and maneuver themselves to take advantage of the system's various cracks, a process that de Certeau calls "reappropriation" (p. 37). I suggest that this reappropriation can also be seen as a part of the complex development of an ex-prisoner's self-agency. The conception of struggle portrayed in de Certeau's work provides a framework for viewing the relations among the participants and the judge and team. Both are being controlled in different ways by one another's actions and by the very system facilitating their interaction.

Critical communication scholars have invoked the work of Michel Foucault for decades, applying his writings to issues of power, dominance, and resistance (Barker, 1993; Chan, 2000; Mumby & Deetz, 1990; Tretheway, 1999, 2000). However, Foucault's 1980 lectures (published in 1993) reveal what he explained as a "change of mind" (p. 203). In these lectures, Foucault marks a transition from an emphasis on systems of power relations and dominance to the creation of ethical agency, what he calls "techniques or technology of the self," by which individuals transform and modify themselves (1980/1993, p. 203). In this context, Foucault provides commentary on concepts of governance, coercion, and power:

> Governing is not a way to force people to do what the governor wants; it is always a versatile equilibrium, with complementarity and conflicts between techniques which assure coercion and processes through which the self is constructed or modified by himself. When I was studying asylums, prisons, and so on, I insisted, I think, too much on the techniques of domination. What we can call discipline is something really important in these kinds of institutions, but it is only one aspect of the art of governing people in our society. We must not understand the exercise of power as pure violence or strict coercion. Power consists in complex relations: these relations involve a set of rational techniques, and the efficiency of

those techniques is due to a subtle integration of coercion-technologies and self-technologies. (pp. 203–4)

Following Foucualt, this chapter argues that the reentry-court communicative processes illustrate this "art of governing" in its "subtle integration" of coercion and self-agency. The power inherent in the interplay of these two forces is revealed in the complex of relations. The ruling relations of the court engage in coercive techniques, but these are not to be regarded as malevolent. On the other hand, the participants are not to be romanticized as resisters of the court system or viewed as empty vessels to be filled by others' ideologies. Rather, the power at work in the court is exercised by both the governors and the participants as we employ what Foucault refers to as "self-technologies"—everyone is engaged in self-construction.

The dynamic process of the court is, therefore, complex and at times ambiguous and ambivalent. Whereas the judge and we, the team, are most often perceived as holding positions of power, we sometimes acquiesce to the power exerted by the ex-prisoners as they increase in self-agency. The dance of power and agency is indeed mysterious, for as Foucault said, "the art of governing" hangs by a thread; it is, at best, a "versatile equilibrium, with complementarity and conflicts between techniques."

To add experiential flesh to these theoretical musings, I turn now to a case study of Ben's nineteen-month journey through the reentry-court program. Let me be clear that I am not investigating Ben but the reentry court and its practices. My work is guided by the following questions: (1) What is Ben's everyday experience in the context of the court, and how is it organized? (2) What are the ruling relations of the court, and how does Ben coordinate his life with those ruling relations? (3) What are the possibilities and constraints for the judge and reentry-court team members to enable the empowerment of self-agency for Ben and other court participants? And (4) What are the communicative dimensions of this delicate dance of coercion and agency? How do the communicative performances of the court's multiple players influence the PSC's outcomes?

"Grab the Line": A Case Study of Ben's Reentry-Court Journey

Ben stepped to the podium when the judge called his name. This was the same judge who had previously sentenced him to twenty-four years in the state prison for eight offenses, including possession of cocaine, carrying a gun without a license, and failing to pay child support. Ben had signed the Participant Agreement, and this was his first day in a reentry-court public session. The judge began the dialogue with a statement and a question: "I remember you from back in the day. Why are you different now?" Ben testified that he had a newfound humility from "knowing the Lord" and went on to say: "My values are different now. I was locked up for eleven years. I know I need structure." In his characteristically blunt manner, the judge asked, "Do you hate my guts?" Ben responded directly but with respect. "No, sir, I'm thankful that I can be in this program and thankful for the things I have learned." The judge told him to follow the rules and look for work in the coming week. He then asked Ben if he had any supporters in the courtroom. Ben's sister stepped forward and said she was proud of him. His eleven-year-old daughter was also present, along with fourteen other people.

The next week, the judge greeted Ben by stating, "You have been a wild guy." The dialogue continued with a series of questions and answers focused on Ben's addiction to cocaine, and then the judge commented, "I recall your dad doing security police. I knew him. He was straight. It's unusual for someone to have a dad like that and go wrong."

Ben explained, "I made mistakes in high school, went into the Marine Corps and would get drunk with the guys. I hit rank of sergeant but a weakness I had was that I hid my anger."

When the judge asked him if he felt he "owed the community," Ben described his participation in a prison program called Straight Talk: "We would go out and talk to youth and the public, tell them about our crimes and how we got to that point. I would like to encourage others not to make the same mistakes." The dialogue continued with a discussion of Ben's job search, and the judge encouraged him to look for an "A" (any) job and not expect a "B" (better) job immediately.[4]

Ben assured him that he had learned the importance of humility, and the judge responded: "This will work. You'll be fine. With age you look at the world differently."

Ben concluded the discussion by stating, "I feel blessed and am trusting you to lead me. There is hope."

The initial reentry-court dialogues between the judge and Ben were built on past discourses that were recorded at the time of his sentencing, eleven years earlier. The judge referred back to the power he used in that action but also began to lay the foundation for a new relationship with Ben in the context of the reentry court by asking him "why things are different now." Ben's reference to his faith, values, time spent in prison, and need for structure demonstrated self-confidence and humble recognition of the help he needed from others, but the tone was one of clear deference to the judge's authority. All the social actors in the court participated in the co-production of power in the months ahead. Those of us who govern the court program shaped Ben's experiences (e.g., his job search), as he navigated court boundaries and surveillance. The goals were for him to become both disciplined and agentic in his path to becoming a contributing citizen. These early conversations reveal Ben's desire to share his experiences with youth to "encourage them not to make the same mistakes," but he would "hit the wall" (the judge's term) in his journey through the court program.

Ben progressed well for the first four months. He found a construction job, reunited with his daughter, began paying child support and attending parenting classes. He moved into his own apartment with one year's free rent provided by grant money from the program. He earned his way off home detention, attended mental-health therapy sessions and Narcotics Anonymous (N.A.) meetings, and paid all the reentry fees that accrued, week after week.[5] But at the end of the sixth month, a surveillance officer saw Ben with a woman who was not on his "approved list."[6] The woman was Ben's former girlfriend, who also had a criminal record and was deemed a "risky contact," that is, one who might lead Ben back to his old lifestyle. When he was questioned about it, Ben denied the report, but he subsequently admitted to lying about the incident and was placed in jail for two weeks. He knew that the team would decide whether he would remain in the program or be sent back to prison. Ben had "hit the wall." In exercising agency, Ben chose to use a "tactic" (de Certeau, 1984) that did not work.

At the next public court session, Ben stood in front of the judge in shackles:

Judge: Ben, you told me you're in love. Wonderful. You can abide by this program or love her from the prison cell. You are accepted back but have to be on home detention. You will be very closely monitored. Do you understand? This is your last chance. I really have a lot of hope for you, but I won't let anyone jeopardize this program. That's where we are. Can you do this?

Ben: Yessir, I believe so.

Judge: First things first. I'm not telling you you can't be in love. I'm telling you that right now this relationship can't be. The choice is yours. Do you understand? Things have to wait in life. It's part of the process of earning your way back.

Ben: Yessir. I apologize to my family. I have opened the door for them to doubt me. I apologize to the other participants and the team. They have reason to question my integrity.

Judge: On behalf of everyone, we accept your apology. Choose wisely.

Ben: I became institutionalized. I have been swimming in my freedom.

Judge: Grab the line this program offers. It'll pull you through it. There are reasons why this program is set up this way. All right. Welcome back.

In the context of this event in Ben's reentry-court experience, we see what Foucault referred to as "coercion-technologies" applied by the judge. The judge's rhetoric reveals his sense of power in his use of the word "choice," in that he makes the word mean what *he* wants it to mean. In reality, Ben is given no choice at all. He can say "yes" to the judge's meaning or go back to jail. The judge did not flinch in his redefining of terms, yet the coercion he employs is, in my opinion, not to be viewed as malevolent. Though in the early stages of the situation Ben may have viewed it as such, the case manager had seen the "red flags" of attraction to this old girlfriend and had warned Ben of the danger. Members of the team and the other participants anticipated that, in time, this man would have complete freedom in his choice of associations, but everyone in the program knows the risky influence of former contacts who continue in their addictions.

In his public address, the judge recognizes the complex relations that empower and constrain Ben. The judge is aware of these conditions because Ben's everyday experiences with the court included discussions with the case manager, jail time, a separate meeting with the judge at which a reentry-court peer spoke on Ben's behalf, a written apology to the team, and the public courtroom dialogue. All of these experiences, intended as means of cultivating behaviors and beliefs, tastes, desires, and needs that would be embodied in Ben, were in turn shared with the judge. The judge did not disregard or ignore Ben's bodily needs and his need to be loved, but at this juncture of Ben's program participation, the rules designed to protect him from the temptations of a drug-addicted lifestyle were violated, and sanctions were imposed. When Ben "hit the wall," he could not move forward. He had lost some of his ability to exercise agency and was forced to coordinate his life with the ruling relations. The team acted on the belief that Ben had personal desire and power to pursue a law-abiding lifestyle, but with the caveat that he could not jeopardize the program. The wall was removed, and Ben moved forward in the program.

The interplay or "subtle integration" of coercion and self-agency in the reentry court's communicative process was demonstrated in a public court session nearly three months later. The judge assigned Ben to read *Character Is Destiny* by Russell Gough (1998) and write an essay about a specific incident applying a principle from the book. Ben read the following in court:

> On June 23rd I had a doctor's appointment. It took an hour and a half. I stressed over this because it cut into my work hours, and I need every hour I can get to make ends meet.
>
> I had gone on to work and finished out my day. At the end of the day came time to fill out my time sheet. It's pretty liberal and done on trust. You would think that after all that I've been through, that it wouldn't be an issue. But, I found myself struggling with putting down my true hours. I was contemplating on writing eight hours, knowing I had only worked six and a half. I really struggled with this even though I knew it was wrong and I was trying to justify why. The thought of "our character is who we are in the dark" hit me. Though it was hard, I wrote down six and a half. Then just as I signed off on it, my boss came in and told me he needed me to work over.

For me that was a confirmation that God was making a way for me. I had made the right decision.

Ben's essay reveals the power inherent in the interplay of Foucault's "coercive technologies" (of the court rulers) and "self-technologies" (of the PSC participants), for Ben is neither a resister of the court system nor forced to accept the ideologies of the judge and team. He asserts that he made the right decision, and it was a faith-confirming decision that impacted his relationship with his employer and his personal "character in the dark."

Another court dialogue focused on Ben's tattoos. Most of the court participants have tattoos covering many parts of their bodies. When they are in front of the judge, the tattoos are not to be visible. The judge claims these images represent a deviant culture, so the participants use "tactics" to identify their ways with his by covering the permanent markings that depict images, attitudes, and ideas. But the judge's insistence that the tattoos not be visible was a nearly impossible task for Ben, who has a tattoo on his bald head. The judge discussed the possibility of having the tattoos physically removed. The ex-prisoners evidenced resistance to the judge's suggestion, and Ben addressed the issue. He sported a large satanic symbol emblazoned on the top of his head and explained that as one converted to Christianity in prison, he wanted to retain the image because it clearly demonstrates his past life and will provide a means of identifying with today's youth. He desires to speak to teenagers about the dangers of drug addiction and the accompanying lifestyle, and the tattoo will be proof of his radically different past, an embodied reminder of how far he has come in his journey back to citizenship.

De Certeau's (1984) imagery of "walking in the city" provides a helpful image for analysis of Ben's interaction with the judge. Those with power execute "strategies" from their places on high, while those like Ben who "live down below" appropriate the "tactics" of those who are "weak." In this example, Ben is "poaching," seizing an opportunity, taking a chance with the judge, and resisting the dominant narrative of "the State" (de Certeau, 1984, pp. 92–93). In this case, the judge acquiesces to the power exerted by Ben as he increases in self-agency.

The discussion of tattoos has not been resumed in court since that day. In fact, in his last three months in the program, Ben expressed his assertiveness in other aspects of his lived experiences. He was finding ways to bond with his daughter. He stated, "I actually have to make things happen for us. I have to create things for us to do and make time." His exercising of agency in this situation had the following self-reported results: "We are both learning and it's definitely not easy for either one of us, but we are finding it very rewarding in our bond that every father and daughter should be able to experience." Ben was out of prison for fifteen months when he offered this observation about establishing his relationship with his daughter.

In his last appearance as a participant in the reentry-court program, Ben read an essay he had written for the court session. The title of the essay reflected the title of the fourth phase of the program: "Establish or Restore Your Rightful Place in Society." Ben described a chance meeting with some "old friends" and confirmed that he had "no desire for that way of life." He then detailed three significant ways he has changed. First, his way of thinking has changed, and he understands that "our thinking affects every area of our lives because our thoughts become our words, our words become our actions, and our actions become our character." His thinking had changed in his now cautionary approach to social contacts with people actively using addictive substances, in his focus on his daughter, and in being honest in recording his correct number of hours of work. Second, he stated, "I have also changed the people I surround myself with. Positive people create positive outcomes. Through this I have gained a better relationship with my daughter. I try to live as an example for her, and it makes me tremble with joy to hear her call me 'Dad' and say 'I love you.'" A third change is his sobriety, which he considers a "huge factor" in giving him a clear mind and the ability to "be accountable and responsible to face any adversity." Sobriety has also meant "employment that is very rewarding and is a career opportunity." Ben concluded his essay by attesting to the value of the reentry-court program:

> The opportunities afforded me from this program have given me life, clarity and understanding. Even in my struggles and trials I have been blessed. They became stepping stones instead of stumbling blocks. Destiny is not by chance . . . it's by choice and I have to make it happen with the right choices. The serenity prayer says it perfect: God grant me the serenity to accept the things I cannot change, the courage to change the things I can, and the wisdom to know the difference.

The judge responded by stating, "There was a time, Ben, when I wasn't sure you were going to make it. Is this the same Ben I put in jail a year ago?" Ben quickly responded, "No!" The judge then rose from his bench, stepped down to the podium next to Ben, and said, "In that year, you mapped out who the new Ben will be. You're not there yet. When people graduate, they are beginning . . . they are in process of changing. The team has voted, and it is my privilege to present to you this certificate of graduation." The two men shook hands and embraced, and everyone in the courtroom applauded. Some cheered. All participated in this ritual of the court, congratulating one who successfully navigated the requirements of the reentry court but who leaves the program with the challenge to continue growing in self-agency.

Ben and I had several personal conversations during and after his participation in the reentry court. Whereas some may see his reliance on and faith in

Jesus Christ as paradoxical to his development of self-agency, Ben states that "apart from Him helping me through all of this, I would not have made it. He is in me, powerfully working, and I am in process of working that all out into my world." Ben's testimony is similar to that of some of the women in the study reported by Nichols (this volume, Chapter Six). His spiritual life was strengthened by the difficulties (e.g., being sent back to jail for lying about his contact with a former girlfriend) as well as by the successes (e.g., being able to establish a relationship with his daughter), and he continually testified to me of God's grace.

Conclusion

The many actors in the reentry court—the participants, judge, social-service providers, and criminal-justice practitioners—are working to reform the reentry process. In answer to my earlier question, I contend that this model is a viable means of men and women redeeming themselves. As they work in the community, vote on election day, and volunteer alongside their neighbors, the stigma of their incarceration can be replaced. I believe it is one means of answering Nichols's call for programs that can be "created and molded to assist this ever-growing, stigmatized population." The ex-prisoners are the ones doing most of the work as they exercise self-agency and are recognized as ones who have restored their rightful place in society. The subtle dance of coercion and self-agency has proven to be one means of assisting men and women reentering their community after imprisonment.

Communication scholars and educators have a wealth of expertise to offer in the arena of social reform and can collaborate with practitioners and those who have experienced incarceration to reform the criminal-justice system. Deetz (2008) encourages us to develop engaged research in our communities in a manner that "puts our knowledge at risk," organizing our scholarship around the needs of the community "rather than our own literature and preferred topics of study" (p. 290). This chapter demonstrates how communication activists can become engaged and offer critical research scholarship in a reentry PSC organization.

Larry Frey (2009) argues that "an alternative approach to making a difference from research is to make a difference through research" and encourages communication researchers to intervene "into discourses to affect them, documenting their practices, processes, and products" (p. 210). Putting our research to work in this way is challenging but has potential for meaningful application to criminal-justice reform efforts. A communicative lens and discursive examination reveal the dialectic interplay of voice, agency, and action. Inquiry of the ongoing talk of the court allows a view of the embodiment of power that is realized in the everyday experiences of the court actors. Most important, we work for justice by extending the lessons learned and the reforms offered through reentry PSCs. As activist scholars, we offer hope and give voice to the men and women who are "doing time" while coming home.

Notes

1. A pseudonym

2. Participants are placed in the county work-release facility when they are brought back to the community by law-enforcement officials. They are housed in work release until they have maintained employment for thirty days.

3. A federal grant, written by a sociology professor on the team, provides funds for one year of free housing for court participants. They choose from a selection of available apartments after being successfully employed for thirty consecutive days.

4. The judge in this reentry court refers to his "ABC job program." The participants are to begin by getting an "A" (any) job, then proceed to find a "B" (better) job, and finally expect to locate a "C" (career) job.

5. Reentry-court participants pay fees for work release, drug screens, mental-health therapy, home-detention fees, and other needs. Very few reentry-court costs are not funded with tax dollars.

6. The case manager works with other law-enforcement officials to approve a list of persons submitted by each participant for social contact.

CHAPTER 6

Life After Incarceration

Exploring Identity in
Reentry Programs for Women

NIKKI H. NICHOLS

Since the 1990s, women have represented the fastest-growing prison population in the United States (United States Department of Justice, 2009). High incarceration rates for women are troubling enough, but what happens once they serve their time behind bars? This chapter, based upon in-depth interviews with formerly incarcerated women, investigates the impact of incarceration on women's identities and explores what happens in their lives after prison. During the interviews, participants offered insights about their identities before, during, and after spending time in prison and revealed the challenges of creating new lives when they are released. The evidence in this study suggests complex layers of identity that defy the unidimensional stigma of "convict" or "felon" that is often imposed on women who have been incarcerated. The women's personal stories convey their perceptions of themselves, their perceptions of how they are viewed by society, and the kinds of resources they need for a successful return to their communities. Thus, in addition to contributing to a more complex understanding of the ways women express and experience their identities after release from prison, this study offers suggestions for transitional programs to better assist women leaving prison in successfully rejoining the communities.

I begin by discussing the challenges women who have been incarcerated face when they leave prison. I then present the research questions and methodology that framed the in-depth interviews I conducted with women in two transitional programs during 2008 and 2009. Next, I explore the identity themes that emerge from the interviews as well as specific needs the women identified as they made their transitions from prison. In the final section, I explore strategies for enhancing the success of women's post-prison experiences.

Challenges Facing Women After Incarceration

Seventy-seven percent of state prisoners are released from prison and return to our communities (Council of State Government Justice Center, 2009). More than 729,200 people were released from federal and state prison in 2009 (Bureau of Justice Statistics, 2011). The average age for a prisoner in the United States is thirty-nine (Federal Bureau of Prisons, 2012). While all people who have been incarcerated face enormous obstacles as they begin their journey back to society, formerly incarcerated women often face additional challenges. For instance, most female prisoners have experienced physical, emotional, and/or sexual abuse and were first abused between the ages of five and fourteen. This abuse is most often sexual abuse perpetrated by a male member of the immediate family (Fletcher, Rolison, & Moon, 1993). In a study of women incarcerated in the Ohio prison system, approximately 95 percent of the 436-person sample reported a history of either physical or sexual abuse (McDaniels-Wilson, 1998).

Additionally, substance abuse is a great concern for women leaving prison. As Fletcher, Rolison, and Moon (1993) note, most female prisoners begin using drugs or alcohol by the time they are thirteen or fourteen years old. Substance abuse, imprisonment, and recidivism are closely linked (Benda & Pallone, 2005; Owen, 1998). In a study by Schram et al. (2006), 38 percent of the women surveyed reported needing assistance with substance addiction. As these statistics suggest, treatment for substance abuse is crucial in reentry programs for women leaving prison.

In addition, approximately four out of five incarcerated women are mothers (Harm, 1992), and two-thirds of mothers in prison have children under the age of eighteen (Snell, 1994). Women who live behind bars have the unfortunate experience of being separated from their children (Greene, Haney, & Hurtado, 2000; Mumola, 2000; O'Brien, 2001). Prisoners who are mothers have the added pressure of worrying about their children and living with limited contact with them while they are in prison. In addition, as Burkhardt (1976) notes, many incarcerated mothers can be labeled "bad mothers," which intensifies the pain of being separated from their children.

Motherhood is also an important concern for many women upon release from prison. Greene, Haney, and Hurtado (2000) document the desperation of mothers wanting to be reunited with their children when they leave prison. The women reported being "good mothers and were determined to overcome the consequences of their traumatic experience and eventually provide homes for their children" (p. 15). These scholars highlight the importance of focusing on motherhood in reentry programs for women, citing the cycles of pain experienced by mothers and how this pain is being passed on to their children. Moreover, O'Brien (2001) found that the transition back into society is smoother when women develop a positive, strong relationship with their children upon leaving prison.

Although physical abuse, substance abuse, and reuniting with their children are the problems most extensively identified in the literature, there are other issues, as well. The interlocking challenges of unemployment, mental health, discrimination, economic stress, and inadequate housing impose enormous obstacles to success as women transition from prison to their communities. Kenemore and Roldan (2006) note that basic needs such as shelter, food, and employment are often denied to former prisoners. In the context of these challenges, the self-perceptions of women leaving prison take on important implications for their successful return to their communities, not the least because a strong sense of self may enable women to overcome the many obstacles they face. Thus the focus of this study is to learn more about the ways women who have been released from prison describe, conceptualize, and enact their identities.

Research Questions and Methodology

This study is an exploration and analysis of women living in two transitional facilities in Ohio. More specifically, this study emphasizes the identities of women who have been incarcerated. The research questions that guided this study are:

(RQ1) How does incarceration affect the lives of women leaving prison?

(RQ2) How do formerly incarcerated women discuss (or communicate) their identities as women?

(RQ3) How do formerly incarcerated women reconcile their self-perceptions with the labels commonly attributed to female prisoners by society?

(RQ4) What are the needs of women after incarceration?

To answer these research questions, I used ethnographic fieldnotes and in-depth, semistructured interviews (McCracken, 1988).

Finding Research Participants and Obtaining Approval

Perhaps one of the biggest challenges of the study was finding the research participants. I set out to conduct extensive research on female-only transitional programs in the Ohio area. After writing letters and emails to program directors, I had face-to-face meetings with several directors and narrowed down possible study sites to two that best fit the scope of the research. The directors at these sites granted me permission to become part of their transitional communities and to interview program participants about their experiences. This process began after I was granted approval from my university's Human Subjects Review Board (HSRB), having ensured confidentiality and free informed consent. Once these procedural matters were in place, I began my research at two different sites, which I call Hope's House and Faith's House. I spent between three and five months at these programs, observing and interacting in the women's daily lives.

Hope's House

Hope's House, a program for women with substance abuse problems located in northern Ohio, housed approximately ten women during my time there. The women came to Hope's House after hearing about the program on the streets, after leaving another substance-abuse treatment program, or after learning about the program while incarcerated. The focus of Hope's House is to aid women with substance abuse; however, I wanted to conduct research there because most of the women in the program had been incarcerated at some time in their lives.

Hope's House is located in an old home in the downtown urban district of a city in Ohio. The house is inconspicuous as a treatment or reentry program, as there are no signs posted on the exterior. In this program, the women spend most of their days in classes, learning about themselves and the process of recovery. I spent one day a week for eleven weeks visiting the program, attending group meetings, and speaking individually with the women. During the last two weeks, I interviewed two of the residents, who had recently been incarcerated. Although I physically spent a great deal of time at Hope's House, I often felt that I was an outsider there and that I never fully gained entry into the community. This feeling of not fitting in at Hope's House was in stark contrast to my feeling of acceptance at Faith's House.

Faith's House

The second program where I conducted research for this project was Faith's House, a faith-based transitional program for women leaving prisons in Ohio. The women enter Faith's House immediately after leaving the walls of prison. Women were admitted into this program after attending Bible study in prison, praying that this was the right path for them, and completing an application. Faith's House is located in an urban, poverty-stricken area of central Ohio and has its offices located in an area church. It includes two residential houses, where the program participants live, and a church where the Faith's House director's office is located and where meetings are held. Four or five program residents and one program coordinator reside in each house at any given time. At the time of my research, Faith's House had nine women participating in its program, which is designed to help formerly incarcerated women succeed in spiritual formation, substance-abuse recovery, employment, life skills, and financial freedom.

I spent one to two days a week for fifteen weeks at Faith's House. My days at Faith's House were spent taking residents to and from work and on other errands that required transportation. I taught computer skills to one resident who had been incarcerated for sixteen years. I had the rare privilege of attending their weekly community meeting where the women vulnerably and openly discussed their feelings and experiences of the past week. I also aided the director with administrative tasks in order to learn more about the program's operations and dealings with the women residents. During my time at Faith's House I often felt like I was a part of the community. The program director made a great effort to put me in constant contact with the program residents and to teach me all she could about how the program operated.

During my time observing and volunteering, I collected approximately forty-five pages of ethnographic fieldnotes. These notes were written in my car, in the directors' offices, in the living room of the residents—anywhere I could write quickly without intruding on the program residents and staff.

After about twelve weeks of spending time with the residents in Faith's House, when I felt that my relationship with program residents had developed, I asked each woman if she would be willing to participate in a one-on-one, audiotaped, semistructured, in-depth interview. A total of eleven women agreed to be interviewed—all of the women who were currently in the program, and two women who had completed it.

All eleven interviews were conducted at the program facilities in a quiet and private place. Each interview was from 60 to 120 minutes in length and was recorded to audiotape. Participants gave written consent before any interviews were conducted, and, given a choice of remaining anonymous or using her real name during the interview process and the written research, all participants requested to have their real first names used in this study. The women who participated in this study ranged in age from their mid-twenties to their late fifties and were from various racial backgrounds (black, white, Hispanic). They had served from one to seventeen years in prison, with some serving a single sentence and others serving as many as four sentences. Their crimes ranged from deadly assault, to drug possession with the intent to sell, to prostitution, to second-degree murder.

In Their Own Words: Emerging Themes

Below I detail four overarching themes that emerged during in-depth interviews with the participants in this study: the impact of prison on the women's lives; identity, or the women's self-perceptions; reconciling society's negative perceptions of women who have been incarcerated; and the needs of the women during reentry. Direct quotes from the women offer insights into each of these themes.

The Impact of Incarceration

Incarceration has had an impact on the women in this study in multiple ways. Perhaps surprisingly, most of the women describe prison as an experience that changed their lives in a positive way. The women's responses clustered around positive and altruistic themes such as "Finding oneself," "Getting closer to God," and "Prison as lifesaving."

Finding Oneself

Lindsey, a young woman in her twenties, who had been incarcerated once, said, "I worked on myself from the time I was there until the time I got out . . . It was the best experience of my life." Julia, who had been incarcerated twice, shared a similar sentiment: "If I could do things different, would I? No, I don't think I would, because I learned so much about me . . . I think that is why I needed to be there, because I needed to sit down and get to know who Julia was—because I didn't know who I was."

Getting Closer to God

Most of the women interviewed at both transitional programs also revealed that while incarcerated, they had experienced a life-changing event by building a strong relationship with God. Kim, a woman who had been in and out of prison all of her life, said that "it was like a safe haven for me because I didn't have to worry about the constant battle with drinking and drugs and I felt good about myself, I felt like I was able to have a relationship with God in prison. I felt separate from him out here [in the free world]."

Prison as Lifesaving

Finally, the participants discussed prison as an experience that saved their lives. Kim explained how, before she went to prison for her fifth and final time, her life had hit bottom, and in going to prison, she got her soul back:

> I had hit all lows, I was just done. I was homeless, I stayed with friends here and there, but I was basically homeless. I had resorted to prostitution as a way of life, as a way to survive. I had no contact with my family and any of my children, and I was just watching everything go by me. I barely existed. I had a spiritual deadness, soul sickness, the emptiest feeling I ever felt.

This comment is similar to many of the women's stories about having hit "all lows" or "the bottom" and prison actually giving them an opportunity to get their lives back.

The three categories revealed in response to the impacts of incarceration are all relatively positive and are representative of most of the responses in this study. The women expressed thankfulness for their time served and the desire to move on in life in a more positive manner. Many of the participants in this study experienced prison as a life-changing positive experience. The notion of prison as a positive and life-changing experience is not new. In his cultural analysis of prison rhetoric in the second half of the twentieth century, Sloop (1996) traces popular representations of prisoners, noting that in the 1950s, people in prison were often depicted as having "the ability to use prison in order to find their way back to a 'normal' state of being" (p. 186).

However, data analysis regarding other interview questions revealed that the women interviewed also perceive society's opinion of their incarceration as a negative element of their identities. This constant tension between their own attitudes about life behind bars and their perceptions of how society views their experience makes it difficult for formerly incarcerated women to "fit in"; they feel ostrasized by society because of the very circumstances that, from their perspectives, made them better, stronger women.

Perceptions of Themselves

Perception is a powerful tool. During the interviews, participants discussed how they viewed themselves now that they have the societal stigma of "prisoner" associated with their identity. In both interviews and casual conversations, it became apparent that the women communicate their identities as (1) women who have felt unloved and empty at various points in their lives (particularly as children), and (2) as survivors.

A Woman Unloved

A prevalent theme that emerged in the women's responses to questions about their self-perceptions is the expereince of being an unloved woman. Nine of the women participating in this study were abused at some point in their lives, in many cases at an early age. The abuse made them feel lonely and unworthy. However, even women who had not been abused expressed feeling unloved. For example, Lindsey, a woman who was adopted at a very early age, said she had never been abused yet she still possessed the feelings associated with not being loved: "Ever since I was young I always remember this emptiness. No matter how much love that I had I just never felt like I belonged anywhere." Melenee, who grew up in foster care after both of her parents died when she was four, described similar feelings. She stated that she was neglected in foster homes, so she ran away. Now, however, the transitional program had offered her a new family. "I had been for so long, so long, without feeling loved, without being happy. They taught me how to love again, they taught me that I was a good person, they taught me to just love and be loved."

Although these two women hailed from drastically different family backgrounds, with one loved abundantly and one experiencing neglect for most of her life, both described feeling alone, empty, and unloved.

A Woman Survivor

While broken relationships and battered spirits were common elements of the women's lives, many participants identified themselves as women who had survived horrific experiences. I asked each participant to describe herself to me, or to use adjectives to describe who she is. Many women used the word *survivor* in their list of adjectives and revealed that they are continuously work-ing to overcome the obstacles they have faced in life, while others described how they are still searching for who they truly are. As Julia stated, "I know who I am and what my goals are now, but I think I am just trying to find a place to fit in. This is me, accept me, and love me . . . I know somebody will."

In the interviews and discussions, the women detail how they see them-selves. Rather than defining themselves as "ex-offenders," they acknowledge the life experiences that may have led them to commit crimes, but they also view themselves as overcoming those circumstances and moving forward with their lives. There is a sense of pride in being a survivor among this group of women; this is not pride in surviving prison per se, but self-respect in surviv-ing the life experiences that led them into criminal activity in the first place, and then making new, more positive lives for themselves.

Reconciling Society's Negative Perceptions

Participants were also asked how they reconcile their own self-perceptions with the labels commonly imposed on female prisoners by society. This informa-tion is pertinent to reentry programming because there is a large disconnect between a formerly incarcerated woman's view of herself and the problematic way she feels society views her.

Participants in this study were very clear that they feel stigmatized by the way society views those who have been incarcerated. Melenee stated this di-rectly: "They think we are shit. They think we are crap." She said the label of prisoner "stays with you. That is an impression that was put on your life and you are going to have to deal with it the rest of your life, so you might as well make it into your life, because it is your life." Trina also described the percep-tion that ex-offenders are untrustworthy: "Society as a whole says that we are unemployable, that we are not trustable, we cannot be trusted, and once this always this, and that is not true."

In contrast to their beliefs about their own identities, the women felt that society continues to stigmatize them and label them as criminals. Sharon said that she had served her time in prison and that the government had said she was redeemed, but society continued to punish her. She asked, "How long do I have to be punished by society?" Many of the women gave examples of the barriers to rights and privileges that they face upon release from prison as well as of their experiences of marginalization: they mentioned difficulty with employment, finding housing, volunteering with certain organizations, and voting. The women also expressed a sense of discouragement about how they fit into society.

The dichotomy between how the women view their own identities versus their experiences of social stigma imposes tremendous stress as they leave prison. While the women in this study are voluntarily participating in reentry programs in hopes of demonstrating that they are upstanding citizens, a difficult tension remains between how they view themselves and their experiences of how society views them.

Combating Negative Stereotypes

The women participating in this study deal with the negative stereotypes associated with their prison experience by attempting to "do the right thing" and prove themselves to others. There are three themes associated with combating the negative stereotypes these women often face: (1) proving themselves, (2) self-acceptance, and (3) giving back to society. Again, this is an area that is important for reentry or transitional programming, because these issues must be addressed in order for formerly incarcerated women to build new lives upon release from prison.

Proving Themselves

Most of the participants recognize that some of their choices hurt many people and expressed their readiness to move forward in life in a positive way. Trina explained how having ten felony convictions may seem like it could hold her back, and in some ways it will, but she expressed determination to overcome her record. "I have four [charges] of aggravated trafficking on my record, and I have ten felonies. It [prison] will always be a part of me, but I can overcome it, because today I believe that there is nothing I can't do."

Self-Acceptance

The second theme revealed that female ex-offenders overcome society's negative stereotypes by working to accept themselves. Kim described how, after being in and out of prison most of her adult life, she felt that she had finally come to a point in her life where she was happy. A mother of four who at one point had lost custody of all her children, she now had three of them back in her life, held a steady job, and was in a program that would help her to one day own her own home. She said, "I am more willing than I have ever been in my life, at peace with who I am now."

Giving Back

Finally, participants also reconciled their own perceptions of themselves with society's negative views of this population by "giving back to society." Every woman interviewed for this study mentioned that her future entailed giving back to society in some form. They described their sense of giving back in various ways. For example, Birdie is a resident director at the transitional program where she once sought help. She lives in one of the transitional homes and serves as a mentor and director to the women currently in the program. Amy said she would like to work with formerly incarcerated women in recovery, but in a unique way, by focusing on nutrition and exercising. "I feel that even when you are incarcerated something is lacking, in incarceration, in treatment facilities, and in transitional homes . . . health and exercise. I kinda want to get something like that started," she said. Trina said she wanted to tell her story to young kids. "In my future I entail [*sic*] to be a motivational speaker for children, to tell my story, to tell my prison life story, and my drug life story because I believe I can get through to them." Lastly, Sharon, a survivor of domestic abuse, said she planned to go into schools and discuss with young girls the importance of having self-respect and healthy relationships. Sharon received an associate's degree in social work while she was serving her sixteen-year sentence. She hoped to obtain further schooling in that area so that she could be an advocate for victims of domestic violence. The women I spoke with had a sense of urgency and duty about giving back to society. The thoughts of proving themselves, self-acceptance, and giving back to society all seemed to help them overcome the negative connotations that society had placed on them.

Identifying Needs After Incarceration

The final piece of this study involved learning from the women about their needs after incarceration. My goal here was to listen to the participants voice their needs for their post-prison lives. This information, which was then relayed to the women's residential programs, can be useful for other transitional programs, as well. While some of the needs expressed by the women participating in this study have been explored in previous literature, there are additional needs discussed here that research has yet to address. These include the needs of community support, mentoring, and a detailed plan upon leaving prison.

The participants in this study clearly felt that the needs of their population were not currently being met. Amy stated, "From what I understand from talking to a couple of ladies, there are a few programs . . . I think they need more help in that area. They get a little bit of treatment while they are in there [prison], but I think they need help when they get out." The themes associated with the needs of female ex-offenders are: (1) the importance of transitional programs, (2) housing and financial assistance, (3) having a plan, and (4) support.

The Importance of Transitional Programs for Women

The study's participants often discussed how their transitional program aided them tremendously, but they also noted that there weren't enough programs in existence to assist other women in the same situation. Melenee explained, "My needs were only met because I came to Faith's House and they cared so much. Basic people's needs aren't met." She added, "Life is really hard when you are booted out of the pen with forty dollars. Life is truly hard." Lindsey observed the harsh realities of women who leave prison but have no place to go:

> I think as women we have different needs from men . . . it is too bad that the prison system doesn't help. If you don't go fight for it, or nobody tells you, just like I found out about Faith's House, then you would never know. I don't think we would have a lot of repeating offenders because there are certain needs that human being need met, and so if you get thrown out on the street and don't have no place to eat or no shelter or whatever, you are going to go back to what you have always done your whole life just to survive, and people have to survive.

In Lindsey's response stressing the need for more post-prison programs, the identity of survivor also emerges in ways that highlight the complexity—and perhaps fragility—of women's experiences as they leave prison. "People have to survive," Lindsay asserts, even if that means returning to old strategies for survival.

A Place to Call Home and Financial Assistance

Transitional programs were described as a temporary solution to one of the basic needs discussed by the participants of this study: housing. Trina explained the critical importance of having a stable place to call home after being released from prison:

> Housing would be an issue for most women, somewhere with stability to come to, be it their own home or places like this [Hope's House], and other places, so that they can get a new life instead of going back to the same old things. Because every time I have gotten out I have went back to the same thing, same old neighborhood, and once you are there in that environment you go right back to doing what you are comfortable with.

As Trina's words attest, a place to call home offers stability that is so essential to the creation of a new life—and identity.

The women also indicated financial assistance as an important need. As Melenee noted above, when women in the state of Ohio leave prison, they are given a small amount of money; in 2008, it was $40. Sharon stated, "My biggest need was just financial. That is my biggest need, because being here [Faith's House], really all of my other needs are met."

A Plan for Success

Housing and financial support alone are not enough to enable a formerly incarcerated woman to reenter society with a hope of succeeding. Another theme that emerged from this study is the need to have a specific plan for the future upon exiting prison. This is a theme not discussed in other literature about women leaving prison. For example, Julia explained how having a plan could enable a woman leaving prison to move forward with her life:

> Where I am from [in] Ohio, we don't have like reentry programming or anything like that. I think if you are going to a bigger community and you are going to a halfway house, and you have a plan . . . if you are just going home from prison and go back to the same old things you knew before, then you probably aren't going to accomplish much.

Sharon also described having a plan—in her case, Faith's House:

> You have to have a plan when you leave prison, you can't just leave prison. Some people might have a supportive family, but the rate of that is so low, a lot of people don't want to be bothered with you anyway. But you have to factor in all of that kind of stuff. Recidivism is so high . . . a lot of the times [people released from prison] go back to doing the same things that they have always done and they think they will get different results. You have to have change in life in order for you to have a life.

In identifying the need for a plan after prison, Julia's and Sharon's comments highlight the importance of a plan for the creation of a new life and a new identity after prison. As they both stress, without a plan after release, the risk of returning to prison looms large.

A Strong Need for Support

A support system after incarceration was the most emphasized need expressed by participants. The idea of support is something that has rarely been reported in the previous literature regarding the needs of women leaving prison. All eleven women participating in this study mentioned the importance of support in their ability to survive after incarceration. For example, Kim said that the acceptance of the community was what kept her in the program. "In the beginning, the acceptance from everyone in the church—people just accepted me and reached out to me. If I wouldn't have had that, I don't think I would have stayed." Kim has now graduated from Faith's House but lives in a rental home across the street; she is enrolled in a program to help her one day own her own home. She explained how being a part of the Faith's House community offered her support, love, and accountability. As Kim's words illustrate, a supportive community also fosters a sense of belonging that enhances her self-perception.

Sharon also offered vivid description of the support she felt when she first arrived at Faith's House:

> I like the fact that when I first came here, people were actually waiting to greet me with open arms. People I didn't even know. I had so much stuff on my bed, clothes and body wash; I had a welcome home party. I was treated like I was coming home, not like I was going to a halfway house.

She continued, "And the fact that there is always somebody to talk to. We have access to talk to anybody about anything . . . it's in confidence and they are going to do what they can to help you." Sharon's comments illustrate the importance of being accepted and feeling a sense of belonging—experiences that also help to lessen the stigma of incarceration. Several studies note that having a safe place to stay is essential for released women (Fletcher, Shaver, & Moon, 1993; O'Brien, 2001; and Kenemore & Roldan, 2006). Moreover, when healthy interpersonal relationships are available upon release from prison, transitioning can be smoother than if these relationships are not present. The findings in this study concur with these authors.

However, the women in this study describe a much stronger need for support networks that exist in multiple forms. Family and friends may provide support for women transitioning from prison to society, but substance-abuse support groups, pastoral mentoring, and mentoring in various other aspects of their lives are essential, as well. The women who participated in this study had spiritual mentors, employment mentors, financial mentors, and substance-abuse support groups. In addition, each woman had a trained volunteer mentor from the community who was assigned specifically to her within the first few days of her leaving prison. A variety of options for ongoing support, as is referenced here, is a relatively new way of thinking about successfully transitioning from prison to society. One reason that multiple forms of support may be essential to the success of women leaving prison is that, in addition to offering emotional and practical support, a strong support network also communicates social acceptance and helps to reinforce women's positive self-images after prison.

Making a Successful Reentry

One of the more practical areas of this study directly pertains to making reentry for women a successful transition from prison to the community. Through interviews and casual conversations with the participants, it was important to learn more about what could be done to improve reentry for this group of women. The participants described areas of programming that they felt helped them the most in their transition, and they also shared areas in which they felt more work could be done. This data can be used to assist prisons and reentry programs in preparing women to succeed upon leaving prison.

The women believed that they had benefited from prisoner programming they experienced while behind bars. Many of the participants said they had completed as many programs in prison as possible. Some of these programs included education (GED and advanced degrees), parenting classes, substance-abuse counseling, agriculture, hairstylist licensing, seeing-eye-dog training, faith-based programs, and specific industrial-skills training. The women expressed the importance of these programs behind bars but also mentioned that such programs were dwindling because of decreased funding. Women who had served ten or more years in prison explained that prisoner programming was once easily accessible but that in the last five years, it has become extremely scarce. Indeed, as a number of scholars note, state and federal governments have drastically reduced funding for prisoner programs (see Garland, 2001; Phelps, 2011; Western, 2006). The reduction of funding for prison programs is especially disconcerting because the evidence is clear that programming behind bars has a variety of benefits (see Bloom, 2006; Chappell, 2004; Winterfield et al., 2009).

Another element that was beneficial to the participants in this study was the structure and accountability built into their reentry programs. Many of the women confessed that they had resisted these elements of programming initially but found that they needed structure and accountability to succeed. The women discussed needing clear, strict rules, with apparent consequences. They also mentioned the importance of having a safe place in which to be held accountable. Accountability was mentioned in several different situations. Trina stated that "the most helpful thing since I have been here is calling me on my behaviors. Calling me on my behaviors so that I can change from my old behaviors." Similarly, Lindsey said that the most beneficial thing about her reentry program is "unconditional love and accountability." She explained, "I enjoy it [accountability] for me because I know I need certain things and that I don't need certain things. And I truly don't want to go back to the way I used to be and if somebody sees me being like that, then I hope they say something out of care and concern."

The final area of programming that was most important to the women's success was having a supportive, safe community. Both of the transitional programs that I worked with for this study tried diligently to provide a sense of community for the women. Many women in transition programs did not have family and friends to turn to upon being released from prison, and the people in the reentry programs were like family to them. A number of steps were taken to provide a sense of community and support: one-on-one mentoring; community dinners where all residents were required to be present and eat together; various types of community support groups; community housing (where the residents live together); and multiple counselors and mentors in various areas to lend support. The feeling of being part of a community was difficult for some women because they were not used to having that sense of love, caring, and belonging; however, all of the women I spoke with expressed the importance of having a safe community in place.

Conclusion: Informing the Reentry Conversation

In this study, formerly incarcerated women presented themselves as survivors who are working diligently to create new lives for themselves after prison. They were striving to move past the stigma associated with their status as former prisoners and reconcile the identities they felt on the inside with their perceptions of the way society views them from the outside. After hearing the women's stories, I am both hopeful and troubled for what life after incarceration means for women in this country. I am hopeful because I witnessed how many women are working jobs to support themselves, taking the necessary steps to rebuild their familial relationships, and attentively doing whatever is necessary to remain out of prison and drug-free.

However, I am also troubled because even though many women are making great strides in their lives after prison, the stigma of incarceration persists. The stigma and mystique often associated with women prisoners have led the media, policy makers, and many other Americans to view those who have been behind bars as evil monsters who should be shunned in our society (see, for example, Chesney-Lind, 1997; Jacobson, 2008; Lebel, 2012). Indeed, as Bill Yousman's work in this volume (Chapter Seven) documents, prisoners' voices are rarely represented in media images of prison, which results in distortions that fuel the stigma of incarceration (see also Mason, 2007; Yousman, 2009; Wilczynski, 1991).

The women who took part in this study reveal complex experiences and complete identities that are rarely represented and often misunderstood. By communicating where they have come from, where they are now, and where they are going, they offer essential information that can be helpful to women who come after them. Just as important, the voices of women leaving prison can challenge the stigma that creates obstacles to building their new lives. It is my hope that the participants' insights highlighted here may inform the work of activists, prison educators, policy makers, and scholars in our ongoing work for justice.

PART III

Working on the Media

Representations of Prisons and Prison Activism

Part Three offers two essays arguing that how Americans think about crime, violence, imprisonment, and the larger social forces that lead to them is shaped in large part by mass-mediated spectacles that teach us to fear stereotypical others and hence to crave heavy-handed efforts by police forces. These chapters argue that a central function of the mass media is to teach us to be afraid and compliant. Rather than simply pointing to the characteristic features of these mass-mediated spectacles, however, these two chapters offer pragmatic proposals for creating a new movement of critical media literacy and community-based productions of alternative forms of media. In Chapter Seven, Bill Yousman offers a roadmap to new forms of grassroots media education, while also showing that grisly images of prison violence are so compelling that they infect the thinking even of prisoners, whose personal experiences might be expected to counter the exaggerated and hysterical images foisted upon the public by mass-mediated corporations. In Chapter Eight, Craig Lee Engstrom and Derrick L. Williams offer a loving tribute to what they call "consciousness-raising hip hop," which they argue amounts to a Ciceronian recipe for sharp-edged political criticism and community-based alternatives to violence. Both chapters draw upon the authors' long-term involvement with underrepresented and underresourced communities, and both chapters offer readers compelling and systematic avenues for becoming engaged in grassroots media movements meant to counter the society of the spectacle with new forms of cultural criticism and community care.

CHAPTER 7

Challenging the Media-Incarceration Complex through Media Education

BILL YOUSMAN

It is a typical night of television in the United States: on HBO a gang of African American prisoners are assaulting another captive, a white man, passing him back and forth and laughing as they abuse him; on NBC a group of black female inmates are wreaking havoc in a hospital emergency room; flip to another channel and a Hollywood film features a group of prisoners hijacking a plane and terrorizing the passengers and crew; over on MSNBC, a reality show called *Lockup* profiles a prisoner who reportedly performed cannibalistic acts; on still another channel, *Law and Order* detectives harshly interrogate an inmate in a small prison meeting room; later in the evening, a similar scene will play out in a rerun of the syndicated program *NYPD Blue*— prime-time fun for viewers of all ages; business as usual for the ratings-driven U.S. television industry.

Focusing on prime-time dramatic television as the most prevalent source of fictional images of violence, crime, and incarceration, in this chapter I address the distorted narratives and images that saturate popular television dramas. I also draw upon interviews I conducted with ex-prisoners to show how media representations of imprisonment, though inaccurate and misleading, shape the perceptions even of those who have themselves been incarcerated. This is a startling finding, for it demonstrates that even prisoners and former prisoners are susceptible to having their thoughts about crime and punishment shaped by the spectacular distractions of mass media. Having established the power of what I hereafter call the media-incarceration complex to warp our thinking about crime, violence, and imprisonment, I then explore ways that media education can offer viewers tools for deconstructing mass-mediated images of prisons and prisoners and, more broadly, help citizens to counter media injustice through grassroots-based media-literacy interventions.

Media Power and "Training in Dependence" in the Carceral State

Beginning with the invention of motion pictures at the end of the nineteenth century, and especially since the rise of television in the 1950s, important social, political, and economic trends are increasingly defined by media images and stories. As Kellner writes:

> Social and political conflicts are increasingly played out on the screens of media culture, which display spectacles such as sensational murder cases, terrorist bombings, celebrity and political sex scandals, and the explosive violence of everyday life. Media culture not only takes up always-expanding amounts of time and energy, but also provides ever more material for fantasy, dreaming, modeling thought and behavior, and identities. (2003, p. 1)

One of the most common of these captivating media spectacles is found in frightening images of dangerous, violent prisoners: men, usually, who are just barely contained by the criminal-justice system. In an era when the massive buildup of the prison-industrial complex is happening without much public scrutiny or knowledge, understanding the role that media images play in shaping our perception of prisons and prisoners is crucial to understanding why policies such as building more prisons and locking up ever-greater numbers of people are accepted as commonsense steps in keeping innocent citizens safe from the predators who are waiting to strike the minute we let our guard down, the minute we go "soft on crime."

Those who question the legitimacy, efficacy, or morality of the incarceration nation we have created are often framed as out-of-touch liberals. As Cusac (2009) points out, during the last few decades the legal system in the United States became increasingly harsh, as more and more prison sentences were handed down and as these sentences became longer and longer. Media stories and images are central to maintaining and legitimating this punitive discourse, thus creating a culture of fear that is among the dominant political forces in the twenty-first century. In regard to television news, for instance, Altheide writes:

> Crime is but one example of a larger array of images that promote the sense that the world is out of control. Helplessness is combined in many reports with a sense of randomness. This promotes incredible anxiety and fear that something might happen (1) which we know about; (2) about which little can be done; and (3) which may occur at any time. The only response we seem to have is to wait and prepare (e.g., get armed, lock doors, build walls, avoid strangers and public places) . . . Moreover, these responses also promote a very strong urge to get help from somewhere, anywhere. This is why audiences seem so willing to accept definitions of what the problem is—the causes of crime, what can be done about it, and how limited our alternatives

are—which usually involves the police and criminal justice system. (2002, pp. 136–37)

For Kellner, Cusac, and Altheide, the fear generated by media images primes viewers to accept and even desire a punitive, carceral state.

Other scholars have documented how this fear has become a key tool for those seeking to justify the ever-expanding prison population, the construction of more and more prisons, and the diversion of more and more funds into the growing prison-industrial complex (Alexander, 2010; Dyer, 2000; Mauer, 1999; Meiners, 2007; Miller, 1996). In fact, a report issued by the National Criminal Justice Commission in the mid-1990s (Donziger, 1996) argued for direct connections among distorted media images of crime, rising public fears, and the severe rise in incarceration, pointing out that the media environment is awash in hyperviolent images of crazed criminals, despite the fact that actual crime has been on the decline for several decades. As Glassner writes about the first decade of the twenty-first century: "In the nation's largest cities, murder accounted for only .2 percent of all crimes, and in the suburbs of those cities, murder accounted for just .01 percent. Yet not only are murder stories a staple of the coverage in those cities, accounting for 36 percent of the crimes reported on the TV news, the newscasts warned suburban viewers that crime was moving to their areas" (2010, p. 230). Thus, rather than thinking of our television and computer screens as windows on reality, a more apt metaphor would be that of the funhouse mirror, as the commercial media display distorted images of crime and violence that have only a tenuous connection to the real world they purport to reflect.

Furthermore, the fear that is generated by these distorted media reports of crime, violence, and chaos is not a generalized or vague anxiety but a focused and specific fear related to gender, race, and class divisions. Scholars have identified how media stories of crime coalesce around the image of the dangerous, predatory, and depraved black male or, less often, the drug-addicted, sexually promiscuous black female (Alexander, 2010; Collins, 2009; Dixon, 2010; Giroux, 2009; Mauer, 1999; Meiners, 2007; Miller, 1996; Shanahan & Morgan, 1999). As Bauman argues:

> The poor are portrayed as lax, sinful, and devoid of moral standards. The media cheerfully cooperate with the police in presenting to the sensation-greedy public lurid pictures of the "criminal elements," infested by crime, drugs and sexual promiscuity, who seek shelter in the darkness of their forbidding haunts and mean streets. The poor provide the usual suspects to be round up, to the accompaniment of a public hue and cry, whenever a fault in the habitual order is detected and publicly disclosed. (2007, p. 28)

The distortions of the commercial media system are thus not simply random inaccuracies, inevitable to any system of representation; rather, we can identify in these images and stories patterns that vilify the poor and people of color by associating them with deviant lifestyles and imagined crime waves.

Despite the media obsession with crime and chaos, experts from across the ideological spectrum agree that the rate of crime (as tracked by government criminal-justice statistics), especially violent crime, has been falling since the mid-1980s (Cusac, 2009; Glassner, 2010; Irwin, 2005; Miller, 1996). Nonetheless, according to public-opinion polls, most Americans believe that the nation suffers from more crime than ever before (Dyer, 2000). And in one peculiar way, they are correct, for while crime in the streets is falling, crime and violence on television is escalating. As George Gerbner has argued, television is the primary storyteller in U.S. culture, and the stories told by the television industry are often stories of intense violence and mayhem. Since the 1960s, Gerbner and his colleagues have presented compelling research suggesting that immersion in the hyperviolent world of television is associated with a fearful emotional state among heavy viewers of television (see Morgan, Shanahan, & Signorielli, 2009, for a comprehensive summary of Gerbner's cultivation theory and research). Furthermore, this fear has important political implications. As Gerbner said (in a 1991 interview) about those who grow up in the cultural environment produced by television:

> You're more insecure, more afraid, more dependent. So this becomes *training in dependence*. This is training to seek protection from the "stronger" members in society. And this is often training in approving repression of other people if you consider that it enhances your security. This represents itself in increasing demands for capital punishment, in approving police action, in approving the army, even foreign wars because they're considered to enhance your chances of survival. (in Closepet & Tsui, 2002, p. 494, emphasis added)

Gerbner thus argues that the scary images of film and television have primed viewers to accept the severe measures advocated by "get tough on crime" politicians for the past four decades. Meanwhile, research has shown that the mainstream news media provide viewers with little information about the massive scale of incarceration or the race- and class-based disparities of imprisonment in the United States (Yousman, 2009), meaning that we are both scared and ignorant, fearful and misinformed.

This alarming confluence of fear and ignorance has been reinforced by two interrelated phenomena: a dearth of journalistic investigation into the current state of incarceration, and a wealth of lurid, graphic images of violent prisoners and criminals on display both in fictional programming and from a degraded television-news industry that is similarly organized around entertainment values and commercial priorities. While the commercial news media tend to ignore what is happening inside U.S. prisons and jails (except for sensationalistic programming, like MSNBC's *Lockup*, which focuses on riots, escapes, and gang wars), incarceration is a significant and recurring theme for the entertainment-media industries. Prison films are abundant, rap musicians refer frequently to life behind bars, and even the video-game industry has created scenarios where the action is played out behind virtual prison walls. In the commercial-entertainment industries, any type of intensely dramatic setting or visually compelling image is good fodder for the corporations whose primary focus is the profit potential behind any text/image. When it comes to stories about the prison-industrial complex, the mythos of danger and deviance associated with incarceration translates easily into media spectacles that are created primarily to captivate audience attention and consumer dollars while simultaneously colonizing our imaginations.

As Guy Debord wrote in 1967: "In societies where modern conditions of production prevail, all of life presents itself as an immense accumulation of spectacles. Everything that was directly lived has moved away into a representation" (1967, p. 42). This is an apt description of the relationship that most viewers have to the images of prisons and prisoners that appear on our screens and monitors. Indeed, because most viewers will not have experienced incarceration directly, media representations become their primary form for imagining prison. Debord explains that "When the real world changes into simple images, simple images become real beings and effective motivations of hypnotic behavior" (1967, p. 42). As I argue below, when viewers mistake violent media spectacles for "real beings," they tend to embrace increasingly severe forms of social control such as increased surveillance, policing, and incarceration (Debord, 1967; also see Kellner, 2003).

Prison Fictions

While television-news investigations of the practices of the U.S. penal system are rare, television dramatic programming is abundant with representations of crime, criminals, and the incarcerated (Rapping, 2003; Yousman, 2009). My examination of popular crime dramas like *Law and Order* and *NYPD Blue*, for example, revealed that nearly all of the episodes included incarcerated characters or those who had been recently paroled from prison. The absence of television-news-media coverage of incarceration, considered in tandem with a wealth of images of the incarcerated in dramatic programming, suggests that fictionalized and sensationalized versions of prisons and prisoners are most familiar to television audiences. However, the story that the television industry tells is one that is vastly different than the reality of incarceration in the United States. For example, my research found that television dramas tend to represent prisoners as violent monsters, with murderers and rapists leading the way, but in actuality the prison boom has not been driven by the incarceration of violent criminals. The majority of prisoners have been sentenced for nonviolent offenses—usually related to the illusory "war on drugs" (Glassner, 2010; Hartnett, 1995; Hartnett, 2000). But as television scholars have argued (see Gerbner & Gross, 1976), violence on television is not meant to be factual so much as generically familiar: the violence must fill genre-driven requirements by creating the compelling visuals, simple dramatic conflicts, and quick resolutions that fuel the assembly line of weekly television-program production. The television industry therefore relies on gruesome tales of murder and mayhem not because anyone involved thinks they are "real," but because they facilitate the production of the formulaic and compressed narratives that attract viewer attention in an increasingly cluttered and fragmented media environment.

While the overrepresentation of violence is one key aspect of television images of prisons and prisoners, an equally significant problem is the mass media's production of racial fantasies. This is why numerous scholars have argued that we cannot fully understand the prison-population explosion without understanding racial politics in America during the twentieth and twenty-first centuries (Alexander, 2010; Davis, 2003; Giroux, 2009; Mauer, 1999; Miller, 1996). For example, scholars have argued that because blacks and Latinos are more likely than whites to be depicted as violent, the severity of the criminal-justice system and the brutal conditions inside the nation's prisons are framed as a necessary and logical response to those savage Others who threaten the racial order (Entman & Rojecki, 2000; Mauer, 1999; Miller, 1996; Yousman, 2009). Brutal state practices are therefore legitimated through narratives that frame the punitive treatment of prisoners as both necessary and deserved. These brutalizing fictions suggest that the penal system is too lenient or soft on these dark Others, that rehabilitation is impossible, that prisoners are dangerous creatures who require severe punishment, and that, ultimately, capital punishment is the only solution. Following on media patterns that date back to the dawn of the nation (Hartnett, 2010; Stabile, 2006), such media images and narratives construct the penal system as just, as a flawed but ultimately functional institution (Cusac, 2009; Meiners, 2007; Rapping, 2003; Yousman, 2009).

My textual analysis of television crime dramas also revealed that imprisoned characters, while a regular part of the cast of prime-time crime dramas, tend to function more as plot devices than as living human beings. In most television crime dramas, the daily conditions of life in the nation's prisons are not germane to the discourse. Crime in the streets is a recurring theme in television drama and the focus of some of the most highly watched programs on television. For example, during the 2010–11 television season, programs like *CSI*, *NCIS*, *Criminal Minds*, *The Mentalist*, and *The Closer* were all ratings leaders, and they all featured dedicated law-enforcement officials hunting down and capturing an endless array of murderers, rapists, and thieves. Despite this focus on crime and punishment, the fates of those who are convicted and sentenced to prison are largely outside of the discourse. In the hundreds of hours of dramatic programming that I examined, scenes of daily life inside prisons were never represented (with the exception of two programs, discussed below). Issues such as the conditions inside the nation's prisons, the fortunes of those who are sentenced to them, and the ripple effect of mass incarceration on communities are seemingly irrelevant to the obsession with crime and policing that these programs both reflect and help to construct. The invisible nature of the nation's prisons and jails held true across all of the television programming I examined, with just two notable exceptions—*Oz* and *Prison Break*.

Oz, which debuted on HBO in 1997, was the first ongoing U.S. television program set inside a prison. TVGuide.com described the program as "a grim and graphically raw drama about life (and often death) in an experimental prison ward called Emerald City at the Oswald State Correctional Facility (nicknamed Oz)." *Oz* was well received by television critics, who praised the program for its realism. However, most of this notion of realism was based on the show's frequent portrayals of extreme violence. In its six seasons, *Oz* pushed television violence to new and bizarre levels, including prisoners burying each other alive, electrocuting one another by shoving each other's heads into television sets, dying on an electric fence, poisoning one another, repeatedly torturing and assaulting other prisoners, attempting to blow up the prison with a homemade bomb, and even being urged to murderous activity by ghostly visitations. As absurd as some of those scenarios are, the overall tone of *Oz* is also at odds with the reality of life in America's maximum-security institutions. On *Oz*, prisoners wander the hallways and recreation areas of the prison at will, with little surveillance or intervention by the guards. They blithely commit havoc over and over again with almost no consequences. In actuality, prisoners in the most severe facilities, like those that *Oz* is supposed to represent, spend most of their time, as much as twenty-three hours a day, alone, locked inside their cells (Abramsky, 2007). *Oz*'s purported "realism" is therefore not only fictional, but fictional in ways that reproduce the worst stereotypes about prisons and prisoners.

The notion that *Oz* presents viewers with a "real" peek into the nation's prisons is thus completely absurd. On one level this is understandable, for television fictions are just that—fiction. Yet HBO works hard to suggest that its programming is different. One of their prominent marketing slogans is "It's not TV: It's HBO." "Reality" has become a key marketing strategy throughout the television industry, ranging from the wild popularity of so-called reality television programs, to the "ripped from the headlines" slogans attached to crime dramas like *Law and Order*, to the emphasis in HBO programs of a gritty look at the underbelly of American culture on programs like *The Sopranos*, *Boardwalk Empire*, and *Oz*. Yet so often in these programs what is considered "real" is simply extreme violence. As Gerbner and his colleagues have argued since the 1960s, this construction of constant violence as a "real" part of ev-eryday existence has debilitating consequences for our social world, for it cultivates mistrust, fear of others, and a willingness to submit to increasingly severe measures of social control.

Oz's use of terror as a commodity, a way to draw viewers to the program's hyperviolent brand image, is therefore politically significant, as viewers who have few counternarratives to draw on may construct their imagination of prisons and prisoners from programs like this, the numerous Hollywood films that represent prisoners in a similar hyperviolent fashion, or the popular Fox television program *Prison Break*, which followed in the wake of *Oz*. *Prison Break* debuted on the Fox network in 2005, becoming only the second U.S. television drama to focus primarily on incarcerated characters as the central protagonists. *Prison Break*, like *Oz*, was both a critical and popular success. Unlike *Oz*, *Prison Break* included many subplots that occurred outside of the prison, yet it also shared many characteristics with the earlier program, including supposed "behind the scenes" glimpses into prison life, bizarre plot twists, unlikely scenarios, characterizations of prisoners as savage (often psy-chopathic) deviants, and an extremely high degree of violence, often leading to death. As Meiners (2007) has written, programs like *Prison Break* are media spectacles constructed from a Manichean worldview, pitting a few innocent heroes against hordes of inherently dangerous and bad prisoners. Meiners asks us to question this construction through a bit of self-reflection:

> And, as we jaywalk, or cheat on taxes, or download songs for free from the Internet, or lie to the boss, or "borrow" paper from the photocopier at work for personal use, or use a variety of legal and illegal drugs, and more, what precisely does this category *innocent* mean? Invoking it is worrisome as it reifies an identity that is not possible, yet fictions still persist. Innocence also exists in a legal and cultural landscape where what is defined as a crime has been, and continues to be, explicitly racialized (2007, p. 179).

Meiners's questions illustrate how the line between innocence and guilt is not as clearly defined as programs like *Prison Break* suggest. In fact, Bohm (1986) argues that as many as 90 percent of Americans have committed some type of illegal offense for which they could have been, might have been, incar-cerated. Yet on television those in prison are defined as alien, completely and totally unlike Us, the innocent viewers. Programs like *Oz* and *Prison Break* fill our homes with images of prisoners (very often black or brown men) as sadistic monsters who are not completely controlled even by today's severe maximum-security institutions. If this is the case, if these creatures are so unlike us, so alien and dangerous, then we must become even more punitive, even more repressive in our approach to criminal justice. Even more polic-ing and surveillance is necessary, even more prisons, even harsher prison environments and sentencing policies; this is all deemed necessary by these narratives of terror.

As Meiners (2007) points out, crime-related fear is often based on an underlying relationship to racial unease, as well, and this is certainly true in both television news and television fictions. To explore this claim, consider the case of England's panic over "mugging" in the late 1970s. As argued in Stuart Hall's landmark text *Policing the Crisis* (Hall et al., 1978), England's news media created the new label of "mugging" to describe street robberies, thus triggering a panic over an imagined crime wave that reflected deep-seated racial fears and anxieties caused by the shifting of long-standing cultural norms in post-imperial England. Hall and his co-authors contend that the crisis that needed to be policed in 1970s Great Britain was not the imagined spike in "muggings" in the streets, but the social pressures that followed from an influx of large numbers of immigrants, the "darkening" of the British population, and the declining economic conditions of the white working and middle classes. "Mugging" was not an actual legal category of crime that had previously existed, but a media/political construction, a peg on which the coat of law and order could be hung, and a rallying cry that provided legitimation for repressive policing and the erosion of civil liberties. "Mugger" became a code word for black youth—the "folk devils" that were the scapegoats for the anxieties of a nation in transition. As Hall and his coauthors argue:

> The Folk Devil—on to whom all our most intense feelings about things going wrong, and all our fears about what might undermine our fragile securities are projected—is . . . a sort of alter ego for Virtue. In one sense, the Folk Devil comes up at us unexpectedly, out of the darkness, out of nowhere. In another sense, he is all too familiar; we know him already, before he appears. He is the reverse image, the alternative to all we know: *the negation.* . . . The "mugger" was such a Folk Devil; his form and shape accurately reflected the content of the fears and anxieties of those who first imagined, and then actually discovered him: young, black, bred in, or arising from the 'breakdown of social order' in the city; threatening the traditional peace of the streets, the security of movement of the ordinary respectable citizen. (1978, p. 161, emphasis in the original)

The British-based "folk devils" created by the mugging craze sound strikingly similar to those racist tropes that have driven U.S. crime policy since the end of the Civil War. Indeed, research has shown that many Americans associate blackness with criminality (Gilliam & Iyengar, 2000) and that the "black image in the white mind," as Fredrickson (1971) put it, is one marked by fear and trepidation. As Alexander (2010), Entman and Rojecki (2000), Giroux (2009), Hartnett (2010), Mauer (1999), Miller (1996), Stabile (2006), West (1994), and many others have documented, in the United States men of

color have long been depicted as threats to the social order by politicians, rep-
resentatives of the criminal-justice system, and media storytellers and pundits.
The image of a scary black or brown man is frequently used as shorthand for
those seeking to consolidate their power, as in the infamous "Willie Horton"
political advertisements that helped George H. W. Bush defeat his Democratic
opponent in the 1988 presidential election by insinuating that Michael Dukakis
favored letting black murderers roam the streets while on parole from prison
(Jamieson, 1993).

While it was not solely men of color who were portrayed as violent in the
programming I examined, television's racial representations must be situated
in the larger historical context of mass-mediated representations of blacks
and Latinos. The construction of violent black and Latino masculinity in the
news, on *Oz* and *Prison Break* and in other dramatic programs, is part of a
long tradition in U.S. film and television that has articulated darkness with
savagery, dating back almost a century to D. W. Griffith's notorious celebration of the rise of the Ku Klux Klan in *Birth of a Nation* (1915) and continuing
on to the overrepresentation of black criminals on television news, the drug
dealers and thugs that inhabited the "blaxploitation" films of the 1970s and
their descendents in urban films of subsequent decades, the villainous figures
on television cop shows (including so-called reality programs), the gun-toting
menaces in "gangsta" rap videos, and the dark monsters that roam the hallways
of *Oz*. Indeed, the histories of U.S. media and U.S. racism align very closely, and
it often seems that the cultivation of racial fear is one of the most consistent
characteristics of U.S. electronic media since Edison first began tinkering with
moving images (Stabile, 2006).

Other Stories, Other Storytellers:
Perspectives of Dissent and Acceptance

Television may be the central storyteller in American culture (Morgan, Shanahan, & Signorielli, 2009), but it is not the only potential source of stories about
incarceration, for those who have lived in America's prisons and jails also have
stories to tell. Thus, in addition to my critical readings of television representations of incarceration, I have spent time speaking with people who have been
incarcerated. I asked them to discuss their own experiences in prisons and
their thoughts on film and television representations of prisons and prisoners.

It is often difficult for researchers to gain access to incarcerated men and
women. However, I was able to locate a community day program that aids
ex-prisoners with their transition back into free society, and they allowed me
to interview any of their clients who were willing to speak to me. While the
twenty-five men and one woman who volunteered to participate in my focus-
group interviews do not constitute a scientific, randomly selected sample, they

do represent a range of prison experiences in terms of the institutions they were imprisoned in and the lengths of sentence they served. In addition, the racial distribution of the volunteers was similar to that of America's prison population: twelve blacks, nine Latinos, and five whites. Their ages also matched the general parameters of most prisoners, ranging from early twenties to early fifties. Meeting in small groups in a conference room at the transitional day program, I asked them to describe their daily routines while incarcerated and their relationships with other prisoners and prison staff. Specific questions focused on concrete situations related to the prison experience: sexual relationships, friendship, violence, privacy, punishment, race relations, drugs, visitation, work, education, recreation and leisure, food, sleep, hygiene, health, safety, and therapeutic and rehabilitative programs. I focused on these topics because much of the vast literature about life in America's prisons—created by historians, sociologists, communication scholars, prisoners, and those educators and activists who work closely with them—has identified these issues as central to the lives of prisoners (for just a small taste of this abundant literature, see Abu-Jamal, 1995; Burton-Rose, 1998; Cleaver, 1968; Conover, 2000; Davis, 2005; Girshick, 1999; Jackson, 1970; Leder, 2000; Prejean, 1993; Rideau & Wikberg, 1992; X & Haley, 1964). Finally, I showed the volunteers a short video clip taken from the program *Oz* and asked them in open and general terms what they thought of it.

The stories these ex-prisoners told were different from the stories I had found in television representations of incarceration. For instance, they described institutions that are much more repressive than those depicted on U.S. television, marked by close supervision and surveillance, limited freedom of movement, and strict daily routines. While they did speak of some violence they encountered in prison, they also tended to refute the hyperviolent construction of prisoners suggested by television. The shows mentioned above tend to focus on rape, murder, and riots, suggesting that these extreme incidents are routine and inevitable due to the natural sadism and brutality of the incarcerated; in contrast, the former prisoners I spoke with provided insights into how prisons and jails *as institutions* encourage rather than discourage violence, are founded in violent principles, and operate based on punitive and violent practices. These perspectives on the relationship between incarceration and violence are consistent with the findings of many other scholars who have written extensively about the dehumanizing effects of the prison-industrial complex (see, among others, Abramsky, 2002; Alexander, 2010; Austin & Irwin, 2001; Burton-Rose, 1998; Conover, 2000; Davis, 2003; Davis, 2005; Girshick, 1999; Hartnett, 2010; Irwin, 2005; Parenti, 2008; Scraton & McCulloch, 2009; Wacquant, 2009).

The ex-prisoners I spoke with also discussed many issues and concerns that were not included in the television narrative of incarceration. They talked about the sorry state of nutritional and health-care services behind bars, and the extremely limited and underfunded educational and vocational programs available to most prisoners. Other issues, such as abusive treatment by corrections staff, the lack of employment opportunities for ex-prisoners, the plight of women in prison, problems caused when prisoners convicted for violent and nonviolent offenses are housed together, and the generally inadequate and often inhumane living conditions in most facilities, came up spontaneously as we talked, yet my textual analysis of both news and dramatic programming had found that these issues are simply not a part of the television discourse about prisons and prisoners (see Abramsky, 2002; Austin & Irwin, 2001; Burton-Rose, 1998; Conover, 2000; Davis, 2003; Davis, 2005; Girshick, 1999; Irwin, 2005; and Parenti, 2008, among others, for analysis of the conditions inside U.S. prisons). Thus the two sets of stories that I examined, stories told by the television industry and stories told by those who have actually lived inside America's prisons and jails, provided very different perspectives on incarceration in the United States. The television story of incarceration is one of a commonsense response to the dangerous savages that threaten our safety, while the stories and experiences of the individuals I spoke with refute this narrative and offer a counternarrative of prisons as punitive, dehumanizing, and ultimately ineffective institutions.

Despite their telling personal life stories that challenged television's representation of incarceration, my volunteers expressed deep involvement with, and belief in, media images of prisons and prisoners. Toward the end of the interview process, we watched a clip from *Oz* and there was general acceptance of the veracity of *Oz*'s representation of incarceration. Even more important, throughout the interviews ex-prisoners frequently brought up other prison-related films and television shows they had seen. These references to mass-mediated images often occurred during discussions of their own personal experiences. Even when I had made no reference to television or film at all, respondents invoked media stories when discussing prison life. And I had been very careful not to mention media myself until the end of the interviews, when we watched the clip from *Oz*. In short, even those viewers whose life experiences were full of firsthand stories and images of life in prison resorted to mass-media representations to make sense of their lives.

These findings mirror the research of Van de Bulck and Vandebosch, who noted in a study of Flemish prisoner responses to media images of incarceration, that

> the expectations of most of the inmates on entering the system were mainly based on television and movie images of prisons in the United States. They realized where they got their information from. They made explicit references to American audiovisual fiction. From it, they seemed to have been led to expect that the majority of inmates would be convicted of very serious

crimes, that the experienced inmates would subject newcomers to an initiation ritual and that rape and violence were part of the daily fare of prison life. (2003, p. 108)

Such media-fueled fears surfaced as well in Angela Davis's work with women in Cuban prisons. Davis (2003) notes that most of the women she interviewed said that their prior knowledge of prison life had come from Hollywood films. During my interviews, as was true of the findings of Davis and Van de Bulck and Vandebosch, ex-prisoners frequently combined media fantasies with real-world experiences, even when I had asked questions specifically about what they themselves had witnessed in prison. For example, Antoine and Miguel (all names used are pseudonyms) engaged in this dialogue after being asked about whether they had seen stabbings while in prison:

> Antoine: Like I said the only one was . . . the one I was telling you about earlier, about the guy with the TV, they were trying to bust him and stabbed him on his head.
> Miguel: It's like they flush you down the toilet if they want to . . .
> Interviewer: They what?
> Miguel: They had a movie just like that. They'll cut you in half, then into little pieces. That shit happens in Puerto Rico.
> Antoine: That's the Puerto Rican jail. That's one jail you do not want to go to. I saw a documentary on that . . . I was watching the Discovery Channel . . . they showed this documentary on . . . the Puerto Rican prison . . . there ain't no COs [corrections officers]. It's like that *Escape from New York* shit. They just throw you in there . . . there ain't no COs . . . like he said, they will hack you up into pieces.

This was a significant exchange, as Antoine and Miguel slid into a discussion of media stories, both fiction and nonfiction, even though I had specifically asked them to discuss their own experiences. Antoine refers to both a television documentary and a Hollywood science-fiction film about a futuristic prison. So although Antoine said he had witnessed only one stabbing while imprisoned, and Miguel referred to no violent personal experiences at all, they quickly turned a discussion about their lives into a replaying of extremely violent images that could have come straight from *Oz*.

In another interview, ex-prisoners began discussing the film *Lockdown*, even though I had asked them to describe their own experiences with corrections officers: "Mike: You seen *Lockdown*? You see how the dude dropped the weights on his chest and broke his arm? And stuff like that can happen. That's why they tried to take the dead weights out of jails now. That can easily happen. That whole room is nothing but metal." Mike had started this discussion by saying that a scene from *Oz*, where prisoners were left unsupervised in a weight room, is unlikely to happen in real prisons. Yet he ended up contradicting himself when he invoked another media narrative. Mike's memory of his own life was thus complicated by images from the mass media, which, in this case, appear to have overpowered his personal experiences of life in prison.

To demonstrate this alarming point in more detail, consider the following example of how closely some prisoners identify with media images:

> Ray: I've watched *Woods*—the movie *Woods*—last week. You saw it, right, Norm? It's about a prison, and this guy . . . was an artist, and at first he was a drug dealer out in the street, and he got in jail . . . and he became an artist. He met this other prisoner, but the prisoner . . . was a white guy, but he was a nervous white guy, so his mother had money, so she owned an art gallery, so he painted the whole story since he been down, and all these COs . . . they were sending him to work in a factory, with asbestos, he was getting . . . cancer . . . and so he found out about it, and he started drawing all this stuff and he told the guy all I want you to do is when your mother comes was to have her put this stuff in her art gallery. So they planned to escape. So the white dude was going to help him escape . . . he backed out at the last moment. So he let him go . . . So they escaped, and one of the guys stabbed the guy . . . The last day that they were going to escape he killed the guy that cut him, while they were escaping. Stabbed him up. So the other guy, he died, his friend, not the guy that stabbed him but his other friend . . . the police shot him because he didn't want to stay alive 'cause everybody else escaped, except him, the one that mapped the plan . . . He charged the fence with a screwdriver, and they blasted him, and that's how it ended. His whole life story in jail was the art gallery and people were looking at it . . . That was a good movie. *Woods*.

This was a lively conversation, with Ray and the other men showing excitement about the particulars of the film and the fate of the characters. Toward the end of his recounting of the film, Ray was obviously emotionally moved by the story. During his long description he seemed to almost lose sight of the fact that he was talking about a film and not a real event that he had experienced or real people that he had personally known.

Psychological research on audience relationships with media figures has labeled this tendency as "parasocial" (Horton & Wohl, 1956). This is the phenomenon, often associated with fans of soap operas, for viewers to so closely identify with the characters that appear in media stories that they speak of them much as they would speak of family members, close friends, or colleagues. As Horton and Wohl observed decades ago:

> One of the striking characteristics of the new mass media—radio, television, and the movies—is that they give the illusion of face-to-face relationship with the performer. The conditions of response to the performer are analogous to those in a primary group. The most remote and illustrious men are met *as if they* were in the circle of one's peers; the same is true of a character in a story who comes to life in these media in an especially vivid and arresting way.

We propose to call this seeming face-to-face relationship between spectator and performer a *para-social relationship*. (1956, p. 215)

As the examples discussed above demonstrate, these parasocial tendencies were apparent in how my volunteers spoke about the incarcerated characters in the films and television shows they had seen. The fact that media images of prison life were influential in shaping the respondents' perceptions of even their own prison experiences should be alarming to activists, educators, and media critics. Indeed, if prisoners' expectations of and memories about prison life are so heavily influenced by their exposure to television stories about incarceration, then we should not be surprised that viewers with no personal experience of the prison system are susceptible to mass-mediated images that push the kinds of extreme narratives and images that make mass incarceration seem like a necessary response to a world of monsters.

Responding: Questioning, Resisting, Working for Change

While media images and narratives are influential in shaping the public imagination, they are not all-powerful. Research into the effects of television, for example, has shown that viewers do not entirely embrace in any direct or simple way the implications of the stories they watch. Viewers can question and resist the distorted picture of incarceration that I have discussed here, and they can work to change the media system that perpetuates these misleading images. In this concluding section I discuss three ways that concerned citizens can work to break the hold that the media industries have over our perception of mass incarceration in the United States: I focus on media-literacy education and the related projects of media activism and alternative media.

While there is much debate among media educators about precisely what media literacy entails (see Yousman, 2008), scholars working in the critical tradition have advocated for an approach to media literacy that does not shy away from questions of power and ideology. Fully understanding the relationship between mass media and mass incarceration thus requires knowledge about the political economy of the media (concentrated corporate ownership, intense profit-orientation, etc.), the social impact of media consumption (media influence on individuals and society, the shaping of perceptions and ideologies), and the activist and alternative movements that are challenging mainstream media norms and practices. As Jhally and Lewis (1998) note, "Media literacy, in short, is about more than the analysis of messages, it is about an awareness of why those messages are there. It is not enough to know that they are produced, or even how, in a technical sense, they are produced. To appreciate the significance of contemporary media, we need to know why they are produced, under what constraints and conditions, and by whom" (p. 111).

This conceptualization of critical media literacy is also advanced by Sholle and Denski (1995), who contend that "Media literacy is not a practice that takes place in isolation. In order to understand the media, one's self, one's relation to it, one must be able to speak (with a voice) and be able to recognize who is speaking in the media and who is not speaking" (p. 27). In the case of media and mass incarceration, my analysis suggests those who have been allowed to speak are primarily apologists, defenders, and engineers of a punitive system of perverted criminal justice that has successfully transformed notions of social justice and a war on poverty into imperatives of social control and war on the poor. Those who are *not* allowed to speak are dissenters from this system and the victims of these trends—the millions of American citizens who are under the control of the prison-industrial complex.

The type of media education that is needed to challenge the connections between mass media and mass incarceration is one that empowers people to ask critical questions about (1) who controls the dominant media industries, (2) the nature of mainstream media images and stories, (3) the social consequences of living in a culture saturated by commercial media, and (4) how people can resist the vast power of the commercial media industries. When it comes to the relationship between mass media and mass incarceration, asking these questions is an essential first step in challenging the dominance of the prison-industrial complex. Thus I will now briefly touch on each of these issues while offering some suggestions for further reading for those who wish to explore these questions in more depth.

1. Who controls the dominant media industries? A political-economic approach to understanding contemporary media focuses on issues of corporate concentration, conglomeration, and commercialism in the media industries and the relationships between these industries and other powerful corporate and governmental institutions. Scholars who have conducted this kind of political-economic research have concluded that the vast majority of the media content that people around the globe watch, read, and listen to is produced by a small and concentrated group of multinational conglomerates, such as Disney, Time Warner, Viacom, General Electric, and the News Corporation. These corporations value profit above all other considerations, and together they control what sorts of stories and images are widely promoted and distributed and what sorts of stories and images are neglected or completely ignored (for further reading, see Bagdikian, 2004; Herman & Chomsky, 1988; Huff, Phillips, & Project Censored, 2010; McChesney, 1999; McChesney, 2004; Meehan, 2005; Schiller, 1989; Schiller, 1996; Wasko, 2001). As Herman and Chomsky (1988) have argued, corporate control of the media industries ensures that most of the stories we have access to amount to little more than propaganda for capitalism and for legitimation of the abuses wrought by

a system of greed and hyperindividualistic self-interest. Which brings us to our second question . . .

2. What is the nature of the media content produced and distributed by these giant corporations? Media images and stories, of course, are varied and sometimes quite diverse. However, media scholars have also uncovered consistent and recurring patterns of stereotypical representations that are sexist, racist, homophobic, nationalist, ethnocentric, and demeaning of the poor. Dissenting and radical perspectives that challenge the status quo, or that raise critical questions about social structures, are usually ridiculed or ignored in mainstream media. As Herman and Chomsky write about those who are allowed to shape and define the news: "In the media, as in other major institutions, those who do not display the requisite values and perspectives will be regarded as 'irresponsible,' 'ideological,' or otherwise aberrant, and will tend to fall by the wayside" (1988, p. 304). Meanwhile, the most consistent message is a celebration of conformity, hypercon-sumption, and material acquisition (for further reading, see Butsch, 2011; Dixon, 2010; Douglas, 1995; Entman & Rojecki, 2000; Gross, 2001; Hall, 2011; Herman & Chomsky, 1988; hooks, 1992; Katz, 2011; Kellner, 2003; Kilbourne, 1999; Parenti, 1992; Parenti, 1993; Said, 1978; Schor, 2004; Wilson, Gutierrez, & Chao, 2003). Overall, the tendency in mainstream media is just that . . . mainstreaming. By *mainstreaming* I mean a narrowing of the range of acceptable discourse, a shutting down of alternative or dissenting perspectives, and a marginalization of those who do not fit neatly into the ideological boxes constructed by the commercial media industries (also see Gerbner, Gross, Morgan, & Signorielli, 1982, on mainstreaming and cultivation). Thus we must ask a third question . . .

3. What are the social consequences of growing up and living in a culture dominated by the commercial media industries? Since the 1930s, there has been a tremendous amount of research into the social impact of mass media. The results of this research have been varied and sometimes contradictory, but certain patterns have been established, such as the tendency for high exposure to violent content to desensitize individuals to the consequences of violence and to make us more fearful of others, the ability of the mass media to set the agenda for what the public deems important and worthy of attention, the tendency for media stereotypes to influence our perceptions and beliefs about people who are not like us, and the detrimental effects of distorted images of beauty on young women's self-esteem and health, to name just a few (for further reading, see Bryant & Oliver, 2009; Gerbner, Gross, Morgan, & Signorielli, 2002; Jhally & Lewis, 1992; McCombs & Shaw, 1972; Pipher, 1994; Postman, 1985; Shanahan & Morgan, 1999; Wolf, 1991). The commercial media industries have in fact amassed enormous profits by making us feel isolated from one another, anxious, unworthy, and, ultimately, very afraid. Alienated

from other people, we thus turn to the myriad products that the consumer society dangles in front of us with promises of fulfillment and salvation. Our last question, then, is crucial . . .

4. How can people work to change and resist the dominance of the commercial media industries? A critical media-literacy approach emphasizes that we do not have to be passive consumers and recipients of media messages. People can and do educate themselves about media, challenge the dominant media industries, work for media reform, and create and consume alternative media outside of the commercial sphere. The rest of this essay focuses on a number of organizations that can provide resources and support for citizens who are fighting back against the abuses of the mainstream media through the three key projects of media education, media activism and reform, and alternative media (for further reading, see Atton, 2002; Duncombe, 1997; Lasn, 1999; McChesney, 2008; Newman & Scott, 2005).

So for those who are interested in learning more about critical media literacy, and spreading that knowledge to others, there are several places to start, including valuable websites such as the one sponsored by the Action Coalition for Media Education (ACME; www.acmecoalition.org). Unlike other media-literacy organizations, ACME eschews corporate funding because they recognize that a true project of media education must be fully independent from corporate influence. On their website, ACME describes their activities in this way: "Using a wide variety of multimedia curricula and resources, ACME helps individuals and organizations gain the skills and knowledge to access, analyze, evaluate, and produce media in a wide variety of forms." ACME's website offers a rich compendium of materials about media and media education, a blog, short videos, curricular materials for educators, and more.

ACME's vision of media education is linked with media activism focused on changing the media industries' priorities and practices. The primary force behind the growing media-reform movement is the nonprofit organization Free Press (www.freepress.net). On their website, Free Press provides a succinct description of their mission: "Free Press is a national, nonpartisan, nonprofit organization working to reform the media. Through education, organizing and advocacy, we promote diverse and independent media ownership, strong public media, quality journalism, and universal access to communications." Free Press is dedicated to changing the corporate media system through lobbying government and educating citizens about media policies regarding concentration of ownership, commercialism, diversity, and access. Free Press works to create a more open and equitable media system. Every two years, Free Press sponsors a National Conference for Media Reform that brings together activists, educators, organizers, media professionals, and citizens to network and debate key issues in confronting the commercial media system. One key area that Free Press focuses on is the relationship between media and civil rights, clearly central to the issues of mass media fueling mass incarceration that I have explored in this chapter.

The media-reform movement led by Free Press also works toward the creation and support of nonprofit media that can provide readers, listeners, and viewers with alternatives to the distortions of the mainstream commercial media. The Media Education Foundation (MEF; www.mediaed.org), for example, is a leading source of documentary films that focus on media and culture and the debilitating effects of the commercial media system. MEF's slogan, "Challenging Media," has a dual meaning, as MEF's goal is to challenge the mainstream media culture that promotes racism, sexism, classism, homophobia, consumerism, and violence, and to do so by producing and distributing challenging media of their own in the form of documentary films, study guides, and other valuable media-literacy resources. Similarly, Paper Tiger Television (http://papertiger.org) and California Newsreel (http://newsreel.org) are nonprofit producers and distributors of alternative documentary films by diverse grassroots filmmakers unaffiliated with the mainstream media industries. Their many films focus on issues of race, gender, class, inequality, resistance movements, and social justice, and they offer a vision of the world that is dramatically different than the one sold to us by the commercial media system.

Focusing on alternative media and information about incarceration is the Real Cost of Prisons Project (RCPP; www.realcostofprisons.org), which offers links to books, videos, and comics, as well as writing and music created by prisoners. RCPP's website functions as a valuable clearinghouse of alternative media that challenges the prison-industrial complex. For people who want to educate themselves about what is really going on in the nation's prisons and jails and the causes and consequences of mass incarceration, RCPP is a great place to start looking for resources. Internet explorers who are concerned about these issues can also discover dozens of documentary films about the prison-industrial complex that offer very different stories and images than those found in commercial television fictions. A YouTube or Google Videos search for "documentaries on incarceration" is a useful start for encountering many different perspectives (admittedly of widely varying quality) on the issues explored in this anthology.

This is a small sample of the wealth of alternative media available for citizens, educators, and activists who are seeking information, images, and stories that challenge the myths promulgated by the mainstream television and film industries. The triad of media education, media activism, and alternative media can offer us a way out of the maze of distortions and delusions perpetuated by commercial media giants who are more interested in spectacular images of fear and violence than in telling real and insightful stories about what is truly an American tragedy.

CHAPTER 8

"Prisoners Rise, Rise, Rise!"

Hip Hop as a Ciceronian Approach to Prison Protest and Community Care

CRAIG LEE ENGSTROM AND DERRICK L. WILLIAMS

> I'm a prison cell six by nine . . .
> I'm the place many fear cause there's no way out
> I take the sun away put misery instead
> When you wit me most folks consider you dead . . .
> —Nas, "Last Words" (1999b)

The United States is addicted to prisons (Walmsley, 2009), and many of the men and women who inhabit these facilities are often abandoned by family, friends, and society. Popular hip-hop artist Nas's lyrics, quoted above, remind us of the stark material reality faced by the nearly 2.3 million prisoners in the United States and 5 million others on probation, on parole, and under house arrest (Pew, 2010; Porter, 2011). As noted in the editors' introduction to this book, this means one in thirty-one adults is under some form of correctional control. This fact captures a depressing truth about the prison-industrial complex: once in the system, there is seemingly no way out. Parolees know this reality well, as they are often denied the right to vote and have increased difficulty finding a job upon release. A significant number—approximately 500,000—of those incarcerated are serving time for nonviolent drug offenses or victimless crimes (Butler, 2009). Regardless of the reason for "doing a bid,"[1] we should be mindful that when we talk about individuals' presence in prison, we are speaking of an absence from families and communities. For many of us, the incarcerated are, as several authors have referred to them throughout this book, our "neighbors." As Eleanor Novek observes in Chapter Ten, it is common for activists, teachers, and those most impacted by the prison-industrial complex to see the incarcerated as "People Like Us," because chances are great that the prison system has directly impacted us. Thus the statistics are likely personal in some way. The absence of our family, friends, and neighbors often continues after incarceration, too, in the form of psychological depression or an inability to support a family, pay taxes, or vote (Pryor, 2010). In short, the prison-industrial complex creates significant social, psychological, and financial costs for families and communities (Fulmer, 1995; Marsh, Fox, & Hedderman, 2009; Mauer & Coyle, 2004).

In this chapter, we argue that the hip-hop movement plays an important role in illuminating the problems of the prison-industrial complex by creating spaces of prison protest and modeling sources of community care. To demonstrate this claim, we explore what we call "consciousness-raising hip hop" as a type of Ciceronian rhetoric that challenges the prison-industrial complex and empowers prisoners and their communities. Our analysis of hip hop focuses on the artists, music, and (life)styles that promote a type of citizen-orator that is Ciceronian in character. Like Cicero, who was as much influenced by poetry as oratory (Enos, 1975a), hip hop speaks to its audience in complex and caring ways. First, we briefly explain why we believe the overzealous growth of the United States prison population is problematic. Without belaboring points already made in the editors' introduction, we want to add resonance to the positions of other chapter authors who address the powerful ways race impacts the prison-industrial complex. Second, we explain how hip hop can be understood as a form of Ciceronian rhetoric. In this section, we define "consciousness-raising hip hop" and explicate how this music (and movement) advocates for prison care and reform. Third, we provide examples of hip-hop advocacy consistent with Ciceronian *ethos* and rhetoric. In particular, we give attention to those hip-hop artists who fit our definition of "consciousness-raising" by providing hope to prisoners and communities working to transform the U.S. criminal-justice system, which, according to hip-hop artist Nas, is a "beast" that has "a fat belly" and "likes to eat dark meat" (DMX, Method Man, Nas, & Ja Rule, 1998).

While mainstream rap artists frequently glorify prison and promote it as a rite of passage, consciousness-raising hip hop addresses issues of mass incarceration and prisoner abandonment. In the concluding section, we provide examples from recently published news and scholarly articles to support our overall claim that hip hop promotes prison protest and community care. We also provide two personal examples that show how hip hop was important in shaping our worldviews and leading us to engage in both prison protest and community care. In sum, we demonstrate how working for justice needs a backbeat, an inspiring soundtrack, a propulsive and empowering aural landscape where America's disenfranchised youth and its wealthy suburbanites come together to think creatively about how the prison-industrial complex perpetuates injustice and racism. Our research, coupled with personal experiences that we share at the close of this chapter, leads us to believe that consciousness-raising hip hop can and does inspire us to take action.

Feeding the Beast: Why Prisons Are Full

The United States has the largest prison population per capita in the world (Walmsley, 2009) and incarcerates more people for victimless crimes than any other Western society (Abramsky, 2002). Three explanations locate the problem within the system itself. First, we live in an increasingly criminalized society. According to former federal prosecuting attorney Paul Butler (2009), the sheer number of laws leaves the average citizen vulnerable to police power. In the United States, anyone can be stopped, detained, and searched for, among other reasons, "spitting on a sidewalk, crossing a street against the light, [littering], [or] forgetting to put on a seat belt" (p. 26). Police use these laws to gain search consent, which is a common way they discover drugs. Such laws are arguably enforced discriminatorily against the poor and minorities (Butler, 2009; Clear, 2007; Mauer, 1999; Mauer & Coyle, 2004; Pager, 2009). In short, increased police surveillance leads to the multiplication of arrests; the nation is not experiencing a crime wave so much as an escalation of the number of citizens caught up in an ever-expanding network of laws governing daily life (Pager, 2009; Silvergate, 2009).

Second, more crimes are being punished with greater severity. Legislatures at the state and federal levels, wanting to appear "tough on crime," have escalated a discourse, in conjunction with the media, that links drug abuse to criminality rather than public health (Larson, 2011) and have thus written laws to dole out lengthy mandatory minimum sentences for low-level drug offenses. In fact, no victimless sociocultural practice has been criminalized more than drug possession (Abramsky, 2002; Clear, 2007), making the "War on Drugs" perhaps the greatest explanation for mass incarceration (Larson, 2011). As Butler (2009) notes, "over 80 percent of the increase in the federal prison population from 1985 to 1995 was due to drug convictions" (p. 46). According to FBI statistics, the most frequent arrests made in 2008 were for drug-abuse violations (approximately 1.7 million). Of these, 82.3 percent were for possession and 17.7 percent were for manufacturing and distribution. Marijuana possession and distribution accounted for 44.3 percent and 5.5 percent, respectively (Bureau of Justice Statistics [BJS], 2008). Such punitive laws are often illogical and have adverse consequences, such as increased social marginalization and addiction (Pryor, 2010). A commonly cited example of legal irrationality was the 100-to-1 sentencing disparity between crack cocaine and powder cocaine. This law adversely affects poorer users and addicts, who choose crack over higher-priced alternatives. The U.S. Congress recently closed the gap by passing the Fair Sentencing Act of 2010, but there is still an 18-to-1 sentencing disparity between the two substances (Public Law 111–220). Whereas increased surveillance has led to more arrests, these enhanced sentencing policies have led to longer sentences for more prisoners, hence driving the dramatic escalation of the prison and parolee population.

Third, several authors (Butler, 2009; Clear, 2007; Natapoff, 2009; Silvergate, 2009)—including some former prosecutors—argue that the latitude of police authority, the proliferation of laws, and the expansion of sentencing have created conditions ripe for snitching. Often low-profile criminals are threatened with punishment if they do not snitch on others; this encourages the practice of suspects providing (sometimes false) information to police on the activities of others, usually in the hope of receiving a plea deal. Police departments' reliance on criminal informants has created a climate of fear and distrust in communities already absent of important social services, making inhabitants of minority and poor communities "ghetto prisoners" (Nas, 1999b). Whereas we argue here for a Ciceronian and hip-hop-driven version of community care, the production of a culture of snitching, or playing the "5K game"—so named after the 5K1.1 section in the Federal Sentencing Guidelines—is among the most damaging consequences of the prison-industrial complex, as a generation of young men has been put in situations where violating trust is a required component of community survival (Brown, 2007; Natapoff, 2009). What is more, there is evidence that based on informants' accounts alone, judges have issued no-knock warrants, which have led to an escalation of wrongful convictions and violent encounters between police and civilians (Brown, 2007; Center on Wrongful Convictions, 2006).

While the encroaching power of the prison-industrial complex knows no racial or class boundaries, the prison population is composed disproportionately of black and brown bodies (BJS, 2010). In 2009, for example, Black non-Hispanic males had an imprisonment rate that was six times higher than white non-Hispanic males (BJS, 2009). This mass incarceration follows the long line of social injustices foisted upon America's minorities and poor (Alexander, 2010). Since the early 1970s, the U.S. prison population has steadily increased at an alarming pace (Pew, 2009).[2] Historically speaking, no group of black men has been more affected by mass incarceration than those of the post–Civil Rights generation (Clear, 2007). Bakari Kitwana (2002) cites this problem as the landmark issue of the post–Civil Rights generation, or what he describes as the "hip-hop generation" (defined as individuals born between 1965 and 1984). Michelle Alexander (2010) and Angela Davis (2003) thus point to mass incarceration as the civil-rights issue of our time. They argue that incarceration is a means of racialized social control. Just as Jim and Jane Crow laws of the late nineteenth and early twentieth centuries existed in the form of poll taxes, literacy tests, denied voting privileges, and legal segregation, laws today are creating second-class citizenship. Disenfranchisement is observable among nonwhites and individuals of low socioeconomic status, who are labeled as

felons for nonviolent drug offenses, serve long prison terms, and lose important democratic powers—such as voting rights, employment opportunities,
and mobility.

In short, the function of prisons, as social theorists in a variety of disciplines
have noted, "has been neither to prevent crime nor to deter violence, but rather,
to reinforce hierarchies of class privilege and political power" (Hartnett, 2000,
p. 200). Because of this political function, minorities and the poor have continued to be ostracized, as they have been for centuries, albeit in more palatable
and media-friendly narratives for the current zeitgeist (Roberts, 2008; Tonry,
2011; Wacquant, 2001). To put the seriousness of this issue in perspective, South
Africa under apartheid was internationally condemned as a racist society. In
1993, just before the end of apartheid, there were 851 black males per 100,000
in South African prisons; as of 2006, in the United States, there were 4,789
black males per 100,000 in prison—a rate 5.8 times higher than that of South
Africa during apartheid (BJS, 2010; Maur, 1994). Clearly, this problem begs
many solutions. Hip hop, as a form of grassroots witnessing and a powerful
language of advocacy, offers some possible solutions.

Hip Hop as Ciceronian Rhetoric:
Justice as Power to the People

As we argued above, the problem of mass incarceration is largely systemic. To
understand how hip-hop culture addresses the system, we now analyze the
rhetoric of politically conscientious hip-hop artists' music. While there is some
critique of rhetoric and rhetorical criticism as being too a-materialistic and
therefore unable to address real structural oppression (e.g., Cloud, 1994), our
analysis is oriented toward constitutive rhetoric (Charland, 1987) and symbolic convergence theory (Bormann, 1972), which treat rhetoric and symbolic
practice as arising from interpretations of institutional realities and therefore
as forces capable of reshaping such realities. We do not deny that power is an
important factor in who gets to shape social practices; however, we believe that
power is always shifting as citizens advocate for multiple and often competing
realities. Barry Brummett (1976) notes that as an intersubjective process of
meaning making, "rhetoric is in the deepest and most fundamental sense the
advocacy of realities" (p. 31). This theory is consistent with Cicero's concern
with how rhetoric creates and sustains social bonds (Micken, 1986). Thus
cultural practices are located within discourse, and rhetoric "is that part of
an act or object that influences how social meanings are created, maintained,
and opposed" (Brummett, 2008b, p. 38). This activist understanding of rhetoric allows us to take a hopeful position, for we believe along with Brummett
(1976), Charland (1987), and Bormann (1972) that if reality is discursively
shared, then it can be changed.

Music and poetry, because of their evocative aesthetics, are highly influential rhetorical forms—so powerful, of course, that even Plato had a love–hate relationship with these arts and Aristotle wrote extensively on the topic. Because of its mass appeal across race, class, and geographical lines in general, and because of its ability to reach urban and marginalized youth in particular, hip hop is a powerful rhetorical medium for drawing attention to and raising awareness about issues related to the prison-industrial complex. As a type of rhetorical folk-poetry (McQuillar, 2003; Wood, 1999), it is a musical genre with activist roots and was developed, in part, by those most impacted by the prison system, giving it a strong ethos among urban ghettoized youth and prisoners (Doggett, 2009; Higgins, 2009; Kitwana, 2002; Pulido, 2009). Often, its themes address the social injustices of mass incarceration and its impact on communities (Darby & Shelby, 2005; Higgins, 2009). In particular, "consciousness-raising" hip hop—in contrast to gangsta rap, for example—calls attention to harsh realities and also evokes a sense of new realities, or new fantasies and visions of how things ought to be and can be (cf. Bormann, 1972).

Hip hop speaks to a broad audience, and even those who do not listen to hip hop likely have a visceral opinion of it. In this sense, hip hop has the power to provoke dialogue. Even if gangsta-inspired rap, which often glorifies criminality, is appalling to many citizens, its presence incites a cultural discussion about criminality. While our bias is toward a more favorable opinion of all hip hop, we hope our reading of the "consciousness-raising" type as Ciceronian in character will allow readers to better appreciate this rhetorical and artistic genre of music in general, and the music that meets our definitions of consciousness-raising hip hop in particular.

Consciousness-Raising Hip Hop Defined

We define consciousness-raising hip-hop artists as those who engage in a sustained effort, both in lyrics and in practice, to create art and other social events that function as political critique and community empowerment. These artists develop critical awareness of our culture by being legitimate (i.e., having "street cred"[3]) and by drawing attention to particular problems. The importance of this definition is twofold. First, such consciousness-raising artists are likely, though not necessarily, to be fashionable and they may, and probably do, raise critical awareness of a particular social problem while problematically contributing to another. For example, because we are focusing on artists who use consciousness-raising rhetoric about the prison-industrial complex but also have broad appeal, we draw on artists who unfortunately at times use misogynistic or other offensive language. While we do not condone this language, we cannot dismiss the fact that these artists' lyrics promote protest and care for the communities most affected by mass incarceration. The unfortunate reality is that artists that take everything on at once, such as KRS-One, may be a Quintilian-type "ideal orator," but they do not often obtain the mass appeal achieved by artists who balance their rapping with the more simplistic, depoliticized, and market-friendly lyrics often selected for airtime by corporate radio stations (Boyd, 2004; Kitwana, 2004, 2005; McQuillar, 2007, 2010). As McQuillar (2007) notes, "Rap music used to be a tool used by inner-city youth to give voice to concerns that weren't acknowledged by mainstream society, inspire positive social change, and reflect hopes and dreams for our future. But as rap became mainstream, the original goals were sacrificed in exchange for a more marketable culture of crass commercialism, sex, class, and violence, with no sense of communal responsibility" (p. 185). Thus hip-hop artists like Tupac, Nas, and Salt-N-Pepa tactically balance political songs with ones more palatable to the general public (Kitwana, 2004; McQuillar, 2007, 2010). This process of balancing political messages and market needs has led some listeners to try to draw a distinction between corporatized rap and what may be called consciousness-raising hip hop.

Second, our definition suggests that artists do not themselves have to be activists, but they do need to address issues related to mass incarceration and the prison-industrial complex in an ongoing manner (e.g., they have multiple songs about the issues, create albums, engage in media interviews about the topic, and use social media to develop awareness). While activism develops "street cred" in certain communities, consciousness-raising artists need not, according to our typology, be consistent and poignant advocates who rap against prisons or for prisoners. What is particular about this point is that consciousness-raising artists may not have activism as their primary goal, although activism may result from their work. In other words, we see building political awareness and presenting messages of solidarity as activism—we are arguing, then, that consciousness-raising hip hop, even when not explicitly political, can play the crucial function of bearing witness to the conditions that lead to crime, violence, and mass incarceration. Moreover, our typology relieves artists of the often didactic burden of directing audiences to act on the information presented within their art. Our position is therefore consistent with the premises of invitational rhetoric (see Ryan & Natalle, 2001), in that hip-hop rhetoric invites audiences into dialogue but does not dictate the ways they must seek change. In many cases, the balancing of messages of advocacy with "pop tracks" and the lack of specific directives enables artists to obtain a broader and larger audience in which to build awareness about issues related to the effects of America's addiction to prisons.

We recognize that our inclusion and exclusion of artists is subjective. We relied, however, as we all do when selecting "great speakers" of any movement, on consensus among scholars of hip hop about those who legitimately raise issues related to social justice and are highly influential among prisoners (e.g.,

Dyson, 2004, 2006, 2009; Kitwana, 2005; McQuillar, 2007). These scholars have already argued at great length about those who are "real" and those who are "wannabes"; from these lists, we selected artists with consistent messages of protest and care regarding issues related to mass incarceration. We also recognize that sustained critique on one issue does not preclude artists (or any rhetor, for that matter) from being flippant or derogatory toward other important matters of social justice (e.g., gender politics). This is not to excuse such behavior, but it is not inconsistent with standpoint hermeneutics, which suggests that people argue from their respective positions, and that we should try to understand others from their own positions (Ryan & Natalle, 2001). Although a listener may disagree with an artist on one issue (e.g., representation of gender), he or she should, from a standpoint-hermeneutics perspective, attempt to dialogue *despite* differences in opinions and seek to find common ground on the issues of shared interest (e.g., prisoner and community care). Taken together, both points of our definition suggest that citizens do not have to like this musical genre or agree with a song's lyrics to be influenced by this art. Indeed, the overall rhetorical orientation of many consciousness-raising hip-hop artists, as we demonstrate in this chapter, critiques the prison-industrial complex, raises awareness about it, offers testimony of hope and care for both prisoners and communities, and therefore *invites activism* against mass incarceration. Thus if we hope to engage with prisoners and those in our communities who are impacted most directly by mass incarceration—and who happen to be disproportionally black, Latino, and poor—then we should know something about what music inspires them. For many of these folks, this music is hip hop (Butler, 2009; Pulido, 2009; Mendleson, 2010).

Toward Justice: Hip Hop as Epideictic, Deliberative, and Forensic Rhetoric

We have drawn upon Cicero to explain why hip hop is a particularly good avenue for advocating for prison reform and described its potential power in making a difference among prison-reform advocates. By drawing on Cicero, we are restoring the notion that arguments always already occur in the public sphere. Hip hop, as a stylistically rich praxis, and in "making a case" about contemporary and historical social injustices, serves political (deliberative), judicial (forensic), and ceremonial (epideictic) ends simultaneously. Hip hop works to subtly change the way listeners view crime, punishment, and our duties as citizens. If nothing else, it keeps the problems and realities of the "inner city" in the minds of suburbanites. Hip hop keeps us deliberating and open to caring. In this section, we explicate how it does so in a manner consistent with Ciceronian rhetoric.

Like most rhetoric in Rome at the time, Ciceronian oratory placed attention on rhetorical substance, yet Cicero did not believe in the restrictive practice of presenting one's argument in a plain style. In Cicero's *De Oratore* we find a more stylistic and pragmatic approach to rhetoric. Returning to Sophistic approaches, Cicero's writing suggests that he thought whatever brings philosophical and moral issues from the heavens to earth—or from the academy to the streets in today's terms—is the style fitting for the occasion (Dugan, 2005; see also Micken, 1986). If political and judicial oratory has to be delivered in poetic form for people to listen, then the savvy orator will use this stylistic approach. Latin poetry developed more than a century ahead of prose, so even the most technical of arguments often had to be poetic (Fantham, 2007). This is why one arguably finds Cicero using his poetic skills in his more formal oratory. In book 3 of *De Oratore*, he offers a positive appraisal of stylistic ornament as originating in poetry. This is also why, given the long tradition of oral history in black and Latino communities, hip hop speaks so boldly to nonwhite minorities in the United States (see, for example, Hallman, 2009, and Pulido, 2009).

Thus, for advocates of prison care, especially for activists and educators who are working directly with prisoners or those who have been incarcerated or impacted by mass incareration, hip hop can become a powerful, Ciceronian way to engage in identification and can offer the common space needed to begin dialogue. For example, according to John McWhorter (2008), hip hop contributes to social deliberation by questioning and encouraging critical thinking. For too long, though, all hip hop has been billed as dangerous persuasion or as simplistic wordplay with no substantive societal value outside of entertainment. Nevertheless, consciousness-raising hip hop, as a rhetorical art, has a philosophical basis (see Darby & Shelby, 2005). Boogie Down Productions' 1988 song "My Philosophy," for example, specifically introduces the idea that hip-hop artists are philosophers. In response to the question "So you are a philosopher?" lead lyricist KRS-One replies, "Yes." Throughout the album containing "My Philosophy," KRS-One embarks on a type of philosophical questioning of violence, racism, social class, government corruption, other artists' *ethos*, and the corporatization of the record industry. Since his start in hip hop, KRS-One has consistently questioned the virtues of life, so much so that he assumed the persona of a "philosophical teacher" within hip-hop circles.

Why Cicero?

Cicero rose to prominence in Rome. Famed as both a practitioner and a theorist of rhetoric (Enos, 1975a), he was a judicial advocate (primarily defense) and a poet, which makes his understanding of rhetoric particularly helpful to our examination of hip hop[4] as a critique of prison and a tool for community care. As a master of style, Cicero united *ethos*, *pathos*, and *logos* in ways that allowed him to speak across differences and to various audiences in a style and "language" that achieved identification with the *polis* (Dugan, 2005). Consequently, Cicero "has been condemned on the grounds of style, called an Asian, a word monger, accused of being fascinated with his own verbosity, [and] a stylistic show-off" (Micken, p. xv). This, of course, is not far from how hip hop is caricatured today. Just consider how Fox News contributor Juan Williams (2007) describes it within a few short paragraphs as "*just* rhyming over beats," with "raw charm," "delightful rhymes," and "nihilistic glorification of the 'thug life'" (p. 126; emphasis added). While Williams provides a legitimate critique of the vulgar and self-hating rap that is an outcome of the corruption of the art by corporate interests, he is dismissive of all hip hop on the basis that "some of the biggest names in rap, such as Tupac, swallow too much of their own poisonous outlaw fantasy and end up in real-life violent confrontations with real-life consequences: prison, death" (p. 126). Moving beyond such simplistic dismissals, Dyson (2006) offers a more complex view of hip hop in general and Tupac in particular, suggesting that Tupac "is one of the most important and contradictory artists to have spoken in and to our culture. Our adoration of him—and our disdain for his image—says as much about us as it does about him" (p. 17).

Like Tupac's multilayered and often contradictory character(s), Cicero was a key defender of a Sophistic rhetoric and (life)style in which thinking, speaking, and social interaction were united (Brummett, 2008a) by a love of aesthetics and persuasion. Cicero's approach to *ethos*, consistent with Roman understanding, suggested that credibility was not merely granted in a particular speech or through the crafting of eloquent words, but in the ongoing lifestyle of an orator consistent in message and practice: "A potent factor in success, then, is for the characters, principles, deeds, and course of life, both of those who are to plead cases of their clients, to be approved, and conversely those of their opponents condemned; and for the feelings of the judges to be won over, as far as possible, to goodwill towards the advocate and the advocate's client as well" (Cicero, *De Oratore*, 2.182).

Consequently, a person with strong *ethos* has to gain such personal credibility over time, through a consistent and empathetic message: "Feelings are won over by a man's dignity (*dignitas*), achievements (*res gestae*), and reputation (*existimatio*) . . . [A] conception of an ethos portrayed only through the medium of a speech was, for the Roman orator, neither acceptable nor adequate" (May, 1988, p. 9). For Cicero, then, ethos was more than just a rhetorical form; it was a lifestyle, a way of being in the world.

Having strong *ethos* and commanding style, in other words, allows an orator to be more effective at constituting understanding among audiences. What made Cicero a powerful orator was his peers' high regard for him as a dynamic speaker. He also used style as a means of persuasion. For example, in his defense of the poet Archias's Roman citizenship, Cicero used a poetic style to defend his client. According to John Dugan (2005), *Pro Archia* was one of Cicero's most elegant speeches. During the speech Cicero transitions from the role of legal advocate using pure forensic rhetoric—the persuasion of guilt or innocence based on statements of historical facts—to one of high tone, using the eloquence fitting an epideictic (ceremonial) approach—that is, one of praise and blame. In this same vein, hip hop often deals with contemporary issues by pointing to historic examples (such as Jim Crow laws); as such, it embodies the interwoven rhetorical style and *ethos* that Cicero practiced and advocated.

For Cicero, an orator's or artist's *ethos* could be enhanced with style, but nothing was more critical to persuasiveness than principle: "wisdom without eloquence does too little for the good . . ., but eloquence without wisdom is generally highly disadvantageous and is never helpful" (Cicero, *De Inventione*, I.i.1). In terms of hip hop, artists who may have a song or two dedicated to ghetto problems, or use the image of prison to only try to enhance their credibility, are often called to account for their inconsistencies. Natapoff (2009), for example, points to the social backlash hip-hop artist Cam'ron faced when he tried to demonstrate in a *60 Minutes* interview that he was in touch with the anti-snitching campaigns in poor neighborhoods by saying he wouldn't turn in a serial killer. He misrepresented the position of the movement, which is to end "5K snitching" to plea down in drug cases, and was thus labeled as a wannabe by his own fans. Because of this, he felt compelled to apologize publicly (see "Cam'ron issues statement . . .," 2007); for Cam'ron, a lack of ethos undercut his attempt to speak authoritatively against the prison-industrial complex.

Drawing upon Cicero, we observe certain similar characteristics in successful artists like Nas, Tupac, Queen Latifah, Salt-N-Pepa, and Wu-Tang (to name a few), who are popular despite their more critical messages (Dyson, 2004). Not all hip-hop artists, particularly those classified as mainstream gangsta rappers, qualify as being Ciceronian-type orators within the hip-hop movement. To qualify, an artist must have "street cred" (practical *ethos*), style, and a civic orientation toward ghettoized communities, which includes prison critique and care (Dyson, 2004). Artists that are able to simultaneously hold street credibility (wisdom) and style will be more persuasive, just as Cicero was as a poet-advocate. In short, to gain credibility, hip-hop artists rap about their time in prison or point to issues relevant to minority and poor neighborhoods. When artists rap about crime, drugs, and prison, they are responding to the rhetorical situation (these things exist in their communities) and are also building their credibility—their lyrics demonstrate how these artists are in touch with the reality of many listeners. For example, T. I. highlights the darkness of prisons in his life when he confesses that "this experience [prison] is truly a pain I have never felt before and that's saying a lot for a nigga who's been down locked up as many times as I have. I see this as a real ass whoopin'" (T.I., as cited in Concepcion, 2010, para. 2). For T. I., this is a courageous comment because it highlights his own vulnerability to the system in two ways, showing (1) that he too is frequently locked up for drug possession (like many black men and other addicts) and (2) that he is vulnerable to depression caused by the system. In making this vulnerable comment, he opens a rhetorical space to talk about mass incarceration and also for talking differently about prison life. In this instance, we can identify two important realizations. First, prison is a depressing and scary place, even for those intimate with the system, which helps to explain why so many people are quick to plea (often requiring them to snitch). Second, depression, perhaps caused by the plight of communities and families already devastated by the effects of mass incarceration, can lead people to try to self-medicate through drug use, which of course increases the risk of arrest, thus furthering the cycle of depression and incarceration (Clear, 2007). T. I.'s confession illustrates how these factors—snitching, depression, fear, and drug use—create a feedback loop of destructive behaviors.

Street credibility cannot be earned from one song alone; it must be developed through the embodiment of a vision that speaks truth while also promising hope, as demonstrated by T. I., or by Nas and Tupac, who have rapped mostly about issues of critical importance to communities of color and who contributed to projects related to these issues (e.g., the *No More Prisons* project). Intriguingly, many consciousness-raising hip-hop artists seem to carry credibility among suburban white listeners, who make up a large portion of the listening audience (Kitwana, 2005). Hip hop's popularity with suburban white audiences also illustrates why style is important. Style, as defined by one of the most respected hip-hop artists, KRS-One, is the ability to appeal to listeners with a sense of authenticity by referring to their own struggles. It is a definition similar to classical style as described by Cicero, uniting *ethos*, pathos, and logos in ways that close the hermeneutical gap between rhetor and audience in rhetorical situations. Nas, for example, has style *and* "street cred" and therefore has become both a mainstream and a consciousness-raising hip-hop artist. He is a master lyricist who uses wordplay, euphemism, irony, and metaphoric language to appeal to mainstream audiences while making important points about social injustices (Daulatzai, 2009; Dyson, 2009). As a multiplatinum-selling performer, Nas is considered by laypeople and scholars alike to offer a compelling critique of urban marginalization. In Queens, New York, where Nas grew up, he is known as "Street Disciple" because his "detailed descriptions, dense reportage, and visually stunning rhymes of the underbelly of the beast . . . capture an urgency and intimacy about life at the tattered edges of the American empire" (Daulatzai, 2009, p. 1). Nas fashions himself as a teacher who cultivates knowledge, as demonstrated in the following outtake from his song "Ghetto Prisoners." This sample, as with those in the following paragraphs (all from the same song), demonstrates why he is a Cicero-like figure in contemporary hip hop:

> [. . .]
> I'm like the farmer, plantin' words, people are seeds
> My truth is the soil; help you grow like trees
> May the children come in all colors, change like leaves
> but hold before you, one of those, prophetic MCs
> [. . .]
> (Nas, 2009a)

This outtake, to outsiders, may appear trite. However, spat over powerfully appealing beats, with the refrain "Ghetto prisoners rise rise rise / Ghetto prisoners . . . get up, wake up, rise," the song received mainstream play upon release and was a call for listeners to overcome adversity by conscious endeavor. Tracked on his autobiographical album *I am . . .*, his fourth full-album release, the song builds upon a consistent theme of raising awareness about the subjugation of urban black youth within "ghetto prisons"—those economically destitute and politically marginalized neighborhoods that fill the prison pipeline. Especially for listeners already familiar with his music, the song furthers Nas's role as a witness to, neighbor with, and advocate for those trapped in communities with little hope for economic or political advancement.

In addition to enabling us to recognize *ethos* as a blend of style and street cred, Ciceronian rhetoric also recognizes the importance of aesthetic communication, such as poetry (and hip hop), as a type of forensic rhetoric that takes place not only in courts but within the *polis*, which is usually considered the space of deliberative rhetoric. We similarly understand forensic arguments as existing outside of court and within popular culture (as citizens advocate for guilt and innocence of people in popular media). Returning to the example above, we see this type of forensic rhetoric as Nas engages in deliberative questioning that points to injustices (which he can do, thanks to his established *ethos*): "Goin' through the same bullshit as our fathers / Readin' history, but who's the authors? For some the game is easy, for most of us the game is much harder" (Nas, 2009a). Nas then makes recommendations about courses of actions and remedies: "never lose faith; through the years just get smarter." Nas leaves open the possibility that one may need to "rise rise rise" in revolution; however, the message suggests that his listeners—ghetto prisoners—need to "rise" to a higher spiritual and intellectual plane: "never lose faith; through the years just get smarter." The song therefore offers hope to "ghetto prisoners"— those who are trapped in poor neighborhoods (of color)—while reminding other listeners that such a world exists and that we need to ask difficult questions about the political forces that sustain it. To offer further evidence of our claim that consciousness-raising hip hop functions both as witness to catastrophe and as call to action, we offer in the following section more examples of how consciousness-raising hip hop both questions the prison-industrial complex and advocates for care of prisoners and those communities affected by mass incarceration.

Examples of Hip-Hop Advocacy

As one of the best-selling genres of music in the world, hip-hop music is known for its boldness, rebelliousness, and often profane lyrics aimed at highlighting the unjust treatment of citizens by governments and corporations (Butler, 2009).[5] It is more than a musical genre; it is also a lifestyle and culture. Consciousness hip hop often takes on themes of social and political significance. With a large nonblack audience (Kitwana, 2005), consciousness-raising hip hop has the potential to make its listeners aware of the injustices suffered in economically destitute ghettos. For example, these hip-hop artists often rap about the effects of mass incarceration in the United States, something that listeners in middle-class suburbs may not, without this kind of hip hop, understand. The late Tupac Shakur, a well-known hip-hop artist who has sold over 75 million albums, was a strong prison-reform advocate. He used his lyrics to address the social injustices of mass incarceration, and he believed in the power of his rhetoric to effect change (see Dyson, 2006): "Too many brothers daily heading for tha big pen / Niggas comin' out worse off than when they went in / . . . There must be another route, way out / . . . Tired of being trapped in this vicious cycle" (Tupac, 1991). As similar assertions echo throughout the movement, hip-hop culture "makes a strong case for a transformation of American criminal justice: it describes, with eloquence, the problems with the current system, and articulates, with passion, a better way" (Butler, 2009, p. 125). Hip-hop artists, in their music and campaigning efforts, both explicitly and implicitly, offer some of the following possibilities: anti-snitching, de-carceration, alternatives to incarceration for nonviolent offenders, such as drug-treatment programs, better policing practices, and jury nullification.

Still, the political power of hip hop derives from its power as critique. For example, in impoverished neighborhoods of color, distrust between community members and law enforcement is long-standing and hard to overcome (Clear, 2007). Consciousness-raising hip hop therefore explores the struggle between community safety and abusive police practices. For example, Chuck D. (1997), the lead lyricist of the influential hip-hop group Public Enemy, once billed rap music as the "black CNN" because it tackles issues other media do not. One area of contribution to investigative reporting vis-à-vis hip hop is police brutality, which was brought to attention by West Coast artists. In particular, Ice-T and N.W.A documented the Los Angeles Police Department's

(LAPD) abusive police practices against young men of color during the late 1980s, which notably came to the wider public's attention following the beating of Rodney King (Dyson, 2004).

Through music and video, hip-hop artists document the tension between police authority and communities of color. The 1982 video of Grandmaster Flash and the Furious Five's "The Message," for example, shows the police arresting the group for just rapping on the street. This example not only highlights the criminalization of nonviolent activities but suggests that the police see hip hop as a threat to their power. Similarly, KRS-One's music is committed to questioning the overuse of police power in communities of color. In his 1989 track "Who Protects Us?," KRS-One opens with a police interview in which he asks, "You were put here to protect us / But who protects us from you?" KRS-One's Ciceronian-like questioning is further backed by his choice to recite the lyrics to the song over an intercom, which gives the impression that he's speaking from a position of authority to a large number of people.

Discriminatory policing in poor communities of color is rampant. According to Alexander (2010), granting unlimited "discretion" and "authorization" to law enforcement has contributed to the high incarceration rate of men of color: "Although prosecutors, as a group, have the greatest power in the criminal justice system, police have the greatest discretion—discretion that is amplified in drug-law enforcement . . . police have discretion regarding whom to target, as well as where to target" (p. 121). Hip-hop artists named the practice of using "probable cause" to authorize discretionary (and likely illegal) searches of individuals in targeted communities as "finding dirt." "Dirt" refers to anything that could lead to additional searches or an arrest—guns, drugs, or parole violations. Most "dirt" is found during "consent searches," whereby individuals give permission to officers to search them (Butler, 2009). As Alexander notes, "so-called consent searches have made it possible for the police to stop and search for drugs [on] just about anybody walking down the street. All a police officer has to do in order to conduct a baseless drug investigation is ask to speak with someone and then get their 'consent' to be searched" (p. 65). In many circumstances, the consenting individual has the legal right to deny speaking to or being searched by agents of the state; unfortunately, the fear of police and lack of legal knowledge contribute to unnecessary searches.

In 2006, Houston-based artist Chamillionaire released a song called "Ridin.'" The song, rapped by lead lyricist Hakeem Seriki and featuring Krayzie Bone, of the group Bones Thugs-n-Harmony, speaks against racial profiling and "unwarranted searches." "Ridin'" gained national prominence and became the first multiplatinum phone mastertone, with over 4 million sales ("RIAA Launches . . .," 2006). Chamillionaire's lyrical advocacy raises awareness about and argues against police harassment in the form of "police fishing," which is the practice of following vehicles until the driver makes a common, though illegal, driving maneuver: "So they get behind me tryin' to check my tags, / look at my rearview and they smiling / Thinkin' they'll catch me on the wrong well keep tryin' / 'Cause they denyin' it's racial profiling." Unfortunately, "there is no meaningful check on the exercise of police discretion [in consent searches], [so] racial biases are granted free reign" (Alexander, 2010, p. 180). "Ridin'" could easily be dismissed as a fun-spirited "hot track" with little to no substance. Chamillionaire's testimonials, however, serve as protest and address real problems that listeners will have to think about the next time they are "ridin.'"

Another common theme in hip hop that identifies how communities have been turned inside-out by mass incarceration is the now highly militarized practice of drug raids, which occur frequently in poorer communities (Butler, 2009). Several hip-hop artists have voiced concerns about police raids (e.g., Nas, dead prez, Jay-Z, Blackalicious, and the Coup). Consequently, artists who take on these themes—especially those who themselves have been incarcerated—provide music of protest and comfort. Wu-Tang Clan's 2000 release "I Can't Go to Sleep," for example, is one of the best demonstrations of lyrical protest against the "War on Drugs" and its negative impact on poor neighborhoods of color. In this song, Wu members comment on the overzealous use of home raids by the FBI. They give a biographical description of being in a constant state of suspicion and fear, documenting both visually in the video and lyrically in the music the feeling of being incarcerated in their neighborhood.

Wu-Tang's track is also comforting. It samples music from Isaac Hayes's legendary song "Walk on By" (1969), a song that has been popular since the Civil Rights Movement. By sampling the track, listeners get a sense of "care-in-mass"—that is, that their struggles are not singular, but communal. Hayes wrote "Walk on By" in the wake of Martin Luther King Jr.'s assassination, and the song came to represent the spirit of black unrest at the time. "I could not create properly," Hayes said of his response to King's death. "I was so bitter and angry. I was rebellious. I was militant" (as cited in Doggett, 2007, p. 156). Peter Doggett notes that the 1969 song ushered in a form of orchestral soul—a sense of black pride. RZA, Wu-Tang's music producer, carefully synchronizes "Walk on By" with lead lyricist Ghostface's rhymes: "I can't go to sleep / Feds jumpin' out they jeeps / I can't go to sleep." Through *pathos*, Ghostface draws on the collective fears of people of color in poor communities—that at any moment federal agents may raid their homes. Simultaneously, Wu-Tang intensifies their *ethos* as an important figure in the current struggle over oppression. "I Can't Go to Sleep" therefore testifies to a collective struggle over community safety. RZA follows Ghostface's verse with a powerful glimpse at American history by mentioning several assassinations of prominent civil-rights leaders, such as Medgar Evers, Dr. King, Malcolm X, and President John F. Kennedy. RZA connects historical oppression with the current unrest of communities: "I'm ready to break this world down. / They got me trapped up in a metal gate. / Just stressed out with hate. / And just, give me no time to relax, and use my mind to meditate." These are images and words that people who do not live inside inner-city ghettos can also identify with.

Although this song may seem depressing, Wu-Tang clearly intends for the song's melancholy imagery to bear witness to a forgotten history of racial oppression and violence, hence offering listeners of all races and ages a necessary history lesson. In this particular song, Wu-Tang explores the politics of misery; it may be the only possibility for people "trapped" in their communities (or "ghetto prisons") thanks, in part, to the War on Drugs and the growth of the prison-industrial complex. Such songs testify about the horrors of living in communities under constant surveillance and present stark reminders of how drastically poverty limits one's life choices: "What should I do? Should I grab a brew? Should I grab a .22 and put this violence in you?" Although these lyrics may seem stark and hopeless, we believe they can also foster dialogues about the harsh conditions of daily life in those communities impacted by crime, violence, and poverty. First, they show that just as power corrupts, so does powerlessness. Not only does this provide one explanation for the cycle of violence, but it says that honest dialogue will be difficult because we all (prisoners and advocates, family members and scholars) have been corrupted by the current system—everyone is implicated. Second, this song asks listeners to examine the historical causes of the current dilemmas of race, class, justice, and violence in America, thus (so we hope) prodding listeners to put the present in deep historical contexts.

Cycling is another powerful theme in hip-hop music. In his book *Imprisoning Communities*, Todd Clear (2007) suggests the continuous cycling of young men going in and out of the prison system has led to communities with little or no stability. As Clear notes, "Because these men stay behind prison bars for only a couple of years at a time, they cycle back into their communities, only to be replaced by other cohorts" (p. 24). T. I. characterizes the demoralizing nature of "cycling": "I don't know what effect this will have on my life moving forward but I'm certainly sick and mother f*cking tired of going to jail, juve, prison, the pen, correctional facilities or whatever else you want to call it. I'd have been better off doing a 5–10 year bid one time than going in time and time again for days, weeks and months for the last 15 years of my life (as cited in Concepcion, 2010, para. 2)."

Here, again, we see a moment in which T. I. gives an honest and vulnerable opinion of the system. Not only should we encourage this honesty, but we should talk about who benefits most from cycling and seek honest solutions, with those actually caught in the cycle, for ending it. Hip hop offers some solutions, such as gaining the courage to learn our rights, to question police practices, and to lobby the courts to nullify laws we do not feel are just (see Butler, 2009).

Tupac, using hip hop's lyrical and visual expression in the 1991 music video for the song "Trapped," illustrates the depressing power of cycling black men in and out of communities and prison. By moving back and forth between shots of himself in a prison cell, and shots of his peers running from law enforcement for no apparent reason, Tupac blurs the distinction between the violence and control experienced on the inside with that experienced on the outside. For Tupac, the "trap" is "Too many brothers daily heading for tha big pen / . . . comin' out worse off than when they went in." He visually represents "cycled communities" with the album cover for the single "Trapped," where it depicts a young girl, with a gloomy look, behind a gated community with her small hands on the bars and the word "trapped" written in the background. Once again, Tupac addresses not only the mass incarceration of black males, but also its impact on the community. As Clear (2007) notes, "for children in these neighborhoods, merely having a parent or brother who has gone to prison elevates their risk of doing the same; in this way, incarceration serves as its own breeding ground" (Clear, 2007, p. 24). Cycled communities are depleted of what Clear describes as "social network" and "social capital": "Men who are behind bars are the missing links in the social network of those who remain behind" (p. 24). While consciousness-raising hip-hop artists highlight the issues discussed herein, they also, as we shall see below, use their credibility and music to remind people of the human dimension of prison, and to give prisoners and communities hope.

Lyrics as Letters and Community Care

There is a long history of the importance of letter writing to those who are incarcerated. While in exile, Cicero and his brother Quintus corresponded with each other through letters. In one letter, Cicero noted that he had fallen into a state of depression and thanked his brother for his continued support: "Your pleas have prevented me from committing suicide. But what is there to live for? Don't blame me for complaining. My afflictions surpass any you ever heard of earlier" (as cited in Haskell, 1964, p. 201). In 1963, after his arrest for civil disobedience, Dr. Martin Luther King Jr. wrote a letter from a Birmingham jail as a response to white clergymen, who condemned his protest strategies. Written on scraps of paper, King's rhetorical advocacy is still felt beyond the confines of a dim prison cell. The prison letter produced one of King's most inspiring and well-known quotes: "Injustice anywhere is a threat to justice everywhere."

Given contemporary incarceration rates in minority and poor communities, most residents of these neighborhoods are likely to have a relative or friend in jail (see Novek, Chapter 10, this volume). The friends and family members of those incarcerated often experience "psychological time," so communication between those physically in and out of jail is critical to maintaining mental health for prisoners and their relatives (Metzl, 2010). As Nelson Mandela (1995) notes in his autobiography, "Communication with one's family is a human right; it should not be restricted by the artificial gradations of a prison system. But it was one of the facts of my prison life" (p. 63). Due to the strict sanction imposed on his communication with the outside world during apartheid, Mandela was allowed to write only one letter every six months. However, as Jennifer Wood notes, "unlike prominent letters written by King, Jackson, and others, most letters written by people who are incarcerated are neither meant for public reading nor designed to further a social movement" (see Hartnett, Wood, & McCann, 2011, pp. 339–40). As Wood further notes, the issue of letter writing is political and can affect both those on the inside and outside—"letter writing requires material goods, . . . [which] are scarce and costly, and can be withheld as a form of punishment" (p. 341). When prisoners are denied opportunities to write, don't have time to do so, or fear that their letters may be screened, they are silenced; and equally so, those on the outside are denied the right to communicate.

The letter-like exchanges between artists and prisoners capture the most intimate space within hip hop. Beyond the hypermasculine posturing often embedded in hip hop, there is a humanistic side to the lyrics of consciousness-raising hip hop. Artists seem to be deeply concerned about the conditions of prison life and its impact on their loved ones. The music, therefore, becomes a compassionate and political plea for change. Through passionate appeals, the rhetorical case against prison is strengthened. A good example of this double-functioning, letter-based argument is found on Nas's classic 1994 album *Illmatic*, where he raps a letter to an incarcerated friend. According to Nas (2007), the song "One Love" is an in-depth letter dedicated to friends, family members, and prison inmates.

Scholar Michael Eric Dyson contributed to a book written about Nas's *Illmatic*. Dyson (2009) notes that "when [he] first heard Nas's 'One Love,' cast in the form of letters to friends locked in prison, [he] thought immediately of [his] brother Everett, who is serving life" (2009, p. 129). Dyson goes on to argue that prison letters bring fans closer to the experiences of prison life and highlight the emotional toil mass incarceration has on families: "Hip hop's roots in the working-class and poor black communities make its artists attuned to the hardscrabble conditions that either become fodder for rap careers or expressway to incarceration. . . . The lyrics of rap artists are flooded by references to prison" (p. 131). Nas's "One Love" begins with writing a letter to a friend serving "a bid." In it, he demonstrates the challenges of expressing sadness and joy, of "being real" yet hopeful. Note how Nas shows empathy toward his friend while also bringing up the delicate, though no less joyful, acknowledgment that his friend has a son:

What up, kid
I know shit hard doing your bid
When the cops came you should've slid to my crib
Fuck it, black, no time for looking back, it's done
Plus congratulations, you know you got a son
I heard he looks like you
Why don't your lady write you?
Told her she should visit, that's when she got hyper

In another line, Nas gives an update about the realities of the streets and community: "Yo, but guess who got shot in the dome-piece [the head]? / Jerome's niece on her way home from Jones Beach / It's bugged / Plus lil' Rob is selling drugs on the dime / Hanging with thugs that all carry 9s." Without being overly preachy, it is clear that Nas is maintaining his credibility by demonstrating he understands the street, though he doesn't approve of what's going on.

Nas was just seventeen years old when he penned most of *Illmatic*. At such a young age, he was able to capture in "One Love" the horrors caused by the prevalence of black men in prison and the absence of black men in communities. To demonstrate just how dire the situation is for many, Nas asks in the letter about other friends doing time in the same prison. Cory McKay, also known as Cormega, a personal friend of Nas who did time, is mentioned in the list of friends locked up: "At night time there's more strife than ever / What's up with Cormega? / Did you see him, are y'all together? / If so, then hold the fort down / Represent to the fullest / Say what's up to Herb, Ice and Bullet."

"One Love" is just one example of many songs that use letter writing as a rhetorical tool for making forensic and deliberative arguments. Another artist who has demonstrated the power of letter writing is AZ. Like Nas, AZ raps both about and to friends and family who have been killed on the streets, who are incarcerated, or who live in the impoverished communities that have suffered the collateral damage of the "War on Drugs" and mass incarceration. While Nas and AZ are on the outside, sometimes the letters of prisoners are sent to those on the outside and published in the lyrics of hip-hop artists. In AZ's "Fan Mail" (2002), for example, he reads a letter from a prisoner. In this song, AZ engages in a dialogue with the prisoner, whose thoughts and words are used in the refrain of the song. The prisoner provides a sense of regret and loss, but also hope: "Peace, Allah, hope tha scribe reach ya hands in good health / As for self, no sense of worrying, my cards been dealt / Sunk in a cell, Fishscale,[6] fifth year of my bid." After deep contemplation, Fishscale makes no excuses about the choices he made, nor does he ignore the emotional pain his incarceration has caused his family, especially his children and their mothers: "Finally got a chance recent to connect with my kids / It's kinda hard thru carelessness I scared they moms / And temporary I was barred voluntary the bond / Nevertheless, it's issues I need to address." Yet he provides hope by sharing his newly found relationship with his children, a serious issue for incarcerated parents.

Through such songs, Nas and AZ expose their audience to the realities of mass incarceration while also giving actual prisoners a space to connect with society. Through this approach, hip-hop artists teach listeners about the conditions of prisons and provide an artistic outlet for incarcerated people. In this regard, hip hop is a form of prison care that is often overlooked, a medium that provides inmates with hope. As it works to transform the outside, letter writing provides an emotional outlet for prisoners. Just as Cicero needed his brother, so do our imprisoned contemporaries need theirs.

From Rhetoric to Action: Hip Hop Matters

As we noted in our introduction, we see rhetoric as action. Consciousness-raising hip hop, as we define it, does not necessarily seek social activism, protest, or confrontation as its primary goal, though it may have this effect. Hip-hop music, like other social-movement and constitutive rhetorics (Charland, 1987), is self- and other-directed—it transforms both speaker and listener. Hip hop, as we've argued, is a Ciceronian-inspired rhetoric that gives authority to artists with a specific and influential *ethos*, who have used their power to create spaces for sharing experiences, for helping listeners develop a critical perspective, and for inviting action. Hip hop sparks reflexive self-oriented and community-oriented dialogue about social justice and prison reform. Consciousness-raising hip hop addresses larger and more public audiences than it ever has, and it has inspired hip-hop classes at major universities, political- and social justice–oriented conventions (e.g., National Hip Hop Convention), specific albums criticizing the prison-industrial complex (e.g., *No More Prisons*), and the publication of anthologies and books discussing the topic.

Still, a skeptic could ask whether hip hop has any positive material effect on society. It is easy to point to gangsta-inspired rap and suggest that it actually promotes violence or glorifies prison. First, we would remind skeptical readers that we have tried to describe consciousness-raising hip hop as a particular type of hip hop that is far more critical. Second, such simplistic interpretations, and the particular type of rap toward which such critiques are aimed, require us to have a social dialogue. When a musician like Eminem, who may not have as much "street cred," pens a controversial song with provocative lyrics about ghettoized neighborhoods, he creates a rhetorical situation for further dialogue. Consciousness-raising hip-hop artists, like those highlighted in this chapter, also provoke; however, they do so in a way that uses rhetorical *ethos* to transform listeners' thinking. This, we believe, leads to caring about prisoners, as is evidenced in the following examples.

More attention has been given to the use of hip hop as a way to assist offenders. For example, Rochester, a Toronto-based rapper, performed in 2010 at the Brookside youth jail in Coburg, Ontario. After his performance, a group of young men performed their music for him. The young men, using only the equipment available to them at the facility, also produced a video. This led Rochester to establish a program for youth offenders to express themselves through hip hop (Mendleson, 2010). When hip-hop artists merge their lyrical advocacy with practice, they not only invoke the Ciceronian spirit, but they help foster spaces of collaboration, growth, and community. Talib Kweli, for example, is a fervent advocate on behalf of political prisoners and a proud supporter of community organizations like the Malcolm X Grassroots Movement (Chang, 2005). Kweli uses his celebrity not only to be heard, but to help others to take action on their own behalf.

Scholars have also engaged in a series of workshops that both advocate and study the use of hip hop as a pedagogical tool (see Hill, 2009; Petchauer, 2011), and researchers have found, for example, that rural (mainly poor white) and inner-city youth (mainly poor black) experience hip hop differently, but that both groups identify with the discussions regarding prisons (Geidel, 2005). As much as inner cities have been impacted by the absence of men who are in prison, rural communities have been adversely impacted by the presence of prisons in theirs. Hip hop has been the voice of reason, according to Geidel (2005), for many rural youth. What is more, hip-hop artists have noticed this theme and, consequently, the "Holler to the Hood" (H2H) program was conceived. H2H is a community arts project started by Amelia Kirby and Nick Szuberla of Appalshop, a regional arts center in Whitesburg, Kentucky. Through this project, rural children and dislocated youth (i.e., those whose families have moved to be closer to their relatives in prison) "explore the power of hip-hop as a force for cultural understanding and social change in central Appalachia" (Geidel, p. 67). This comingling of urban and rural has impacted hip-hop style, as tracks now frequently include samples of banjos and fiddles.

Hallman (2009) shows that hip hop is a critical bridge in student learning, which has provided hope for pregnant and single-parent teens. The power of hip hop is captured in a letter written by one of her students as part of a literacy program:

Dear Tupac,
   You speak to me.
   Your music makes me remember the good times when life wasn't hard and there weren't responsibilities.
   But even now you tell me that I can do it and be a good mom.
   I miss you. (LaTasha, as cited in Hallman, p. 36)

Pulido (2009) has also documented the power of hip hop as pedagogy. One of her ethnographic interviewees—Ernesto, a twenty-two-year-old Puerto Rican—so powerfully substantiates the claims we have made in this chapter that we feel it important to cite his comments in their entirety:

> It [hip hop] was introducing White America to the rest of society, it showed them the life of the inner-city . . . and then as KRS-One and Chuck D . . . started using it as a tool to politicize the youth, like hip hop started, hip hop was just, was just a tool that could be used as a revolutionary tool, as a tool for consciousness, for education or just to convey common stereotypes of the day . . . It introduced America to the culture of inner city youth, they had no choice but to listen and to accept reality. They could either study and learn from it or they could go on with their assumptions. (p. 67)

As the above examples demonstrate, using hip hop pedagogically can help improve the psychological state of underserved or at-risk youth. Hip hop may therefore mitigate the risk of criminal offense by making educational success more likely.

Perhaps no evidence is more powerful than one's own. Therefore, we provide our own stories to demonstrate just how powerful hip hop is in promoting a way of life that leads to prison care, community empowerment, and protest against the prison-industrial complex. When I (Derrick) was growing up in Birmingham, Alabama, I was heavily influenced by the early hip-hop artists during what is now known as the "golden era." As hip hop developed more during the mid-1990s, my brother and I noticed a change in artists' narrations. More and more artists began to describe the harsh realities of urban decay. Artists such as Biggie, Nas, and Jay-Z became the rhetorical voice of an urban generation of black youth trying to appropriate the vestiges of the "War on Drugs" and its impact on our communities. The theme of prison became common as artists began to speak about mass incarceration. Through hip hop, I was made aware of the realities of fatherless men, and this motivated me to become a community organizer. And so I, along with some fellow activists, started Progressive Masculinities Mentors (PMM) at Southern Illinois University Carbondale in efforts to mentor young men who have been impacted by mass incarceration.

I (Craig) am a volunteer for the Prison Entrepreneurship Program (PEP), a nonprofit organization based in Houston, Texas (www.pep.org). As a business-plan advisor, twice a year I assist future parolees through an entrepreneurship boot camp. Though it graduates over 100 men a year, the program has a single-digit recidivism rate (see www.pep.org). PEP not only helps incarcerated men; it also transforms the hearts and minds of business executives, who often give or find these men a job upon release. My technical expertise in entrepreneurship allows me to assist PEP participants. My passion, however, grew out of my hearing about the pain and suffering of incarcerated men through hip-hop music. I grew up in Rawlins, Wyoming, home of the Wyoming State Penitentiary. The reality of this place, though, was far from my mind until, in 1995, one of my friends handed me "One Love" (1994) by Nas and said, "This is how I feel with my father just south of town." Nas's powerful music, coupled with the influence of hip-hop rock artists Rage Against the Machine, fueled my passion for de-carceration and community engagement.

The above examples illustrate the importance of hip hop in inspiring activism and transforming lives. They also show that hip hop plays a role in the debate about mass incarceration, but also, and more important, that it is a voice of compassion and care for prisoners and parolees, who are often overlooked by those who live beyond the wall. Hip hop has saved lives and provides a medium and outlet for social activism, as hip-hop artist and "raptivist" Capital-"X" shows in his new album *305375: The Voice of the Voiceless, Volume 1*. As a parolee, "X" now spends most of his time traveling across the world speaking and performing to educate and enlighten the masses on what he considers the truth about a corrupt and unjust legal system. In the spirit of Ciceronian and constitutive rhetoric, he also describes his experience with an eloquence that gives him *ethos* while developing *pathos* for those still trapped, as he was, in the web of the criminal-justice system.

While we hope that this chapter will inspire action beyond listening, we believe that by having gained a new understanding of consciousness-raising hip hop, readers will be inspired to turn up the beats and listen. As a present-day Ciceronian rhetoric, hip hop invokes a new way of thinking about our oppressive criminal-justice system and, at the very least, inspires listeners to care.

Notes

MUSICAL NOTE: To listen to a wide sampling of the artists and tracks discussed in this chapter, please select the "Consciousness-Raising Hip Hop" button on the PCARE website, at http://priscare.blogspot.com.

1. Hip-hop slang for "doing time."

2. Refer to the editors' introduction for a more nuanced discussion of the shifting prison populations since 1972.

3. Many artists within hip hop are faced with the complexity of establishing trust with listeners, or "street cred." Street cred is the authority granted to artists by community members. As a perception of others' interpretation of one's character, street cred must be maintained, and may be revoked.

4. Having defined *consciousness-raising hip hop*, from this point forward in the text any reference to hip hop without qualification should be understood as "consciousness raising." We do not want to burden the text with the overuse of this qualifying adjective. In certain circumstances, we will want to draw attention to the specific nature of consciousness-raising hip hop as something quite different from mainstream rap. In these cases, we will add the qualifier.

5. *Rap* refers to the cultural product of hip hop (culture), which combines the artistic elements of emceeing and deejaying. As a cultural movement, hip hop is a lifestyle that, through music and other cultural practices, challenges the status quo. Rap, on the other hand, is a commodity and can be produced and consumed with little attachment or understanding of hip hop.

6. "Fishscale" is the pseudonym of the inmate.

PART IV

Working on the Futures
of Prison Activism

Part Four offers two essays urging scholars and activists to think more creatively about ways not only to oppose mass incarceration, but to imagine new forms of engaged and compassionate citizenship. In Chapter Nine, Bryan McCann explores the paradox of life without parole in the death-penalty-abolitionist movement. While the concept of life without parole has helped to end the death penalty in a number of states, McCann believes it also obscures the fact that capital punishment is only the most grisly element of the entire failed prison-industrial complex. If activists are serious about abolishing mass incarceration, McCann argues, they need to take a position that humanizes the incarcerated and challenges the structures of inequality that enable the state to rationalize execution and life incarceration in the first place. In Chapter Ten, Eleanor Novek identifies racism as a major cause of the nation's stratospheric incarceration rates and tracks the intersections of crime, fear, and social inequality. She argues that prison activists must organize a new civil-rights movement based on *agape*, or compassionate love. In the egalitarian structure of the Alternatives to Violence Project, an international volunteer organization that teaches nonviolence in prisons and conflict zones, Novek finds a model of human connection that activists can use to confront the destructive impact of racism and to help heal those communities targeted by the prison-industrial complex. McCann and Novek believe that the prison abolition movement can succeed only by opposing the racialized fears and entrenched inequalities that have rationalized the state's prerogative of violence and legitimized the prison-industrial complex in the public mind. To do this, they contend, activists must call on love and imagination as first principles.

CHAPTER 9

"A Fate Worse than Death"

Reform, Abolition, and Life without Parole in Anti–Death Penalty Discourse

BRYAN J. McCANN

Over the past decade, citizens and public officials in the United States have begun to turn against the death penalty. The first indication that capital punishment may be reaching its twilight years came in 2003, when George Ryan, the Republican governor of Illinois, commuted every death sentence in his state following a moratorium and institutional review of his state's death-penalty apparatus. The findings convinced Ryan (2003) that "the Illinois capital punishment system is broken" (para. 110) due to its arbitrary application and a startling number of exonerations over several decades. In the years following Ryan's controversial decision, New Jersey, New Mexico, New York, and Illinois have abolished their death-penalty statutes ("New Mexico Gov.," 2009; Richburg, 2007; Scott, 2008; Stern, 2011). Many other states recognize that the death penalty has no demonstrative deterrent impact on crime and is a money pit of public policy. For example, California, which houses the nation's largest death row, spends approximately $250 million for every execution. Texas, the state that executes more inmates than any other, spends three times the cost of a life sentence for every death-penalty case ("Facts about the Death Penalty," 2008; "Switching Off the Death Penalty," 2010). In a particularly damning gesture for state-sanctioned killing, the American Law Institute (ALI), whose 1962 Model Penal Code functioned as the intellectual framework for performing executions in America, abandoned its own standards "in light of the current intractable and structural obstacles to ensuring a minimally adequate system for administering capital punishment" (Liptak, 2010a, para. 7). Abolitionist William McAuliffe commented that the ALI's gesture is "a recognition and a furtherance of a shift in the culture" of American criminal justice, in which a prestigious legal body has now made clear "they don't want to have a role in legitimizing the use of the death penalty" (Hoppe, 2010, para. 6). In the spring 2007 edition of her organization's newsletter, National Coalition to Abolish the Death Penalty (NCADP) executive director Diann Rust-Tierney declared, "Quietly but definitively, brick by brick, the foundation of the death penalty system is crumbling across the country" ("A Welcome Trend," 2007).

Even in the domain of public opinion, abolitionists have cause to be optimistic. According to the most recent Gallup poll on the death penalty, 65 percent of American respondents supported capital punishment; this is far lower than the peak years of the late 1980s and early 1990s, when support reached a staggering 80 percent. Furthermore, in 2006, respondents were more likely to support life imprisonment without the possibility of parole (henceforth, LWOP) than execution when given a choice between the two (Newport, 2009). It is this final statistic that propels the argument of this chapter. In a widely read and influential essay on the death penalty and public opinion, executive director Richard Dieter (1993) of the Death Penalty Information Center (DPIC) argued, "The public wants to be sure that murderers will not, in fact, be released after a few years and that the families of victims are compensated for their tragedy. As these ingredients become standard in the country's sentencing schemes, the death penalty may once again become a minority position in this country" (Dieter, 1993, para. 111). In other words, Dieter saw in the growing prevalence of LWOP an opportunity to have his abolitionist cake and eat it, too: Americans need not do the grisly work of executing the most dangerous criminals to remain confident that the criminal-justice system will prevent such individuals from doing harm again.

In this chapter, I draw from literature theorizing the death penalty's place in the prison-industrial complex, rhetoric of anti–death penalty activists, and my own experience as a grassroots abolitionist organizer to critique the prevalence of LWOP in the death-penalty abolitionist movement. Specifically, I argue that while the alternative of LWOP serves as an understandable rhetorical strategy to spread the anti–death penalty gospel to more ambivalent audiences, it undermines what I believe should be a central organizational posture of the abolitionist cause: understanding capital punishment as only the most macabre expression of a colossal and broken prison-industrial complex. Far too many anti–death penalty activists partake in what I am calling a corporeal myopia that emphasizes the body of the condemned rather than its location within the prison-industrial complex as a whole. Instead of viewing LWOP as a cruel and problematic expression of mass imprisonment in its own right, abolitionists regard it as a reasonable alternative to exterminating the condemned body. In addition to bypassing the structural intricacies of the prison-industrial complex, too heavy a reliance on LWOP results in messages emanating from the abolitionist movement that are troublingly similar to the discourses that sustain mass incarceration in the United States. Like my fellow author in this section, I believe that any worthwhile investigation of our nation's prison system must not only consider the deeds of the incarcerated, the nature of a singular punishment, or the sophistic possibilities of the moment, but also account for questions related to recidivism, the experiences of inmates' families, and, in this case, the broader project of prison abolition. Ultimately, I argue in this chapter that the rhetorical choices play a direct, structural role in shaping public discourse on controversies (see Stewart, Smith, & Denton, Jr., 2001). If death-penalty abolitionists desire, as I believe they should, to encourage critical analysis of the American prison system as a whole, then we must begin to question many of our allies' dependence on LWOP in making public arguments.

In order to clarify this position, I will first describe the historical relationship between death and imprisonment in the United States. Specifically, I demonstrate that execution and incarceration are fundamentally similar expressions of the punitive impulses that drive our carceral society. Such an analysis, I argue, highlights the problematic nature of an abolitionist discourse grounded in LWOP. Next, I engage recent examples of discourse from prominent anti–death penalty rhetors to illustrate the movement's heavy reliance on LWOP as a rhetorical strategy and argue that this approach supports the prison-industrial complex. Finally, I offer a sketch of a death-penalty abolitionism more firmly rooted in a vision of a society that relies on neither executions nor mass imprisonment to respond to crime.

Death, Incarceration, and America

In his canonical *Discipline and Punish*, Michel Foucault (1977) traced the evolution of punishment from grotesque public displays of torture and execution to subdued regimes of docility; punishment departed the public eye and citizens transformed into self-surveilling subjects. A central lesson of his work is that the form of punishment is not nearly as salient as the structures of power whose discursive practices justify multiple forms of punishment and define the boundaries between citizens and criminals, between the lawful many and the monstrous few. Thus, on a fundamental level, the drawing and quartering that famously opens Foucault's influential book is different only in form from the inconspicuous prison that seeks to rehabilitate the offender, for both partake in a regime of discipline invested in producing docile bodies and rationalizing prevailing systems of social control. Indeed, a consideration of the history of crime and punishment in America demonstrates that the prison and the execution chamber are inextricably bound to each other.

Stuart Banner (2002) notes in his history of capital punishment in America that citizens could scarcely imagine an anti–death penalty politics were it not for the emergence of the prison as a site for warehousing criminals. As the eighteenth century drew to a close, many states simultaneously abolished the death penalty for crimes other than murder and treason, and erected prisons as sites for forced labor and rehabilitation. Indeed, with the birth of the Republic came numerous lively debates on the efficacy of capital punishment (Hartnett, 2010b). Influential thinkers like eighteenth-century Italian philosopher Cesare Beccaria (2009) envisioned the prison as a source of personal transformation and reflection. While he posed arguments about the morality of executions and the right of the state to kill its citizens, his position was fundamentally utilitarian: he felt prisons would better punish criminals through long periods of agonizing incarceration. Further, Beccaria worried that the spectacle of public punishments risked provoking volatile crowds in ways that would threaten the state's monopoly on violence. Similarly, Michael Meranze (1996) observes in his history of crime and punishment in early nineteenth-century Philadelphia that ritualistic public punishments constituted a gamble on the part of the state that required the cooperation of the condemned (through their confession and penance) and the populace (through their attendance and capacity to absorb the punishment's pedagogical injunction to follow the laws of the land). He writes, "The instabilities of public punishment marked the limits of public authority, demonstrating the dependence of the governors on those they governed" (p. 54).

Beccaria (2009) saw courts and prisons as institutions that would persuade citizens to more directly identify their own interests with those of the state. In a particularly telling passage, Beccaria writes, "Let verdicts and proofs of guilt be made public so that public opinion . . . acts as a brake on powerful human passions" (p. 38). In other words, the courts and the prison, Beccaria believed, were more capable of producing rational allegiances to the state than the gallows or the whip. Hartnett (2000) explains, "This shift from a form of social control based on the violent spectacle of often arbitrarily assigned bodily torture to 'rational' discourse grounded on a formalized and universal set of laws indicates a dramatic transformation in the exercise of political authority from a dependence on outright terror to what we call today 'ideology'" (p. 205).

Thus, the purpose of punishment did not change with the prison. It remained a project committed to the enforcement of property laws and the complicity of the citizenry. As property rights came to transcend the norms of feudal culture and capitalist accumulation began to take shape, the courts and the prison represented a new social contract in which incarceration served to mediate new social relations between propertied and nonpropertied classes (also see Linebaugh, 1991).

Obviously, the death penalty did not vanish from the American landscape. Rather, questions of who is killed and who is imprisoned are tethered to broader social anxieties regarding race, gender, sexuality, property, and nationhood (Gottschalk, 2006; Hartnett, 2010b). Banner (2002) argues that capital punishment serves a strongly symbolic function where citizens can claim allegiances, identify enemies, and express misgivings about contemporary law enforcement. Support for the sanction and who is most deserving of it operates at a multidimensional intersection of social factors. The administration of death, in other words, was one of many ways America came to know itself—albeit a highly contingent sense of self.

As the death penalty continued into the nineteenth and twentieth centuries, opponents leveraged arguments against executions. As I demonstrate below, contemporary arguments against the death penalty engage in utilitarian arguments virtually identical to those of Beccaria and his contemporaries. These rhetors advance LWOP not only as a more virtuous sentence than the death penalty, but also as a more effective one. In order to clarify why this is deeply problematic, I turn below to the political and economic implications of the nation's addiction to incarceration. While the history of the American prison and the accompanying rhetorics that rationalize it is vast, I focus here on the "War on Crime" approach to criminology during the twentieth century.

The War on Crime and Social Control

While crime has always been an important part of American public culture (see, for example, Gottschalk, 2006), the latter half of the twentieth century was a watershed period for crime rhetorics. Most scholars trace the turn toward a "War on Crime" to the successful presidential campaign of Richard Nixon in 1968. Amid the political flames of the era associated with the Vietnam War, Black Power, gender struggles, and other movements, Nixon assumed a posture of "law and order" and offered himself as a source of stability in tumultuous times (see Perlstein, 2008). Accepting the 1968 nomination of the Republican Party, Nixon (1968) declared, "Let those who have the responsibility to enforce our laws, and our judges who have the responsibility to interpret them, be dedicated to the great principles of civil rights. But let them also recognize that the first civil right of every American is to be free from domestic violence. And that right must be guaranteed in this country" (para. 64). With an unambiguous appropriation of Civil Rights Movement rhetoric, Nixon began to transform the systems of meaning that had previously shaped public policy. Whereas the language of Civil Rights functioned primarily to promote racial equality, Nixon's revisionist discourse envisioned a state that protects its citizenry from a racialized underclass.

Jonathan Simon (2007) claims that the ascent of the "War on Crime" coincided with the erosion of New Deal liberalism. As the role of the government in managing economic affairs waned, crime control emerged as a preferred expression of state power and articulation of social anxieties. Furthermore, Julilly Kohler-Hausmann (2011) argues that late twentieth-century discourses of crime and punishment "came to imagine cities as urban jungles wherein public safety must be guarded" through overwhelming, militarized force (p.

44). Nixon and his allies moved public deliberation and policy regarding crime away from the wrongdoings of the individual criminal toward a state imperative to protect the people from ravenous criminal threats. Markus Dubber (2004) elaborates: "The crime war is fought on behalf of the community of actual and potential victims against a community of actual and potential offenders, where the boundaries between the two track familiar, and politically potent, American socioeconomic friend-foe distinctions of race and class" (p. 50). While Faris and Nichols use their chapters (Chapters Five and Six, this volume) to eloquently illustrate how incarcerated individuals are products of complex, often destructive familial and other sociological arrangements, this new war on crime thrived on a stark division between the peaceful populace and ravenous criminals.

The "War on Crime" took shape in earnest during the 1980s and early 1990s when Presidents Reagan, Bush, and Clinton enacted a series of "tough-on-crime" policies rationalized with the discourse of war. For example, the Reagan administration invested considerable energy and capital into waging a "War on Drugs" most forcefully targeted at the sale and consumption of crack cocaine in predominantly black urban areas. Areas like South Central Los Angeles quickly became fodder for sensationalistic political and popular discourse, as young people of color became the embodiment of public anxieties about crime (see Brown et al., 2003). Sociologist Doris Provine (2006) writes of this period, "A punitive drug war would play well among middle-class suburban voters concerned that their children might be attracted to drugs. The human costs of enforcement would be borne by people with whom they did not identify or sympathize" (pp. 280–81). Thus Reagan continued to wage the war that Nixon helped inaugurate by establishing a bright line between those who perpetrated heinous crimes and those who required state protection. Reagan's successor to the White House, George H. W. Bush, would similarly pursue a fervent crusade against criminal threats. By the time Bush entered office in 1989, 63 percent of Americans identified drugs as the most serious problem facing society. In 1985, only 1 percent of respondents felt this way (Provine, 2006). In one noteworthy, even comical, instance, Bush's staff arranged for a drug dealer to sell crack to a Secret Service agent across the street from the White House so that the president could proclaim to an alarmed national audience that drugs had contaminated even the most sacred realms of American governance (Reed, 1990). Daniel Larson (2011) argues that, in the wake of the Cold War and before the national hysteria following 9–11, "the drug war filled a gap in our national consciousness by offering Americans a new series of enemies to be feared and pursued by the military, and to be punished and incarcerated by the prison-industrial complex" (p. 75). Indeed, Reagan, Bush, and their allies had created what Stuart Hall and his colleagues call a moral panic (Hall et al., 1978; also see Reeves & Campbell, 1994).

The Bush presidency would also wage the "War on Crime" in other ways. During his successful 1988 presidential campaign, supporters of the elder Bush aired the notorious "Willie Horton ad." The advertisement noted that Bush's Democratic opponent, then–Massachusetts governor Michael Dukakis, opposed the death penalty and oversaw a prison furlough program (although Dukakis's Republican predecessor inaugurated the latter policy). Willie Horton was an African American man who, while out on furlough, kidnapped a young couple. He robbed them after "stabbing the man and repeatedly raping his girlfriend" ("Willie Horton," 1988). Dukakis was never able to recover politically from the stigma of unleashing a racialized sexual predator on the populace and refusing to endorse the state-sanctioned killing of the most heinous criminals (see Jamieson, 1993; Simon, 2007). Bush had effectively channeled the fears of a voting populace through the twin threats of Willie Horton and crack cocaine.

After Dukakis's humiliating defeat, the Democratic Party regrouped to, among other things, articulate a firmer stance on crime. Arkansas governor Bill Clinton would successfully carry this strategy into the White House by firmly expressing his support for capital punishment and other tough-on-crime measures. Clinton famously suspended his 1992 presidential campaign to oversee the execution of Ricky Ray Rector, a mentally disabled African American. Following his election, Clinton signed the Omnibus Crime Bill and the Anti-Terrorism and Effective Death Penalty Act. These pieces of legislation expanded the federal use of the death penalty, made the death-penalty appeals process significantly more difficult for defendants, and instituted so-called three-strikes laws that mandated a life sentence for a defendant's third violent offense (Selfa, 2008).

Clinton's crime policies were accompanied by rhetorical strategies similar to those of Reagan and Bush. In addition to emphasizing the importance of law and order, Clinton and the Republican legislature passed laws like the Personal Responsibility and Work Opportunity Reconciliation Act of 1996. The legislation placed significant limits on welfare benefits and mandated strict welfare-to-work programs, the latter often forcing poor Americans—a disproportionate amount of whom are people of color—into low-wage service-sector labor that did little to improve their socioeconomic status (Collins & Mayer, 2010; Selfa, 2008). Elaine Brown (2007) writes, "[What] Clinton policy became, and what America began to embrace, was the notion that any suffering arising from poverty or from degradation, oppression, or repression—in fact, any problems existing within the black community—was not the fault of the government or larger society. These problems existed because something was wrong with black people ourselves" (p. 44). Thus the reputably liberal Clinton did little to distinguish himself from his conservative predecessors on matters of crime and punishment, or on issues of poverty and labor so deeply connected to crime (see Faris, this volume, Chapter Five; Hartnett, 2008). Continuing to enact policies that disproportionately incarcerated African Americans, the Clinton administration leveraged the "War on Crime" to rationalize social inequality and pit victims against predators.

By the time of the Clinton White House, crime had become a preferred wedge issue for members of both parties (Simon, 2007). This period also saw the highest public approval for capital punishment in the post–Vietnam War era (Newport, 2007). However, Banner (2002) argues, "The death penalty by the end of the twentieth century was less a method of punishing criminals than a terrain of cultural argument, within which one could declare one's allegiance either with the criminal or with the law-abiding majority" (p. 284). While the literal act of execution obviously inflicted irreversible violence upon the condemned body, those who sought political power in the final decades of the twentieth century were far more concerned with the sanction's political and cultural capital. The rhetors who expanded and promoted capital punishment also justified long prison sentences for drug crimes and other offenses. Thus, much as before, different forms of punishment functioned to support familiar regimes of social control based on stratifications within the body politic. I turn now to the failure of many in the anti–death penalty movement to recognize this deep structural connection between otherwise distinct punitive measures.

LWOP and the Corporeal Politics of Abolition

The widespread use of life sentences without the possibility of parole is relatively new in the history of American criminal justice. While "true life sentences" have always existed to one degree or another, they have proliferated at a rapid rate over the past two decades. The prison reform organization the Sentencing Project writes, "In particular, support for LWOP sentences grew out of the same mistrust of the judicial process that birthed sentencing guidelines, mandatory minimums, and 'truth-in-sentencing' laws to restrict parole eligibility" (Nellis & King, 2009, p. 5). We can, of course, add to this list the expansion of the death penalty during this era. In short, the "War on Crime" that shaped so much of political discourse at this time helped motivate a turn toward LWOP. According to the same report, one of every eleven prisoners (140,610) in the state prisons and federal penitentiaries is serving a life sentence. Of this group, 29 percent (41,095) have no chance of parole (p. 3).

One can understand why those invested in a "War on Crime" discourse support LWOP. It is but one mechanism among many to exercise the state's authority to punish in the name of the victimized and the vulnerable. Far more curious is the investment many members of the anti–death penalty movement display in this sentencing option. As I note above, in 1993, prominent abolitionist and DPIC director Richard Dieter (1993) drafted an essay titled

"Sentencing for Life: Americans Embrace Alternatives to the Death Penalty."
In the essay he writes,

> Since its reinstatement in 1976, the death penalty has brought little but frus-
> tration to both proponents and opponents alike. The evidence of racism, of
> innocent defendants, of costs and delay continue to plague this country's
> recent experiment with the punishment of death. The failure of executions
> to achieve more than a spectacle has raised the question: Could America
> live without the death penalty? Are there alternatives to deal with the type
> of criminals who are currently sentenced to death? Would the American
> people be satisfied with those alternatives? (para. 3)

A key challenge to taking advantage of this ambivalence toward executions,
Dieter claims, is a lack of public confidence in the reliability of prison sentences.
Who, after all, is to say that a heinous murderer sentenced to life imprisonment
will not be released on parole simply to kill again? Dieter continues, "One of
society's best kept secrets is that the length of sentences which people would
support over the death penalty are already in place and functioning in most
of the United States" (para. 5). Dieter's rationale is that if abolitionists made
the public more aware of the availability of LWOP and other long sentences,
support for capital punishment would drop considerably. Furthermore, Dieter
notes that many juries across the country have returned death sentences out
of ignorance regarding sentencing alternatives. To Dieter, the lesson for abolitionists is simple: "To the extent that support for the death penalty continues,
it is because the public in general, and jurors in capital cases in particular, are
still unaware of this fundamental change in U.S. sentencing practice" (para.
110). Thus Dieter introduces a new rhetorical strategy for the death-penalty-
abolitionist movement: activists, he believes, should promote alternative means
of punishing criminals in hopes of rendering the death penalty irrelevant.

Since Dieter's article, the death-penalty-abolitionist movement has placed a
heavy emphasis on the availability of LWOP as an alternative to capital punishment. For example, the NCADP, the nation's largest abolitionist organization,
lists ten reasons why Americans should oppose capital punishment. Among
them are racism, lack of deterrence, arbitrary application, and other common
arguments targeting the institutional flaws associated with the death penalty.
The organization concludes its list of ten with the position that "Life without
parole is a sensible alternative to the death penalty," explaining, "Unlike decades
ago, a sentence of life without parole generally means exactly what it says—
convicts locked away in prison until they die." The NCADP continues, "Unlike
the death penalty, a sentence of life in prison without parole allows mistakes
to be corrected or new evidence to come to light" ("Facts and Figures," 2010,
para. 27). This final rationale for opposing capital punishment is undoubtedly
written with the potential death-penalty supporter in mind. Drawing directly

from Dieter's (1993) abolitionist playbook, the NCADP assures the ambivalent citizen that LWOP allows civil society to confront the death penalty's heaviest albatross, the risk of executing an innocent, without compromising the imperative to protect a fearful citizenry from society's monsters.

An NCADP-affiliated group, New Yorkers for Alternatives to the Death Penalty (NYADP), leverages LWOP to counter one of the most common arguments in favor of capital punishment: offering closure to victims' families. While Peterson, Cohen, and Smith (Chapter Four, this volume) eloquently detail the impact of "courtesy incarceration" on inmates' families, the vast majority of death-penalty discourse in the United States solely emphasizes the needs of victims' relatives. Whereas death-penalty advocates typically claim that nothing less than an execution is necessary to bring closure to these devastated families (see McCann, 2007; Wood, 2003), NYADP argues the exact opposite. On their webpage, they share the words of Sandra Place, a murder victim's daughter:

> Nearly eight years since the jury delivered the verdict of death, I am still forced to focus on my mother's killer. If the killer were given life without parole, *and I mean a true life sentence*, I would not be here. I would not be forced to discuss the killer and the verdict and the ways in which my life has been affected. Each court date, each appeal, each write-up in the newspaper, revisiting and revisiting the pain, each event keeping me that much further from the curative process I and my family so greatly deserve. ("Victims/ Survivors," 2010, emphasis added)

Drawing upon the same protracted appeals process that "War on Crime" advocates invoked to justify LWOP, the abolitionists of NYADP argue that the only true hope for victim closure is a definitive life sentence.

Similarly, in the biographical documentary *At the Death House Door*, former Texas death-row chaplain and prominent abolitionist Pastor Carroll Pickett invokes LWOP when his adult children question him at the dinner table regarding his opposition to capital punishment. When asked if he would change his position were his daughter brutally raped and murdered, he replies, "Give him life without parole and put him in solitary for the rest of his life." In response, his daughter exclaimed, "Ouch! That's worse than death." The pastor explains, "That's right! That's what they all holler about. They would rather be executed than have life without parole. You're in a cell twenty-three hours a day. You have no hope" (Gilbert & James, 2008). In Pickett's estimation, LWOP is preferable not only because it is a reversible sentence and avoids a painful appeals process, but also because those most traumatically impacted by homicide can find purification through the pain of the incarcerated. Death, indeed, would be far too generous a sentence for society's monsters.

Above, I have noted instances of death-penalty abolitionists wielding LWOP in a manner that reproduces the discourses endemic to the "War on Crime."

In some instances, abolitionists deploy LWOP to assure skeptical citizens that those heinous murderers their culture has taught them to fear will remain behind cold steel bars for the remainder of their days. Others appropriate the prevalent pro–death penalty narrative of victims' rights by arguing that life imprisonment is the only certain mechanism for closure amid grieving. The measure of such strategies, of course, is in their resonance with the public and individuals in positions of power. Much of the abolitionist activism surrounding LWOP is premised on the observation that survey respondents tend to favor the sentence over the death penalty. But what of those who are making policy decisions regarding the state's prerogative of violence vis-à-vis the death penalty? An examination of recent discourses surrounding the death penalty in states that have made significant moves against capital punishment reveal that LWOP has enabled these leaders to respond to the grievances of death-penalty opponents without sacrificing a "War on Crime" rhetorical posture.

Former Illinois governor George Ryan helped set the current momentum against the death penalty into motion when he commuted most of his state's death sentences to LWOP in 2003 (Vock, 2003). During his now-famous address announcing the decision to clear death row, Ryan went to great lengths to justify his opinion. He noted that the Land of Lincoln had exonerated more innocent individuals (thirteen) than it had executed presumably guilty individuals (twelve). The governor also noted the socioeconomic and racial disparities that tainted the Illinois system. Nonetheless, he assured constituents that he had not grown "soft" on crime. He claimed that at least one condemned inmate had written him directly, begging the governor not to commute any death sentences to LWOP. Ryan (2003) elaborated: "They'll be confined in a cell about six feet by 12 feet. Usually double-bunked. Our prisons have no air conditioning, except at one of our supermax facilities where inmates are kept in their cell 24 hours a day, and in summer months, the temperature gets as high as 100 degrees. It's a stark and dreary existence, and they can think about their crimes for the rest of their life. Life without parole has even, at times, been described by prosecutors as a fate worse than death" (para. 46). Just as Pastor Pickett assured his family members, LWOP would be no walk in the park. While Ryan may be eliminating the state's ability to execute the potentially innocent, he nonetheless retains its prerogative to exercise sustained misery on the presumably guilty.

Four years after Ryan emptied his state's death row, New Jersey became the first of the states to ban its death penalty through a legislative vote. While most states with death-penalty statutes rarely, if ever, execute criminals, few have taken the largely symbolic step of striking it from their legal code (see Hartnett & Larson, 2006). The state legislature and Governor Jon Corzine justified this unprecedented legal move on the basis of three perceived flaws in the New Jersey system: a lack of evidence that the death penalty deters crime, the high cost of capital cases compared to those involving life without parole, and the looming risk of executing an innocent person (Richburg, 2007). In addition to enlisting these common arguments in the death-penalty-abolitionist repertoire, Corzine and his government turned to LWOP to soften the legislation's blow to their perceived "toughness" on crime. Speaking on the occasion of signing the abolition bill (flanked by prominent abolitionist Sister Helen Prejean), Governor Corzine put to rest any doubts that the state government was committed to anything less than the harshest approaches to crime: "Now, make no mistake: by this action, society is not forgiving these heinous crimes or acts that have caused immeasurable pain to the families and brought fear to society. The perpetrators of these actions deserve absolutely no sympathy and the criminals deserve the strictest punishment that can be imposed without imposing death. That punishment is life in prison without parole" (vanden Heuvel, 2007, paras. 33–35). The governor added, "Let me repeat: this bill does not forgive or in any way condone the unfathomable acts carried out by the eight men now on New Jersey's death row. They will spend the rest of their lives in jail. And to that end, last night, I signed an order commuting to life without parole the death sentences of the eight persons currently on death row. This commutation action provides legal certainty that these individuals will never again walk free in our society" (paras. 37–40). In other words, while those convicted of capital murder will not die by the needle, they will nonetheless die under state confinement and surveillance. The "War on Crime" narrative in which the state takes the side of victims against a ravenous criminal threat remains intact.

The next state to eliminate capital punishment was New Mexico. Like Ryan and Corzine before him, Democratic governor Bill Richardson justified his decision to sign the abolition bill by emphasizing the inefficient costs of capital punishment, its failure to prevent crime, and the terrifying possibility of executing an innocent. However, by signing the bill, Richardson also made LWOP the law of the land in New Mexico for the first time. The governor assured his critics: "While today's focus will be on the repeal of the death penalty, I want to make clear that this bill I'm signing actually makes New Mexico safer. With my signature, we now have the option of sentencing the worst criminals to life in prison without the possibility of parole. They will never get out of prison" ("Governor Bill Richardson," 2009). Richardson's rhetoric, then, continues the work of delineating the citizen-victim from society's offenders. A flawed form of punishment may be cast aside, but Richardson is nonetheless able to alleviate public concern with the promise of harsh and certain punishment for the "worst of the worst." Governors Ryan, Corzine, and Richardson thus abolished the death penalty while invoking the same pro-punishment logic supported by Beccaria (2009) three centuries ago, when he too advocated for a transition from the instantaneous pain of the gallows to the slow pain of prison. In this sense, supporters of LWOP enact what Foucault (1977) described as "the transition from one art of punishing to another" (p. 257).

Toward an Abolitionist Imagination

I should be clear that I do not take recent advances against the death penalty lightly. For instance, many abolitionists correctly note that a wrongful life sentence is reversible, while an execution of an innocent clearly is not. For example, my friend Kenneth Foster is currently serving a life sentence in a Texas prison after a grassroots campaign succeeded in halting his impending execution hours before it was to take place in the summer of 2007. As I write, he and his family continue exploring legal avenues for his release, something that would be impossible if not for the governor's option of replacing his death sentence with one of life (see Asenas, McCann, Feyh, & Cloud, 2012). Furthermore, LWOP has created openings among constituents who might otherwise doubt that death-penalty abolition is a wise course for public policy. Victims' families, as noted above, are among the most salient of these constituencies. In short, LWOP provides an avenue for reform that is profoundly meaningful for what Erica Meiners (2007) calls "real bodies who need immediate assistance" (p. 169).

However, while I remain mindful of the short-term gains associated with LWOP and the horrific acts that most of the condemned have committed, I believe that no social movement can be guided solely by utilitarian pragmatism. Instead, abolitionists must also partake in a kind of radical imagination that fuses the death penalty with other expressions of the prison-industrial complex and works toward nothing less than a society without prisons. To begin the work of situating the death penalty within the broader structural violence of the prison-industrial complex, it is essential to note the role of LWOP in sustaining the same race, class, and other inequities as the death penalty. In their lengthy report on life sentences, the Sentencing Project found startling racial imbalances. Nationally, two-thirds of those serving life sentences in the United States are nonwhite (Nellis & King, 2009). Indeed, this percentage is higher than that of minorities who sit on the nation's death rows ("Facts about the Death Penalty," 2010). Furthermore, while the Supreme Court recently imposed limits on the practice, courts may still sentence juveniles to life terms without the possibility of parole for murder (Savage, 2012). Seventy-seven percent of juveniles who receive LWOP sentences in the United States are youth of color (Nellis & King, 2009). While a life sentence does not exercise the same immediate violence upon the condemned body as an execution, it nonetheless partakes in the same structural violence as its more forthrightly macabre counterpart.

Beyond the structural inequalities that LWOP helps to sustain, I have spent the majority of this chapter documenting the ways an abolitionist rhetoric too dependent on LWOP partakes in the same discursive strategies as those who would seek to sustain capital punishment. For activists partaking in this strategy, a focus on the corporeal differences between execution and incarceration comes at the expense of critiquing the prison-industrial complex in its totality. This tension between the prison and the gallows is as old as the Republic itself, with the former typically replacing the latter as the preferred mode of punishment whenever state killing fell out of fashion. Nonetheless, the crude narrative that posits the state as the rightful protector of a class of victims against fearsome villains continues, carrying with it a litany of corrosive discourses and structural inequalities. Indeed, in what I believe to be one of the finest articulations of the death penalty's ideological character, legal scholar Austin Sarat (2002) identifies the sanction as "*part of a strategy of governance that makes us fearful and dependent on the illusion of state protection, that divides rather than unites, that promises simple solutions to complex problems*" (p. 247, emphasis added). Capital punishment is but one of many forms of governance that participates in this spectacular regime of fear.

An anti–death penalty movement constrained by corporeal myopia regarding executions is bound to continue the organizational strategy of privileging LWOP over the death penalty. However, a movement that is mindful both of the *kairotic* opportunity in today's prison crisis and the structural relations that fuse the prison and the execution chamber together has an opportunity to imagine alternatives beyond the prison-industrial complex (see Moore, 2009; "Rough Justice," 2010). Rather than seeking to replace one form of punishment with another, death-penalty abolitionists can partake in what Kent Ono and John Sloop (1992) have called a *critical telos*: one that envisions a society no longer dependent on the "War on Crime" narrative to manage social anxieties about instability. This, of course, is no small task. I agree with Hartnett's (2008) observation that "shutting down the prison-industrial complex will require nothing less than a social revolution" (p. 511). In other words, a successful antiprison politics will entail incremental confrontations with the vast tapestry of ideological and structural forces that help rationalize mass incarceration. It will also require programs and strategies, such as those my colleagues in previous chapters advocate, that attend to the reentry needs of the formerly incarcerated and the "courtesy incarceration" of their families. Such a revolution is possible only if abolitionists broaden their gaze from its narrow focus on the grisly rituals taking place in execution chambers across the country to the systemic factors that make such a ritual possible. We must, in short, do "the creative work of reinventing the nation" (Hartnett, 2011, p. 5).

In her book *Are Prisons Obsolete?*, Angela Davis (2003) laments that while the prospect of abolishing the death penalty holds a respectable place in civil society, the notion of prison abolition is downright alien to most citizens. She notes that "the prison is considered an inevitable and permanent feature of our social lives" (p. 9). Meiners (2007) adds that the ingrained discourses of "victim" and "perpetrator" that rationalize mass incarceration make mentions of abolition perplexing, if not infuriating, to most audiences. Thus, orienting the public toward anything remotely resembling a prison-abolitionist politics will first require efforts to humanize the incarcerated and condemned, as well as rhetorical strategies that call the efficacy of modern penal policies into question (on humanizing the incarcerated and condemned, see Asenas et al., 2012; Hartnett 2010a; Tannenbaum, 2000). This will mean taking part in movements for social justice that focus more broadly on social ills that specific policies like capital punishment sustain and enact. I agree with Meiners's (2007) argument that "working toward [prison] abolition means creating structures that reduce the demand and need for prisons" (p. 168). Indeed, grassroots campaigns against racism, economic exploitation, unfair housing practices, police brutality, and other community-based concerns strike at the very core of the prison-industrial complex. For it is the desperate and disenfranchised sectors of society that most often occupy America's prisons and death rows. The body of the condemned, in other words, is a synthesis of inequities that abolitionists would be wise to confront on their own terms.

Thus, while we should continue advocating for death-penalty abolition and organizing around key capital cases, the movement for abolition must also explore coalitional possibilities with mobilizations that engage the very structures of inequality enabling the state to rationalize capital punishment. A particularly ingenious example of this model of organizing came in February of 2012 when activists associated with the Occupy Movement participated in a national "Occupy for Prisoners" demonstration. Drawing on Occupy's galvanizing advocacy for the "99 percent" of working Americans in an age of reckless finance capitalism and agonizing austerity measures, the demonstration vocally confronted matters including race and imprisonment, exploitative prison labor programs, and the entrenched interests of finance capital in the prison-industrial complex. Consisting of prison and death-penalty abolitionists, as well as organizers around causes less explicitly connected to criminal justice reform, this singular event constitutes an example of how abolitionists can confront the macabre excesses of the criminal-justice system in ways that illuminate their entrenchment in broader structures of inequality (see Kunichoff, 2012). Such an approach holds a great deal of promise to build solidarity with other realms of struggle and articulate a politics better suited to confront the prison-industrial complex in its totality.

This chapter is not intended to function as a sectarian tract that will separate the abolitionist wheat from the reformist chaff. Scholars and activists with such intentions do our movement a disservice (see, for example, Rodríguez,

2006). However, debate is a precondition for any healthy movement, and I believe the prevailing character of anti–death penalty arguments that circulate in the public sphere lacks the imagination required to comprehensively engage capital punishment. For (formerly) elected officials like Jon Corzine and Bill Richardson, the prospect of anything other than LWOP as an alternative to the death penalty would have been political suicide. For many death-penalty abolitionists, LWOP is a strategic posture on the road toward broader carceral reforms. To the condemned facing the executioner's needle, the salience and immediacy of death are obviously unbearable. However, the ideologies and institutions that rationalize the state's prerogative of violence stretch far beyond the small, sterile constraints of the death chamber. Addressing these nuances of our carceral society will come only from debate among a community of activists not beholden to the careerist objectives of our elected officials. It will require citizens with the radical imagination to widen the parameters of what we mean when we speak of abolition.

CHAPTER 10

"People Like Us"

A New Ethic of Prison Advocacy in Racialized America

ELEANOR NOVEK

Mass imprisonment has failed to reduce crime and poverty and has undermined America's most fundamental values of liberty and equality. Reproducing the worst patterns of racial discrimination, the population of the nation's overflowing prisons is more than half black or Hispanic. Black men are 6.5 times more likely to be in prison than whites, and 2.5 times more likely than Hispanics (Sabol, West, & Cooper, 2009). Young African American men in particular are targeted for arrest, investigation, and incarceration (Alexander, 2010; Mauer, 1999; Tonry, 2011; Western, 2007), while the cycle of marginalization imposed on their communities affects succeeding generations of the urban poor (Gandy, 2009; Wacquant, 2001). Decades of selective targeting have created a permanent underclass of presently and formerly incarcerated people of color who have been legally excluded from social, political, and economic participation in society (Alexander, 2010; Davis & Rodriguez, 2000; PCARE, 2007; Reiman, 2004). The evidence gathered by prison scholars and activists has had little influence on policy makers or public discourse, however, for despite its profound impact on American society, the mass imprisonment of Americans in general and African Americans in particular continues to be regarded with general indifference by broad segments of the public. With political discourse framing the system's brutality as deserved punishment, and with the media exploiting it as sensational entertainment, public support for mass incarceration endures.

As an educator who has worked with incarcerated men and women since 2001, I have come to believe that the racialization of the prison-industrial complex is propped up by the self-serving manipulation of public fear on the part of repressive social structures. I agree with Hartnett's (2000) assertion that the contemporary prison functions "neither to prevent crime nor to deter violence, but rather, to reinforce hierarchies of class privilege and political power" (p.

200). To change this system, nothing less than a revolution of the spirit is required. The antidote to the prison crisis is not only radical justice, but love.

This chapter begins by exploring public discourse on prisons and detailing the intersections of crime, fear, and social inequality that reinforce the racism of the prison-industrial complex. Next, it sketches the parameters of an inclusive vision of community safety based not on punishment, but on ethics of nonviolence, care, and compassionate love. Drawing from experiences of personal engagement, the chapter introduces a number of activist models of this approach and offers a close look at one in particular, the Alternatives to Violence Project. The chapter concludes by urging activists to reframe the prison-abolition movement as a new civil- and human-rights effort, a broad-based multiracial and cross-class coalition of people partnered in peacemaking actions that support healthy communities through their unswerving commitment to inclusion and reconciliation.

Loathing and Love: The Case for Transformation in the Public Mind

Public attitudes toward incarcerated people encompass a wide spectrum of attitudes, from dread to derision to compassion. This section will explore three distinct fields of those attitudes: fear of the incarcerated as dangerous beings "not like us," beyond all redemption; distanced pity for those whose social struggles and personal flaws have contributed to their imprisonment; and solidarity for the incarcerated as "people like us," members of families and communities whose imprisonment is precipitated by the historic, economic, and political factors that define crime and punishment in contemporary U.S. society.

In his work on social stratification, Massey (2009) observes that people judge members of other social groups and categorize them along the dimensions of emotional warmth and competence (p. 13). People are most likely to esteem others whom they perceive to be like themselves. "People like us" are seen as likeable, competent, and worthy of respect; they are accepted as members of our own social category. People "not like us" are categorized into social out-groups that may generate responses of envy, pity, or other feelings of difference. When an out-group is despised and its members are seen as neither congenial nor capable, they may trigger emotions of disgust, contempt, or outright fear (p. 14). Following Massey's typology, I argue that the prison-industrial complex is a machine of loathing, an institution that perpetuates cycles of fear and otherness that populate our world with ever growing numbers of people perceived to be "not like us." The most negative mainstream views of imprisoned men, women, and youth acknowledge no human value; to many, a person who commits a crime is not a human being, but an evil creature without potential for redemption, deserving neither mercy nor understanding. If a prisoner is also a man of color, he is twice despised, his status re-inscribed by social institutions with a history of racially discriminatory outcomes and mass-culture mythologies of criminality. While incarcerated African American and Hispanic men may have "strong desires to perform as fathers, supportive lovers, and productive, autonomous workingmen" (Nandi, 2002, p. 8), they are not seen in these ways by socially dominant groups.

On the contrary, men of color are viewed through the highly racialized lens of public culture in the United States, which has historically defined them as primitive and savage (Hall, 1995, p. 19). Numerous scholars (including Dixon, 2010; Ferber, 2007; Stabile, 2006) point to the long-standing cultural tradition of sensationalistic narratives about crime and punishment that portray African American men as dangerous brutes and predators, dark-skinned criminals "from a pariah group still considered alien to the national body" (Wacquant, 2001, p. 98). Dixon (2010) argues that, for decades, local and national television news coverage has overrepresented black men as criminal suspects and underrepresented them as victims of crime. By promoting "a black criminal stereotype that associates African Americans with criminal behavior," television news activates the audiences' racist stereotypes and leads viewers to "endorse punitive measures to address the so-called problems with African American crime" (p. 119). In entertainment media, too, Yousman (2009) finds plentiful evidence of the image of the dark-skinned criminal—"the savage OTHERS who are roaming our streets, merely waiting for an opportunity to strike if nothing is done to stop them" (p. 171). The dominant cultural image of men of color is that they are violent, out of control, "inherently dangerous and in need of civilizing" (Ferber, 2007, p. 20), leading many to accept "repressive, humiliating and even violent practices by the state in keeping these inmates under control" (Yousman, 2009, p. 91). Mass incarceration thus seems a taken-for-granted outcome for those dangerous Others who are "not like us."

Some contemporary views of the prisoner out-group are more nuanced. Massey (2009) notes that people may evaluate members of out-groups as likeable but not competent, which evokes the emotion of pity. This dimension can be seen in the views of those who see prison as a valid response to crimes triggered by poverty, mental illness, drug addiction, or other social problems. Circumstances and struggles may lead people to imprisonment; this perspective acknowledges that young people get caught up in bad decisions, or that people in poverty may be driven to desperation. Rather than defining offenders as evil predators, this viewpoint sees them as flawed people who need socially imposed discipline in order to mend their ways and reform. This view, according to Garland and Sparks (2000), was typical of twentieth-century criminology, which defined crime as a social problem in the form of individual criminal acts carried out by "delinquents" whose distant childhood experiences and psychological conflicts led them to act out in antisocial ways.

Crimes were "the surface signs of underlying dispositions, usually to be found in poorly socialized or maladjusted individuals . . . For modern criminology, the maladjusted delinquent was the problem and correctional treatment was the solution" (Garland & Sparks, 2000, p. 194). Illustrations of this view can be found in numerous mainstream criminal-justice journals, such as *Criminology*, *Crime & Delinquency*, and *Criminal Justice & Behavior*, which feature research addressing the psychological, social, and policy issues related to incarceration. While this perspective is more moderate than the fear-saturated attitudes previously discussed, it, too, is based on a foundational belief that the current criminal justice system "works." Notably, this worldview rarely critiques the racialized practices of the current system, which locate the social problems of poverty, addiction, and violence in communities of color while largely glossing over the presence of the same concerns in predominantly white neighborhoods.

Fear also shapes this view, which maintains the stigma associated with crime and expects imprisonment to maintain public safety, protecting society ("people like us") from offenders ("people not like us"). In recent years, although policy makers have begun to acknowledge racially based sentencing inequities, pollsters continue to find public support for lengthy prison terms as a response to crime (Cook & Lane, 2009; Maruna & King, 2009; Roberts & Hough, 2005). With young black men culturally constructed as "the worst offenders," public opinion still supports their exclusion from society (Green, Staerklé, & Sears, 2006, p. 447). The net effect of mass incarceration has been similar to that of intertribal warfare on other continents: it has led to the wholesale oppression of entire classes of people while constructing a state of racial hatred and fear (Alexander, 2010; Tonry, 2011).

A third perspective makes minimal distinction between lawbreakers and the rest of society: all are "people like us." In this view, offenders are embedded in the social fabric of their families, neighborhoods, communities, and nation. They are sons and daughters, parents, brothers and sisters, friends and neighbors; they are wage earners and taxpayers. They have been convicted of breaking the law and sentenced to prison, but they are still a vital part of the social, political, and economic life of the nation. In contrast to Garland and Sparks's (2000) description of the individual delinquent as the locus of crime in modern criminology, this view sees definitions of crime as fluid and historically situated, reflecting the values of society's elites. Reiman (2004) emphasizes that people in the United States are more likely to be killed or disabled by occupational industries and diseases than by aggravated assault or homicide, and more likely to lose money through price fixing, monopolies, consumer deception, and embezzlement than through robbery or other property crimes defined by the FBI. "The workplace, the medical profession, the air we breathe, and the poverty we refuse to rectify lead to far more human suffering, far more death and disability, and take far more dollars from our pockets than the murders, aggravated assaults, and thefts reported annually by the FBI," he asserts (Reiman, 2004, p. 93). Yet the criminal-justice system comes down more frequently and more harshly on the poor and the dark-skinned *"after most of the dangerous acts of the well-to-do have been excluded from the definition of crime itself"* (p. 94, emphasis in original).

The dialectical interplay between these views of crime is made visible in the way that some behaviors are deemed serious offenses to the social order while similar behaviors are seen as acceptable, depending on who commits them. The early history of drug-sentencing policy in the United States may be seen as an example of this discrepancy. Marijuana was a controlled substance as early as the 1920s, and criminalized in the 1950s with the Boggs Act of 1952 and the Narcotics Control Act of 1956, which imposed mandatory sentencing and fines for convicted users. But public policies became less punitive as use of marijuana became popular among white college students, with milder penalties and lax enforcement becoming the norm in many communities (Sentencing Project, 2009). In contrast, the "War on Drugs" hysteria over crack cocaine use, perceived to be a "black crime," led to the wholesale targeting and incarceration of low-income African Americans for drug offenses (Larson, 2011; Porter & Wright, 2011). Media rhetoric and political posturing during this period created a siege mentality that played upon deep-rooted racial stereotypes to color-code drug users as black and Other (Larson, 2011). This dynamic fostered a political climate in which mandatory penalties for crack-cocaine offenses resulted in sentences longer than those for possession of powder cocaine, methamphetamine, or heroin, perceived to be the choices of white drug users (Sentencing Project, 2009). Crack also became the only drug to carry a mandatory prison sentence for a first-time possession offense.

The point, Mauer (1999) argues, was not the potential harm inherent in any of these drugs, but "how the public perception of the appropriate societal response was shaped by the composition of the user population" (p. 134). Drug policy in the United States offers a clear example of contingent definitions of crime that shift according to social, political, and economic contexts. Here, prison is a mechanism of social control aimed at targeted groups, particularly racial minorities, the young, and the poor; as Parenti (2000) argues, "nothing produces crime and violence like sending young people to prison" (p. 47).

There are milder and harsher interpretations of the system's intent. Wilson (2009) argues that the workings of the criminal-justice system may produce "an impact on racial group outcomes, even though they are not explicitly designed or publicly discussed as matters involving race" (p. 4). On the other hand, Wacquant (2001) asserts that prison is an invasive punishment structure that serves the interests of neoliberal globalization by carrying out a mandate to "surveil, train, and neutralize the populations recalcitrant or superfluous to the new economic and racial regime" (p. 97). Regardless of intent, Magnani and Wray (2006) point to the country's deeply rooted racism and classism as the ultimate cause, arguing that racial animus is at the root of both the over-incarceration of people of color and the widespread indifference to it among whites (p. 33). People who hold this latter view do not believe that the current criminal-justice system corrects, protects, or rehabilitates. Rather, they see prisons as a tool of violent suppression and exploitation of African American and Hispanic communities. They understand incarcerated people to be capable of reconciliation with their communities and deserving of inclusion in their society. Such critics call for society to find other ways of dealing with the social problems now being consigned to the prison-industrial complex for containment and control (Alexander, 2010; Davis & Rodriguez, 2000; Kivel, 2002; Magnani & Wray, 2006; Mauer, 1999; PCARE, 2007; and many others).

The three perspectives described here are politically and philosophically worlds apart, but U.S. corrections policy and public opinion contain strains of all three. To mobilize public opposition to the prison-industrial complex, activists need to find ways to make the fears and consequences of these inter-pretations transparent and to reconcile their most polarized elements. One way to begin this reconciliation is to engage the public in explicitly antiracist dialogue about the origins and impacts of the prison-industrial complex.

The Prison Crisis and Systemic Racism

As the prison population in the United States tripled over the last thirty years (Sabol, West, & Cooper, 2009), people of color were disproportionately af-fected (Alexander, 2010; Gandy, 2009; Mauer 1999; Reese, 2006; Sentencing Project, 2009; Sudbury, 2005; Tonry, 2011; Western, 2007; among many others). Despite recent legislative attempts toward more equitable sentencing, more than half the nation's overflowing prison population is still black or Hispanic (Sabol, West, & Cooper, 2009). In the late 1990s, one in fourteen adult black males was locked up on any given day (Mauer, 1999); now, among young African American men, the rate is one in nine (Pew Center on the States, 2009). Not only have racist drug policies eroded community–police relations in urban areas, reinforcing the mistrust felt by many black people toward law enforcement as a mechanism of white domination (Gandy, 2009), but they have also strengthened the tendency of dominant groups to equate blackness with criminality (Wacquant, 2001).

Critical scholars (including Alexander, 2010; Mauer, 1999; Roberts, 2008; Wacquant, 2002) have traced the connection between the current mass incar-ceration of blacks and Hispanics and the nation's historic practices of chattel slavery and Jim Crow segregation. Roberts (2008) argues that the nation's criminal-justice system "has always functioned, in coordination with other institutions and social policy, to subordinate black people and maintain the racial caste system . . . racism is engrained in the very construction of the system and implicated in its every aspect—how crimes are defined, how suspects are identified, how charging decisions are made, how trials are conducted, and how punishments are imposed" (p. 262).

Wacquant (2001) finds an unbroken narrative of social control in the history of the racial separation and labor exploitation of African Americans in the United States—from the chattel slavery that began in the 1600s to Jim Crow segregation in the Reconstruction era to the urban ghetto of the twentieth century to the current phenomenon of mass imprisonment. Where social institutions like segregation explicitly imposed confinement and control on the basis of racial identity, he asserts, today's prisons function as "a substitute apparatus for keeping (unskilled) African Americans 'in their place,' i.e. in a subordinate and confined position in physical, social, and symbolic space" (p. 97). From this perspective, the prison-industrial complex of today may be seen as the culmination of centuries of racism.

Thus what Wideman asserted in 1995 is truer than ever today: in an environment characterized by historically biased attitudes, actively hostile legislative practices, and sensationalistic cultural representations, "to be a man of color of a certain economic class and milieu is equivalent in the public eye to being a criminal" (p. 505). The racialized approach to public safety (as identified by Rose, 2002; Wacquant, 2001; and others) has defined blacks and Hispanics as "dangerous classes," anticipating crime in advance among these groups rather than addressing its occurrence after the fact. Criminal suspicion, Rose (2002) asserts, no longer focuses on the individual suspect, but on where race and class place him on the "continuum of dangerousness" (p. 197). In his analysis of a number of cases of racial profiling (anticipating the shooting of Trayvon Martin and numerous other contemporary occurrences), Rose (2002) observes that defendants were stopped by police not because they had been involved in criminal activity, but because they "looked like" criminals—their skin color "identified them as part of a population subgroup which might be deemed more likely to be involved in crime . . . The result is to replace considerations of individual criminal fault with predictions of dangerousness and safety management" (p. 197).

While drug policies may be modified here or there, the nation's public-safety apparatus continues to focus mainly on the management and exclusion of blacks and other so-called "dangerous populations" rather than any efforts at rehabilitation or reintegration (Rose, 2002, p. 199). The routine uses of racial profiling, stop-and-frisk, disproportionate sentencing, and mass over-incarceration make plain "the political deployment of the concept of race" (Winant, 2000, p. 186), in which the dominant racial meanings encoded in social structures support practices of oppression. These meanings and practices have entrenched the perspective that African Americans and Hispanics are dangerously "not like us." They have led to the wholesale oppression of people of color and have bred a climate of racial hatred, suspicion, and fear that has damaged the nation.

Civil Rights and the "Movement of Love"

To confront the racism driving the prison-industrial complex, activists face two challenges. The first is the need to engage the public in explicitly antiracist discourse about prisons. A number of scholars (among them Michael Tonry, Michelle Alexander, and Marc Mauer with the Sentencing Project) are doing excellent work in making the relationship between racial animus and mass incarceration incontrovertibly clear to the public. Activists can support and advance this work by publicizing, extending, and applying it in their own advocacy. The second struggle is the need for a revolution in public sentiment extensive enough to bring about policy change. Society has clear responsibilities to its imprisoned members: to afford them human rights and protections; to provide education, health care, and shelter; to refrain from torture or abuse; and to restore them to full citizenship once their sentences have been served. But ending mass incarceration and healing the dreadful wounds it has caused will depend not only on a change of policies, but on a change of heart. Thus activists must do nothing less than reframe public discourse on prisons into a moral movement for the civil and human rights of the incarcerated. To support this argument, I describe a number of related ethical principles: the ethics of nonviolence, community, care, and compassionate love.

Sally King (1998) uses the term "transformative nonviolence" to describe the kinds of thought and action that can transform the self, community, and society at large peacefully (p. 4). Christians (2007) asserts that nonviolence is an ethical imperative; he argues that the principle applies not only to intergovernmental bodies and global politics, but to "peaceful coexistence in community life," as well (p. 6). In a nonviolent social system, great importance is placed on "the worth of every individual and the belief that he can change" (Sharp, 1959, p. 47). Similarly, in their exploration of Gandhi's precepts of nonviolence, Starosta and Shi (2007) observe that human beings are obliged to see the good in one another, even in moments of conflict or harm. "Something can be found in the Other," they assert, "that will lead him or her toward Truth" (p. 9).

King, Christians, and Starosta and Shi argue, in short, that when people regard one another as worthy and valuable, they can coexist without doing violence to one another. In a similar vein, Gilligan (1982) hypothesized an "ethic of care" that could structure a society based on relationships. She imagined "a world that coheres through human connection rather than through systems of rules" (p. 29). At the heart of this ethic is "the vision that self and other will be treated as of equal worth, that despite differences in power, things will be fair; the vision that everyone will be responded to and included, that no one will be left alone or hurt" (p. 63). From this perspective, a person's identity is defined by her responsibility to and connection with others; Garver and Reitan (1995) name this form of interconnectedness "community in the moral sense" (p. 28). This is not a community based on family, neighborhood locale, or shared interest, but "a dynamic state" characterized by a group of people who consider each other's needs and interests to be important and who act to satisfy one another's interests and needs as well as their own. In such a state, every member of a community is valuable, everyone is perceived as "someone like us."

Certainly some prison advocates do the work they do because of the caring relationships they have formed with the incarcerated; the ethic of compassionate love helps describe their experience of finding humanity in an inhumane space. Dr. Martin Luther King Jr. (1963) pointed to the divine commandment to love one's neighbor as the "invisible, inner law which etches on [our] hearts the conviction that all men are brothers and that love is mankind's most potent weapon for personal and social transformation" (p. 28). Craig and Ferre (2006) note a number of faith traditions with an obligation to selfless love, a steadfast responsibility toward others and a regard for their value, no matter who they are or what they have done. Selfless love, also called *agape*, includes a deep-seated commitment to fairness and a spirit of nonreciprocal giving that embraces even the unlovable and unlikable (p. 129). Similarly, Sprecher and Fehr (2005) call compassionate love a spirit of "caring, concern, tenderness, and an orientation toward supporting, helping, and understanding" other people (p. 630), particularly when they are seen to be suffering or in need. Jovanovic and Wood (2004) describe a way of seeing the world "that embraces and loves the other" regardless of the person's qualities or the outcome of the interaction; the focus of action is "not on what I want to achieve but what the other needs of me" (p. 331). While Dr. King's view was that of a Christian theologian, in his speech at the University of California, Berkeley (1957) he insisted that people of other faiths, or of no faith, could also sense this deep power of the connection among human beings and be governed by "something in the universe that unfolds for justice" (para. 6).

Engaging these principles may help activists begin to reframe their challenge to the prison-industrial complex as a movement of love. In his death-penalty activism, Conquergood (2002) critiques the "distanced perspective" that characterizes much scholarly research in the social sciences. He advocates instead an embodied approach that involves "active, intimate, hands-on participation and personal connection: 'knowing how,' and 'knowing who.' This is a view from ground level, in the thick of things" (p. 146). Many activists and scholars who work directly with incarcerated people find themselves deeply moved and changed by the inspired moments of human connection they have experienced under these unlikely conditions (Anderson, 1996; Hartnett, 2010; Novek, 2005; Pompa, 2004; Valentine, 1998; and in this volume, Shailor; Coogan; Hinck, Hinck, & Withers). For these scholar/activists, the sense of wonder that drives their work folds into what I am calling the ethic of caring, wherein working for justice is seen as an act of love.

What have we learned in "the thick of things" about prisoners? As a volunteer at three correctional facilities since 2001, I have been privileged to get glimpses into the lives of many incarcerated men and women. As a white woman, I have beheld the face of the system's racial targeting; in fact, the vast majority of the hundreds of prisoners I have met over the years have been people of color. Prisoners have taught me that the hospitality of the state affords the same degree of anguish and fear to all, whether an individual has committed a petty crime or a serious one. And overall, I have been a witness to the struggles of the human spirit to find forgiveness and meaning, even as human lives are condemned to be warehoused and wasted.

Because we work in the "thick of things," prison teachers and activists see firsthand that imprisoned people are still husbands and wives, mothers, fathers, sons, and daughters; they are artists, workers, protectors, and lovers, with desires for companionship and caring, with elements of spirituality and compassion. Both male and female prisoners struggle to forge proactive identities that may redeem them in the eyes of their families and society. Wallace, one of the men I have worked with in recent years, wrote in an essay, "With age comes wisdom, and a little late I've come to realize that one must accept responsibility for his own actions. Only then can one begin to atone for his actions and begin to build for himself a better life." Tina, a student in my prison journalism class, wrote, "I am thankful for this chance to sit back and sort out what went wrong and how I can make it better, not only for myself, but for the people I love the most. This 'chance,' as I call it, is my opportunity to find myself, because somewhere I lost me." Based on my interactions with Tina and hundreds of imprisoned learners like her, I believe that transforming the prison-industrial complex depends on our pursuing an ethic of care that helps prisoners claim their rightful places within our civic life.

In a contemporary culture based on competition and status, the principles described here may seem better suited to theology than to policy. But over the last thirty years, American society has lost—has been willing to cast aside—millions of its sons and daughters. If the public is to reject the physical, emotional, and economic brutalities imposed by the prison-industrial complex, it must come to know and value the individuals affected by it. Allen (2004) maintains that public opinion on prisons, based largely on second-hand knowledge and media sensationalism, would change if more people were personally involved in some aspect of the criminal-justice system (p.

65) and experienced its contradictions for themselves. When teachers and activists encounter prisoners, they experience them not as monsters, but as complicated and valuable people with abilities, emotions, concerns, and love. They also witness the human suffering that takes place in our overcrowded correctional institutions: the humiliations, confrontations, and outrages that make up daily life behind bars, and the damage left behind in prisoners' home communities. In affirming the worth of incarcerated human beings and their potential for redemption, moral reasoning demands that we find alternative ways of engaging with prisoners and begin treating people whom we now fear, marginalize, and condemn as "people like us." The Civil Rights Movement of the twenty-first century therefore calls upon teachers and activists to embody an ethics of care, to work for justice by practicing *agape*.

Putting the Ethics of Love into Action

"People like us" ethics inform numerous nonprofit groups and organizations that mobilize on behalf of incarcerated people and their families. These may be local individual or state efforts, such as educational, religious, or arts groups that operate in particular correctional facilities, or they may be organizations that are national or international in scope and seek systemic change. National examples include the Sentencing Project, based in Washington, DC, a national organization that promotes sentencing reform and alternatives to incarceration (http://www.sentencingproject.org/template/index.cfm) by focusing public attention on inequities in the criminal-justice system with research, aggressive media campaigns, and strategic advocacy for policy reform. According to the group's website, "The Sentencing Project is dedicated to changing the way Americans think about crime and punishment" (The Sentencing Project, 2010). Similarly, Families Against Mandatory Minimums (2009) works to change mandatory sentencing laws by educating legislators at the federal and state levels about the need for sentencing reform. The organization, also Washington-based, participates in precedent-setting legal cases involving mandatory minimum sentencing and works with the media to humanize the problem by highlighting individuals affected by these policies (http://www.famm.org/).

The Prison Activist Research Center (http://www.prisonactivist.org/) and Critical Resistance (http://www.criticalresistance.org/), both based in Oakland, California, and the Real Cost of Prisons Project, run from Northampton, Massachusetts (http://www.realcostofprisons.org/), are prison abolitionist organizations that work to expose the negative consequences of mass incarceration and to build "safe, healthy communities that respond to harm without relying on prisons and punishment" (Critical Resistance, 2011). These groups compile research and information; make resources available to prisoners, the formerly incarcerated, and their families; and create action networks with other activist groups and communities. They call for social and economic reforms, not the brutality and racism of the prison system, to address social and economic problems (Alexander, 2010; Davis & Rodriguez, 2000; Magnani & Wray, 2006). The abolitionist approach seeks an end to capital punishment and police brutality, a moratorium on prison construction, the release of nonviolent offenders, and repeal of harsh mandatory drug sentences. Advocates note that funding currently apportioned to the prison system could be redirected to rebuild low-income neighborhoods devastated by the prison crisis and help residents "build local institutions, support social networks, and create social citizenship" (Roberts, 2008, p. 285).

The national organizations described above share a spirit of solidarity with imprisoned people but may not necessarily interact and build relationships with them. Other organizations involve direct contacts and relationships with the imprisoned; their efforts involve ethics of care and of compassionate love. For example, Inside-Out, based in Philadelphia, Pennsylvania (http://www.insideoutcenter.org/home.html), creates partnerships between institutions of higher learning and correctional systems, bringing college students together with incarcerated men and women to study together behind prison walls. The program seeks to create a paradigm shift for participants, encouraging transformation and change as they work for justice. Prison arts programs, including small individual efforts as well as established endeavors around the nation like the Prison Creative Arts Project in Ann Arbor, Michigan (http://www.lsa.umich.edu/english/pcap/), the Shakespeare Prison Project of Parkside, Wisconsin (http://shakespeareprisonproject.blogspot.com/), Prison Performing Arts in St. Louis, Missouri (http://www.prisonartsstl.org/), and Rehabilitation through the Arts in Katonah, New York (http://www.rta-arts.com/), bring incarcerated men and women together with educators, students, and arts professionals for development through performance, creativity, and self-expression. And, led by curiosity, compassion, or faith, countless individuals volunteer their talents at prisons as educators, mentors, or coaches, sharing their skills, energy, and time with the imprisoned.

A particular example of a volunteer effort involving direct relationship between members of the public and incarcerated people is the Alternatives to Violence Project (AVP), based in St. Paul, Minnesota (http://www.avpusa.org). AVP is a national and international volunteer organization that uses experience-based workshops to promote nonviolence. It offers direct witness of the prison experience in a deeply transformative way. I will offer a detailed description of the program below to show how prison activists can call on love as a transformative dynamic to begin addressing the racialized fear and exclusionary impact of the prison-industrial complex.

A Safe Community: The Alternatives
to Violence Project

In the spring of 2006 I took part in a series of workshops sponsored by the Alternatives to Violence Project. Although I became an active volunteer facilitator for AVP in the intervening years and have led many workshops myself, I still remember those early sessions in a stifling prison gymnasium with broken windows and cracked floorboards, because they left me with strong sense memories like these:

I am sitting with 23 other people, mostly young men of color in their early 20s. Our chairs are arranged in a circle facing out, so that our backs are to each other. We are asked to close our eyes and then call out any expressions we can remember hearing from parents or authority figures when we were children. The room is silent for a few minutes. Then the voices begin: "Dummy." "Bastard." "Just like your father, you'll never be no good." "I wish you were dead." "You have shit for brains." "Stop crying or I'll give you something to really cry about." "I should have had an abortion instead of having you." "Get the belt." "Get out." The pain in the room is palpable. Then the voices begin again, answering back what we could not say as children: "I need you." "I'm scared." "Please don't hurt me."

The workshop facilitator, an older White man, climbs up on a folding table and crosses his arms over his chest. He asks for volunteers, and then steps to the very edge of the platform. Turning around, he closes his eyes and flings himself backward off the table. Seven young men in prison uniforms lunge forward to catch him as he falls, steadying his body carefully, and then slowly lowering him to the floor like a precious porcelain vase, their hands on his limbs a patchwork of light and dark browns. Later, incarcerated men are paired up; one closes his eyes while the other leads him around a room filled with chairs, steps, uneven surfaces and other people milling about. Although they were strangers to each other not 24 hours ago, the men now trust their partners to lead them to safety, and no one runs into a wall, falls down, or gets hurt.

In a paired-discussion exercise, a prisoner named Tariq looks at me, struggling with the idea of forgiveness. When he was an adolescent, he says, his father rejected him. "I don't have time for you. You're not good enough to be my son," his father said. But now that Tariq is serving a long sentence, the man is trying to make contact. "Why should I open my heart now?" he asks. "When I really needed him, he wasn't there. I don't want to open my heart again just to have it hurt." Another day, a small group of men sit in a circle of plastic chairs while a prisoner named George shakes his head and strokes the neatly trimmed beard on his chin. "When I was on the street, my cousin and I were tight—we did everything together. That was my boy. But now I'm up in here, he don't send me no money, no kite [letters]—nothing."

He just hung me out to dry. I can't forgive that." He shakes his head again and blinks his eyes. Another man in the group shares a similar experience, but describes how he has let go of his anger: "I feel free, you know? Relieved. I didn't do it for them. I did it for me."

In a circle, a group of young men throw a ball back and forth in an intricate pattern. A facilitator adds another ball, then another. Soon half a dozen balls are whipping across the circle. Suddenly the facilitator tosses in a beanbag teddy bear too. Then a floppy kitty. The first man to catch one of these drops it in confusion—"What's this?" The circle erupts in laughter.

These activities were not idiosyncratic, but were typical of interactions that take place in AVP workshops all over the world. In one-on-one conversations and small-group discussions, participants share personal pains and triumphs and recognize their own experiences in the stories of others. Activities that create experiences of trust may lead participants to reflect on which is more challenging: learning to trust someone else, or being responsible for another's trust. When participants hear that other people have overcome anger or let go of resentment, they begin to envision that they can, too. Exercises like role-plays and scenarios offer physical and verbal explorations of the possible responses to friction, including avoidance, competition, or cooperation. These interpersonal experiences build insight into which approaches work best under what conditions. They allow participants to practice nonviolent responses to conflict, encouraging them to speak, breathe, and move in ways that suggest what a situation might look and feel like if it were moving toward a mutually satisfactory ending, instead of a fight.

The Alternatives to Violence Project (AVP) began in 1975 at Green Haven Prison in Beekman, New York, after the Attica prison riots. According to the organization's creation story, a group of prisoners concerned about increasing numbers of young offenders in the criminal-justice system sought the support of local Quakers and began developing a program to teach youth the skills of nonviolent conflict resolution. They were assisted by a consultant who had led training workshops for people planning to participate in nonviolent civil disobedience with Dr. Martin Luther King. The program expanded, first to other prisons and then to communities; today, AVP workshops are held in prisons in thirty-one states, as well as in more than fifty nations and conflict zones around the world. Last year more than fourteen thousand people participated in the U.S. program (AVP, 2010). Although the majority of workshops are held in prisons, they are also offered at businesses, churches, community associations, halfway houses, and women's shelters, and in other settings.

The mission of AVP, "to empower people to lead nonviolent lives through affirmation, respect for all, community building, cooperation and trust" (AVP, 2010), does not explicitly identify racial equality as a goal, yet the organization's bedrock commitment to respect and human connection resonates with the philosophies of civil-rights and human-rights activists everywhere. The three-day experiential workshops offered by AVP are grounded in egalitarian attitudes and practices. Workshops are built around a series of structured exercises, discussions, games, and role-plays that help participants connect with each other and practice new, nonviolent ways of dealing with conflict. The guiding philosophy of AVP, called "transforming power," is akin to Craig and Ferre's (2006) notion of selfless love and Gandhi's concept of *satyagraha*, the soul force that people can apply to the joint pursuit of truth.

According to Aspey and Eppler (2001), transforming power involves an attitude of mind in which a person values and identifies deeply with all of humanity, even someone who seems hostile or threatening. When approaching a stranger, no matter how antagonistic, Apsey and Eppler (2001) say, "If we reverence their potential, we can break down the barriers which prevent us and them from influencing each other. Are we willing to learn . . . to relate ourselves sympathetically to those of whose actions we disapprove—militarists, bigots, materialists, delinquents, and those whose race, religion, or ideology differ from our own? Until we do this, their minds are closed to us" (p. 6). Participants in AVP workshops are asked to reach inside themselves for the energy that builds genuine regard for others and precludes the use of violence.

The social relations that reduce antagonism are simple but profound: affirmation, respect, trust, empathy, cooperative problem solving. During sessions, participants work on learning habits of mind that accept the possibility of change and forgiveness. These relationships are not only developed during the exercises of each workshop, but they are also built into the organization's essential principles and modeled by workshop facilitators. Thus sessions are led cooperatively by teams of facilitators that consist of both civilian volunteers and prisoners; no one person is "in charge." There is no hierarchy of leaders and followers. All participants, including facilitators, are present to learn from each other, decisions are often made by consensus, and all feedback and suggestions are welcome.

Activities take place with participants sitting in a circle, or clustered in small groups. Much energy is spent on establishing norms of affirmation, respect, and equality. Intermittent games promote teamwork, cause laughter, and encourage humility and empathy. Throughout the workshop, civilian volunteers may eat, talk, and mingle freely with prisoners as equals. AVP operates in this manner because, as Garver and Reitan (1995) observe, "When members of a group respect and care for one another, they are more apt to cooperate in solving problems, and to deal with conflicts in a nonviolent way; when individuals feel they belong to a group, they are more likely to work cooperatively with other members of the group; when they feel safe, they are less likely to lash out with violence" (p. 24). This is true in small groups and workshop sessions behind bars, but also when the program operates in larger social networks and communities outside—even in parts of the world where genocide and intergroup conflict have devastated communities, as in AVP's work in Rwanda, Burundi, Congo, Kenya, Uganda, Colombia, El Salvador, Nicaragua, Guatemala, Indonesia, and the West Bank (http://avpinternational.org/index).

In prison workshops, people with resources mingle with people who have none, and whites, African Americans, Hispanics, and people of other races and ages come together. Among civilian and prison participants alike are a number of people with little prior close contact with other races, but they suddenly find themselves full partners with these "others" in learning and social change. AVP participation offers a visceral encounter with a nonviolent, nonracist society—not a theoretical abstraction, but an embodied lived experience. During the twenty-four hours that make up a three-day workshop, participants build and maintain a different kind of community.

For some participants, this weekend is the first time in their lives that community means trust and acceptance, not struggle, suspicion, or fear. On the street, young men may see each other as competitors locked in desperate conflict, with violence the only possible means of overcoming their disadvantage. This value system may be seen as parallel to the larger society's focus on individualism and competition. But in the AVP workshop, they see the similarity of their own struggles with those of others, and they learn that trust and cooperation are possible. A spirit of cooperation and nonaggression emerges. Similarly, middle-class volunteers, the majority of whom, according to Tewksbury and Dabney (2005), are likely to be white, middle-aged or older, educated men, may have never associated closely with poor blacks and Hispanics, who make up a majority of the incarcerated. In an AVP workshop, they find their fears of dark-skinned criminality, stoked by media stereotypes, dissolving through the reality of human connection. A shared mood of empathy and generosity develops.

A common critique of nonviolence motivated by *agape* is that it is a spiritual position, too "soft" or passive to be successful when applied to persistent violent conflict. On the contrary, Mahatma Gandhi saw it as one of the ingredients needed "to build a new social and economic order" in the intensely racist climate of his nation (Sharp, 1959, p. 58). He, and Dr. King after him, believed that political action grounded in nonviolence was "more effective than other means of action for opposing aggression and oppression, in particular more effective than violence" (Martin & Varney, 2003, p. 215). Nor is *agape* an artifact of the past; it shows up in "second-track diplomacy," a relatively recent model that uses unofficial actions of groups and individuals outside government to "build understanding and to restore broken relationships" between groups in conflict (Wehrenfenning, 2008, p. 359). As in AVP, political concerns are set aside in favor of the growth of understanding, empathy, and relationships of equality. A variety of contemporary human-rights movements (from

Czechoslovakia's "Velvet Revolution" to the Arab Spring to Liberia's Women in Peacebuilding Network) have appreciated the political utility of nonviolence and human connection. These dynamics suggest that *agape* is sturdy enough for the prison-abolition movement to use in addressing the racialized fear and exclusionary consequences of the contemporary criminal-justice system.

Conclusion

As Michelle Alexander (2010) notes, "Since the days of slavery, black men have been depicted and understood as criminals, and their criminal 'nature' has been among the justifications for every caste system to date. The criminalization and demonization of black men is one habit America seems unlikely to break without addressing head-on the racial dynamics that have given rise to successive caste systems" (p. 240). Thus activists who oppose the prison-industrial complex are obliged to address the system's pervasive, deep-seated racism if we are to make any progress in decommissioning the prison-industrial complex. Harsh policing and sentencing policies continue to target men of color and to re-inscribe the racialized fear widely held by white citizens and lawmakers. Public opinion in the United States still shows pervasive support for prison as a response to crime, while media messages persevere in exploiting the racist stereotypes of the past with ever more violent iterations. Racial animus continues to be one of the factors that dehumanizes the poor, keeps arrest and conviction rates of blacks and Hispanics disproportionately high, and intensifies the suffering of the incarcerated.

The sentencing-reform and prison-abolition movements already acknowledge that the War on Drugs is a failed social policy (Larson, 2011; Mauer, 2006) and that the violence and injustice of the prison system make it a poor solution to social problems (Davis & Rodriguez, 2000; Hartnett, 2010; PCARE, 2007). Clearly, the movement to end the prison-industrial complex must be a civil-rights movement; to establish alternative visions of community safety and build public support for the elimination of the prison-industrial complex, we must eliminate the racism that permeates its very foundations. I have argued here that a first step is learning to see prisoners as "people like us," with intrinsic human value and rights that were not forfeited when they were incarcerated. The Alternatives to Violence Project and other volunteer efforts offer citizens direct engagement with incarcerated people on a face-to-face level that enables the growth of personal relationships of solidarity and equality and reduces the racial animus that breeds fear.

Extending from the personal to the political requires a more explicitly antiracist discourse of the spirit, one that can be built upon these transcendent experiences of connection with incarcerated people and their families. Alexander (2010) agrees that the movement to end mass incarceration must include a frank discussion of race: "We must stop debating crime policy as though it were purely about crime. People must come to understand the racial history and origins of mass incarceration—the many ways our conscious and unconscious biases have distorted our judgments over the years about what is fair, appropriate, and constructive when responding to drug use and drug crime" (p. 238). Magnani and Wray (2006) also add a plea for forgiveness as part of the dialogue, to foster healing and encourage a "fundamental change in how people within the community see one another—particularly the way they view those who are struggling or outcast, or who harm themselves and others" (p. 157).

Like the Civil Rights Movement of the 1950s and 1960s, the prison-abolition movement must develop a multiracial and cross-class coalition that goes beyond activist groups on the left to encompass churches and other faith-based organizations, students, lawmakers, and public advocates from all sides of the political spectrum. We must make it clear that our nation's desire for safe communities can never be achieved by ever larger battalions of police and ever more prison beds. A society that recognizes and values the humanity of all of its members, including its demonized outcasts, would not impose "law enforcement," but create "community safety." It would work to provide opportunity to individuals and groups of all races and to mitigate the consequences of social problems contributing to crime, such as poverty and mental illness. The funding that now feeds the prison system would be redirected to rebuild the low-income neighborhoods devastated by the prison crisis and help residents "build local institutions, support social networks, and create social citizenship" (Roberts, 2008, p. 285). The radical force behind such actions would be generated by an unswerving commitment to inclusion and reconciliation, fairness and love.

The African American child is still small when the street begins to beckon him, and it is here that the society he was born into expects him to join the ranks of the violent, as victimizer, victim, or both. We must intervene, as Dr. King urged, "because he is a part of me and I am a part of him. His agony diminishes me, and his salvation enlarges me" (p. 29). Instead of profiling, incarcerating, disenfranchising, and excluding young black and Hispanic men, the nation must learn to see them as "people like us." This is the most urgent step we can take toward dismantling the prison-industrial complex. The healing of the nation's political and economic conscience begins with rejecting mass incarceration and embracing the full participation of all citizens of color.

Bibliography

Abbott, J. H. (1998). In the belly of the beast. In H. B. Franklin (Ed.), *Prison writing in 20th century America* (pp. 187–99). New York: Penguin. (Reprinted from *In the belly of the beast: Letters from prison*. 1981. New York: Random House.)

Abramsky, S. (2002). *Hard time blues: How politics built a prison nation*. New York: Thomas Dunn Books.

Abramsky, S. (2007). *American furies: Crime, punishment, and vengeance in the age of mass imprisonment*. Boston: Beacon Press.

Abu-Jamal, M. (1995). *Live from death row*. New York: Avon Books.

ACMHE: The Association for Contemplative Mind in Higher Education. Available from www.acmhe.org. A welcome trend: Coast to coast the death penalty system is on the defensive. (2007, Spring). *Lifelines*. Retrieved August 21, 2010, from http://www.ncadp.org/index.cfm?content=14

Alexander, B. (2010). *Is William Martinez not our brother? Twenty years of the Prison Creative Arts Project*. Ann Arbor, MI: University of Michigan Press.

Alexander, B. (2011). "A piece of the reply": The Prison Creative Arts Project. In S.J. Hartnett (Ed.), *Challenging the prison-industrial complex: Activism, arts, and education alternatives* (pp. 149–78). Champaign: University of Illinois Press.

Alexander, B., & Paul, J. (2005). *Doing time, making spaces*. Ann Arbor, MI: PCAP.

Alexander, M. (2010). *The new Jim Crow: Mass incarceration in the age of colorblindness*. New York: The New Press.

Allen, F. A. (1981). *Decline of the rehabilitative ideal: Penal policy and social purpose*. New Haven, CT: Yale University Press.

Allen, R. (2004). What works in changing public attitudes: Lessons from "Rethinking Crime and Punishment." *Journal for Crime, Conflict and the Media*, 1(3), 55–67.

Alternatives to Violence Project (2010). *Annual Report*. St. Paul, MN.: AVP USA.

Alternatives to Violence Project (2011). AVP/USA bylaws. Adopted January 1993, last amended 2012. Available at http://avpusa.org

Altheide, D. L. (2002). *Creating fear: News and the construction of crisis*. Hawthorne, NY: Aldine de Gruyter.

Altheide, D. L., & Johnson, J. M. (1998). Criteria for assessing interpretive validity in qualitative research. In N. K. Denzin & Y. S. Lincoln (Eds.), *Collecting and interpreting qualitative materials* (pp. 283–312). Thousand Oaks, CA: Sage.

Alvesson, M., & Kärreman, D. (2000). Varieties of discourse: On the study of organizations through discourse analysis. *Human Relations*, 53, 1125–49.

Anderson, S. (1996). Ethnography as advocacy: Allowing the voices of female prisoners to speak. In P. M. Spacks (Ed.), *Advocacy in the classroom: Problems and possibilities* (408–21). New York: St. Martin's Press.

Andrews, D., & Bonta, J. (2003). *The psychology of criminal conduct* (3rd ed.). Cincinnati, OH: Anderson Publishing.

Andrews, D., Bonta, J., & Hoge, R. D. (1990). Classification for effective rehabilitation: Rediscovering psychology. *Criminal Justice and Behavior, 17,* 19–52.

Angermeyer, M. C., Link, B., & Majcher-Angermeyer, A. (1987). Stigma perceived by patients attending modern treatment settings. Journal of Nervous Mental and Mental Disease, 175(1), 4–11. Retrieved August 31, 2012, from http://journals.lww.com/jonmd/pages/default.aspx

Applegate, B. K. (2000). *Specifying public support for rehabilitation: A factorial survey approach.* Washington, D.C.: U.S. Dept. of Justice. Retrieved January 20, 2011, from http://www.ncjrs.gov/pdffiles1/nij/grants/184113.pdf

Applegate, J. L., & Morreale, S. P. (1999). Service-learning in communication: A natural partnership. In D. Droge & B. O. Murphy (Eds.), *Voices of strong democracy: Concepts and models for service-learning in communication studies* (pp. ix–xiv). Washington, DC: American Association for Higher Education.

Archibold, R. C. (2010, March 24). California, in financial crisis, opens prison doors. *New York Times.* Retrieved April 22, 2012, from www.nytimes.com/2010/03/24/us/24calprisons.html

Arrigo, B. A. (1997). Transcarceration: Notes on a psychoanalytically-informed theory of social practice in the criminal justice and mental health systems. *Crime, Law, and Social Change, 27,* 31–48.

Asenas, J., McCann, B. J., Feyh, K., & Cloud, D. (2012). Saving Kenneth Foster: Speaking with others in the belly of the beast of capital punishment. In. L. R. Frey & K. M. Carragee (Eds.), *Communication activism, volume 3: Struggling for social justice amidst difference* (pp. 263–90).

Ashforth, B. E., & Kreiner, G. E. (1999). "How can you do it?" Dirty work and the challenge of constructing a positive identity. *The Academy of Management Review,* 24(3), 413–34. Retrieved August 30, 2012, from http://www.aom.pace.edu/amr/

Aspey, L., & Eppler, K. (2001). *Transforming power for peace* (4th ed.). Alternatives to Violence Project and the Quaker Press of Friends General Conference. Plainfield, VT: OMlet Publications.

Associated Press. (2009, December 9). Prison population up, despite drop in 20 states. *New York Times.* Retrieved April 22, 2012, from http://www.nytimes.com/2009/12/09/us/09prison.html

Astin, A. W. (1996). Involvement in learning revisited: Lessons we have learned. *Journal of College Student Development, 37,* 123–34.

Astin, A. W., Sax, L. J., & Avalos, J. (1999). Long term effects of volunteerism during the undergraduate years. *Review of Higher Education, 22,* 187–202.

Astin, A. W., Vogelgesang, L. J., Ikeda, E. K., & Yee, J. A. (2000, January). How service learning affects students. Los Angeles, CA: Higher Education Research Institute. Retrieved January 13, 2007, from http://gseis.ucla.edu/

Atton, C. (2002). *Alternative media.* London: Sage.

Austin, J., & Irwin, J. (2001). *It's about time: America's imprisonment binge* (3rd ed.). Belmont, CA: Wadsworth.

AZ (Performer). (2002). "Fan Mail." On *Aziatic.* New York: Motown.

Baca, J. S. (1999). Coming into language. Reprinted in B. G. Chevigny (Ed.), *Doing time: 25 years of prison writing* (pp. 100–106). New York: Arcade.

Baca, J. S. (2002). *A place to stand.* New York: Grove.

Bagdikian, B. (2004). *The new media monopoly.* Boston: Beacon Press.

Bales, W. D., & Mears, D. P. (2008). Inmate social ties and the transition into society: Does visitation reduce recidivism? *Journal of Research in Crime and Delinquency, 45,* 287–321. doi: 10.1177/0022427808317574

Bandura, A. (2002). Selective moral disengagement in the exercise of moral agency. *Journal of Moral Education, 31,* 101–19.

Banner, S. (2002). *The death penalty: An American history.* Cambridge, MA: Harvard University Press.

Barber, B. R. (1992). *An aristocracy of everyone: The politics of education and the future of America.* New York: Oxford University Press.

Bargh, J. A., McKenna, K. Y. A., & Fitzsimons, G. M. (2002). Can you see the real me? Activation and expression of the 'true self' on the internet. *Journal of Social Issues, 58,* 33–48. doi: 10.1111/1540–4560.00247

Barker, J. R. (1993). Tightening the iron cage: Concertive control in self-managing teams. *Administrative Science Quarterly, 38,* 408–37.

Barnett, C., & Mencken, F. C. (2002). Social disorganization theory and the contextual nature of crime in nonmetropolitan counties. *Rural Sociology, 67,* 372–93.

Baro, E. (2009). Nowhere holy. *Captured Words/Free Thoughts, 7,* p. 20.

Bauman, Z. (2007). *Consuming life.* London: Polity Press.

Baumeister, R. F. (1986). *Public self and private self.* New York: Springer-Verlag.

Baxter, L. A. (1990). Dialectical contradictions in relationship development. *Journal of Social and Personal Relationships, 7,* 69–88.

Baxter, L. A., & Montgomery, B. M. (1996). *Relating: Dialogues and dialectics.* New York: Guilford Press.

Bayer, R. (1981). Crime, punishment, and the decline of liberal optimism. *Crime and Delinquency, 27,* 169–90.

Beasley, W., & R. Forman (Producers) & Weir, P. (Director) (1993). *Fearless* [Motion Picture]. United States: Warner Brothers Pictures.

Beccaria, C. (2009). *On crimes and punishments.* New Brunswick, NJ: Transaction Publishers.

Becker, D. J., & Corrigan, M. D. (2002). Moving problem-solving courts into the mainstream: A report card from the CCJ-COSCA Problem-Solving Courts Committee. *Court Review, 39,* 4–7.

Belenky, M. F., Clinchy, B. M., Goldberger, N. R., & Tarule, J. M. (1986). *Women's ways of knowing: The development of self, voice, and mind.* New York: Basic Books.

Belmont Report (1979). *The Belmont Report: Ethical principles and guidelines for the protection of human subjects of research.* Washington, DC: Department of Health, Education, and Welfare. Retrieved April 8, 2012, from http://ohsr.od.nih.gov/guidelines/belmont.html

Benda, B., & Pallone, N. (Eds.). (2005). *Rehabilitation issues, problems, and prospects in boot camp.* New York: Haworth Press.

Bernburg, J. G., Krohn, M. D., & Rivera, C. J. (2006). Official labeling, criminal embeddedness, and subsequent delinquency: A longitudinal test of labeling theory. *Journal of Research in Crime and Delinquency, 43,* 67–88. doi: 10.1177/0022427805280068

Birenbaum, A. (1970). On managing a courtesy stigma. *Journal of Health and Social Behavior, 11,* 196–206. Retrieved August 31, 2012, from http://hsb.sagepub.com/

Blomberg, T. G., & Lucken, K. (2010). *American penology: A history of control* (2nd ed.). New Brunswick, NJ: Aldine.

Bloom, D. (2006). Employment focused programs for ex-prisoners: *What have we learned, what are we learning, and where should we go from here?* New York: National Poverty Center.

Bohm, R. (1986). Crime, criminal and crime control policy myths. *Justice Quarterly*, 3(2), 193–214.

Bolen, J. S. (1984). *Goddesses in everywoman: Powerful archetypes in women's lives.* New York: HarperCollins.

Boogie Down Productions (Performer). (1988). "My philosophy." On *By all means necessary* [CD]. New York: Jive Records.

Bormann, E. G. (1972). Fantasy and rhetorical vision: The rhetorical criticism of social reality. *Quarterly Journal of Speech, 58*, 396–407.

Boyd, T. (2004). Check yo self before you wreck yo self: The death of politics in rap music and popular culture. In M. Forman & M. A. Neal (Eds.), *That's the joint!: The hip-hop studies reader.* New York: Taylor and Francis.

Braz, R., & Williams, M. (2011). Diagnosing the schools-to-prisons pipeline: Maximum security, minimum learning. In S. J. Hartnett (Ed.), *Challenging the prison-industrial complex* (pp. 126–47). Champaign: University of Illinois Press.

Brooks, J., & Bahna, K. (1994). "It's a family affair"—The incarceration of the American family: Confronting legal and social issues. *University of San Francisco Law Review, 28*, 271–308. Retrieved August 31, 2012, from http://www.usfca.edu/law/lawreview/

Brown, E. (2007). *Snitch: Informants, cooperators, and the corruption of justice.* Jackson, TN: PublicAffairs.

Brown, M. K., Carnoy, M., Currie, E., Duster, T., Oppenheimer, D. B., Shultz, M. M., & Wellman, D. (2003). *White-washing race: The myth of a color-blind society.* Berkeley: University of California Press.

Browne, M. A. (2003). Derailed! The schoolhouse to jailhouse track. *Washington, DC: Advancement Project.* Retrieved September 17, 2006, from http://b.3cdn.net/advancement/c509d077028b4d0544_mlbrq3seg.pdf

Brummett, B. (1976). Some implications of "process" or "intersubjectivity": Postmodern rhetoric. *Philosophy & Rhetoric, 9*, 21–51.

Brummett, B. (2008a). *A rhetoric of style.* Carbondale: Southern Illinois University Press.

Brummett, B. (2008b). *Uncovering hidden rhetorics.* Thousand Oaks, CA: Sage.

Bryant, A., & Charmaz, K. (2007). Grounded theory in historical perspective: An epistemological account. In A. Bryant & K. Charmaz (Eds.), *The Sage handbook of grounded theory* (pp. 31–57). Los Angeles, CA: Sage.

Bryant, J., and Oliver, M. B. (2009). *Media effects: Advances in theory and research.* New York: Routledge.

Bureau of Justice Statistics. (2008a). *Justice expenditures and employment extracts, 2006.* Retrieved August 26, 2012, from http://bjs.ojp.usdoj.gov/content/glance/tables/exptyptab.cfm.

Bureau of Justice Statistics. (2008b). *Key facts at a glance: Correctional populations.* Retrieved August 26, 2010, from http://bjs.ojp.usdoj.gov/content/glance/tables/corr2tab.cfm.

Bureau of Justice Statistics. (2008c). *Parents in prison and their minor children*. Washington, DC: U.S. Department of Justice.

Bureau of Justice Statistics. (2008d). *Persons arrested*. Retrieved August 31, 2012, from http://www.fbi.gov/ucr/cius2008/arrests/index.html.

Bureau of Justice Statistics. (2009a). *Prisoners in 2007*. Washington, DC: U.S. Department of Justice—see Appendix tables 11 and 12.

Bureau of Justice Statistics (2009b). *Prisoners in 2009*. Retrieved August 31, 2012, from http://bjs.ojp.usdoj.gov/content/pub/pdf/p09.pdf

Bureau of Justice Statistics. (2010). *Total correction population*. Retrieved August 31, 2012, from http://bjs.ojp.usdoj.gov/index.cfm?ty=tp&tid=11

Burkhardt, K. (1976). *Women in prison*. New York: Popular Library.

Burton-Rose, D. (Ed.) (1998). *The celling of America: An inside look at the U.S. prison industry*. Monroe: ME: Common Courage Press.

Butler, P. (2009). *Let's get free: A hip hop theory of justice*. New York: The New Press.

Butsch, R. (2011). Ralph, Fred, Archie, Homer, and the King of Queens: Why television keeps re-creating the male working class buffoon. In G. Dines & J. M. Humez (Eds.), *Gender, race, and class in media: A critical reader* (pp. 101–9). Los Angeles: Sage.

Cacoyannis, M. (Producer & Director). (1964). *Zorba the Greek* [Motion Picture]. United States: 20th Century Fox.

Campbell, J. (1949, 2008). *The hero with a thousand faces*. Novato, CA: New World Library.

Campbell, J. (1959, 1962, 1964, 1968, 1991). *The masks of god (volumes 1–4)*. New York: Penguin.

Cam'ron issues statement concerning *60 Minutes* appearance. (2007, April 26). Retrieved August 31, 2012, from http://www.xxlmag.com/news/latest-headlines/2007/04/cam%E2%80%99ron-issues-statement-concerning-60-minutes-appearance/

Casey, T. (2004). When good intentions are not enough: Problem-solving courts and the impending crisis of legitimacy. *Southern Methodist University Law Review, 57*, 1459–69.

Center on Wrongful Convictions. (2006). How snitch testimony sent Randy Steidl and other innocent Americans to death row. Chicago: Northwestern University School of Law. Retrieved August 31, 2012, from http://www.innocenceproject.org/docs/SnitchSystemBooklet.pdf

Chan, A. (2000). Redirecting critique in postmodern organization studies: The perspective of Foucault. *Organization Studies, 21*, 1059–75.

Chang, J. (2005, October). An uplifting voice of hip-hop. *Progressive, 69*, 42–44.

Chappell, C. A. (2004). Post-secondary correctional education and recidivism: A meta-analysis of research conducted 1990–1999. *Journal of Correctional Education, 55*(2), 148–69.

Charland, M. (1987). Constitutive rhetoric: The case of the Peuple Québécois. *Quarterly Journal of Speech, 73*, (1987), 235–50.

Charmaz, K. (2000). Grounded theory: Objectivist and constructivist methods. In N. K. Denzin, & Y. S. Lincoln (Eds.), *Handbook of qualitative research* (2nd ed., pp. 509–35). Thousand Oaks, CA: Sage.

Chesney-Lind, M. (1997). *The female offender: Girls, women and crime*. Thousand Oaks, CA: Sage.

Chödrön, P. (1991). *The wisdom of no escape*. Boston: Shambhala Publications.

Christians, C. (2007). Non-violence in philosophical and religious ethics. *Javnost—The Public*, *14*(4), 5–18.

Chuck D., & Jah, Y. (1997). *Rap, race, and reality*. New York: Delacorte Press.

Cicero, M. T. (1970). De Oratore (J. S. Watson, Trans.). In J. S. Watson (Ed.), *Cicero on oratory and orators*. Carbondale: Southern Illinois University Press.

Cicero, M. T. (2004). *De Inventione* (C. D. Yonge, Trans.). New York: Kessinger.

Clear, T. R. (2007). *Imprisoning communities: How mass incarceration makes disadvantaged neighborhoods worse (Studies in Crime and Public Policy)*. New York: Oxford University Press.

Cleaver, E. (1968). *Soul on ice*. New York: Dell.

Clemmer, D. (1958). *The prison community*. New York: Rinehart.

Closepet, R., & Tsui, L. (2002). An interview with Professor George Gerbner. In M. Morgan (Ed.), *Against the mainstream: The selected works of George Gerbner* (pp. 492–99). New York: Peter Lang.

Cloud, D. (1994) The materiality of discourse as oxymoron: A challenge to critical rhetoric. *Western Journal of Communication*, *58*, 141–63.

Cohen, L. (1992). *Anthem*. From the album *The Future*. Sony Music Entertainment.

Coley, R., & Barton, P. (2006). *Locked up and locked out: An educational perspective on the U.S. prison population*. Princeton, NJ: Educational Testing Service.

Collins, J. L., & Mayer, V. (2010). *Both hands tied: Welfare reform and the race to the bottom of the low-wage labor market*. Chicago: University of Chicago Press.

Collins, P. H. (2009). *Another kind of public education: Race, schools, the media, and democratic possibilities*. Boston: Beacon Press.

Collinson, D. (1994). Strategies of resistance: Power, knowledge and resistance in the workplace. In J. M. Jermier, D. Knights, & W. R. Nord (Eds.), *Resistance and power in organizations* (pp. 25–68). London: Routledge.

Comfort, M. (2008). *Doing time together: Love and family in the shadow of the prison*. Chicago: University of Chicago Press.

Concepcion, M. (2010, November 19). T. I. "sick and tired" of jail, says letter from prison. Retrieved August 31, 2012, from http://www.billboard.com/column/the-juice/t-i-sick-and-tired-of-jail-says-in-letter-1004128084.story#/column/the-juice/t-i-sick-and-tired-of-jail-says-in-letter-1004128084.story

Conference of Chief Justices. (2003). *Policy statements and resolutions: Resolution 13 in support of the national drug court evaluation*. Retrieved January 30, 2010, from http://ccj.ncsc.dni.us/InternationalResolutions/resol13NatlDrugCourtEval.html

Conover, T. (2000). *New jack: Guarding Sing Sing*. New York: Random House.

Conquergood, D. (2002). Lethal theatre: Performance, punishment, and the death penalty. *Theatre Journal*, *54*, 339–67.

Conroy, P. (1976). *The great Santini*. Boston: Houghton Mifflin.

Cook, C., & Lane, J. (2009). The place of public fear in sentencing and correctional policy. *Journal of Criminal Justice*, *37*(6), 586–95.

Cooper, D. D. (1998). Reading, writing, and reflection. In R. Rhoads & J. Howard (Eds.), *Academic service learning: A pedagogy of action and reflection* (pp. 47–56). San Francisco, CA: Jossey-Bass.

Corbin, J., & Strauss, A. (1990). Grounded theory research: Procedures, canons, and evaluative criteria. *Qualitative Sociology*, *13*, 3–21. doi: 10.1007/BF00988593

Corey, F. C. (1996). Personal narratives and young men in prison: Labeling the outside inside. *Western Journal of Communication, 60*, 57–75.

Correctional Association of New York. (2009, January). *Education from the inside, out: The multiple benefits of college programs in prison*. Retrieved March 31, 2012, from http://www.correctionalassociation.org/press/advisories/1-28-2009_CA_Higher _Education_Report.htm

Correia, M. G., & Bleicher, R. E. (2008). Making connections to teach reflection. *Michigan Journal of Community Service Learning*, 41–49.

Council of State Government Justice Center. (2009). *Community Supervision*. Retrieved March 23, 2012, from http://reentrypolicy.org/Report/PartII/ChapterII-E/ PolicyStatement26/ResearchHighlight26-1

Craig, D., & Ferre, J. (2006). Agape as an ethic of care for journalism. *Journal of Mass Media Ethics, 21*(2&3), 123–40.

Craig, R. T. (1989). Communication as a practical discipline. In B. Dervin, L. Grossberg, B. J. O'Keefe, & E. Wartella (Eds.), *Rethinking communication* (pp. 97–122). Newbury Park, CA: Sage.

Critical Resistance. (2011). Retrieved August 31, 2012, from http://www.criticalresistance.org

Crowther, B. (1964, December 18,). Zorba the Greek [Film Review]. *The New York Times*. Retrieved April 1, 2012, from http://movies.nytimes.com/movie/review? res =9B04E1DE1F3FEE32A2575BC1A9649D946591D6CF

Cullen, F. T., & Gilbert, K. E. (1982). *Reaffirming rehabilitation*. Cincinnati, OH: Anderson Publishing.

Cullen, F. T., Wright, J. P., Gendreau, P., & Andrews, D. A. (2003). What correctional treatment can teach us about criminological theory: Implications for social learning theory. In R. L. Akers & G. F. Jensen (Eds.), *Social learning theory and the explanation of crime* (pp. 339–62). New Brunswick, NJ: Transaction Publishers.

Cummins, E. (1994). *The rise and fall of California's radical prison movement*. Stanford, CA: Stanford University Press.

Currie, E. (1998). *Crime and punishment in America*. New York: Henry Holt.

Cusac, A. (2009). *Cruel and unusual: The culture of punishment in America*. New Haven, CT: Yale University Press.

Cutrona, C. E., Suhr, J. A., & McFarlane, R. (1990). Interpersonal transactions and the psychological sense of support. In S. Duck & R. Silver (Eds.), *Communication of social support: Messages, interactions, relationships, and community* (pp. 30–45). London: Sage.

Darby, D., & Shelby, T. (Eds.). (2005). *Hip hop and philosophy: Rhyme 2 reason*. Chicago: Open Court.

Daulatzai, S. (2009). Illmatic: As it was written. In M.E. Dyson & S. Dailatzai (Eds.), *Born to use mics: Reading Nas's illmatic*. New York: Basic Civitas Books.

Davis, A.Y. (2003). *Are prisons obsolete?* New York: Seven Stories Press.

Davis, A. Y. (2005). *Abolition democracy: Beyond empire, prisons, and torture*. New York: Seven Stories Press.

Davis, A., & Rodriguez, D. (2000). The challenge of prison abolition: A conversation. *Social Justice, 27*(3), 212–18.

Davison, W. P. (1983). The third-person effect in communication. *Public Opinion Quarterly, 47*(1), 1–15. doi. 10.1086/268763

De Certeau, M. (1984). *The practice of everyday life*. Berkeley: University of California Press.

Debord, G. (1967). *Society of the spectacle*. Detroit: Black and Red.

Deetz, S. (2008). Engagement as co-generative theorizing. *Journal of Applied Communication Research, 36*, 289–97

Denzin, N. K., & Lincoln, Y. S. (2000). Introduction: The discipline and practice of qualitative research. In N. K. Denzin & Y. S. Lincoln (Eds.), *Handbook of qualitative research* (2nd ed., pp. 1–28). Thousand Oaks, CA: Sage.

Derlega, V. L., & Chaikin, A. L. (1977). Privacy and self-disclosure in social relationships. *Journal of Social Issues, 33*, 102–15. doi: 10.1111/j.1540–4560.1977.tb01885.x

Derlega, V. L., Metts, S., Petronio, S., & Margulis, S. T. (1993). Privacy and self-disclosure in social relationships. *Journal of Social Issues, 33*, 102–15. doi: 10.1111/1540–4560.00247

Dieter, R. C. (1993, April). Sentencing for life: Americans embrace alternatives to the death penalty. Death Penalty Information Center. Retrieved August 21, 2010, from http://www.deathpenaltyinfo.org/sentencing-life-americans-embrace-alternatives -death-penalty#sxn12

Dines, G., & Humez, J. M. (Eds.). *Gender, race, and class in media: A critical reader* (pp. 81–84). Los Angeles: Sage.

Dixon, T. (2011). Teaching you to love fear: Television news and racial stereotypes in a punishing democracy. In S. J. Hartnett (Ed.), *Challenging the prison-industrial complex: Activism, arts, and educational alternatives* (pp. 106–23). Champaign: University of Illinois Press.

DMX, Method Man, Nas, and Ja Rule (1998). Grand finale. On *Belly (soundtrack)* [CD]. New York: Def Jam Records, 1998.

Dodge, M., & Pogrebin, M. R. (2001). Collateral costs of imprisonment for women: Complications of reintegration. *The Prison Journal, 81*(1), 42–54. doidoi:10.1177/ 0032885501081001004

Doggett, P. (2007). *There's a riot going on: Revolutionaries, rock stars, and the rise and fall of the 60s*. New York: Canongate.

Donziger, S. R. (Ed.) (1996). *The real war on crime: The report of the National Criminal Justice Commission*. New York: Harper Collins.

Douglas, S. J. (1995). *Where the girls are: Growing up female with the mass media*. New York: Three Rivers Press.

Droge, D., & Murphy, B. O. (1999). *Voices of strong democracy: Concepts and models for service-learning in communication studies*. Washington, DC: American Association for Higher Education.

Dubber, M. K. (2004). Criminal justice process and war on crime. In C. Sumner (Ed.), *The Blackwell companion to criminology* (pp. 49–67). Malden, MA: Blackwell.

Dugan, J. (2005). *Making a new man: Ciceronian self-fashioning in the rhetorical works*. Oxford, UK: Oxford University Press.

Duncombe, S. (1997). *Zines and the politics of alternative culture*. London: Verso.

Dyer, J. (2000). *The perpetual prisoner machine: How America profits from crime*. Boulder, CO: Westview Press.

Dyson, M. E. (2004). *The Michael Eric Dyson reader*. New York: Basic Civitas Books.

Dyson, M. E. (2006). *Holler if you hear me*. New York: Basic Civitas Books.

Dyson, M. E. (2009). "One love," two brothers, three verses. In M. E. Dyson & S. Dailatzai (Eds.), *Born to use mics: Reading Nas's illmatic*. New York: Basic Civitas Books.

Eakin, P. (1999). *How our lives become stories: Making selves.* Ithaca, NY: Cornell University Press.

Edinger, E. F. (1972). *Ego and archetype.* Boston: Shambhala.

Ehrenhaus, P., & Owen, A. S. (2004). Race lynching and Christian evangelicalism: Performances of faith. *Text and Performance Quarterly, 24,* 276–301.

Enos, R. L. (1975a). Cicero's forensic rhetoric: The manifestation of power in the Roman Republic. *The Southern Speech Communication Journal, 40,* 377–94.

Enos, R. L. (1975b). The epistemological foundation for Cicero's litigation strategies. *Central States Speech Journal, 26,* 207–14.

Entman, R., & Rojecki, A. (2000). *The black image in the white mind: Media and race in America.* Chicago: University of Chicago Press.

Estés, C. P. (1992). *Women who run with the wolves: Myths and stories of the wild woman archetype.* New York: Random House.

Eyler, J. (2002). Reflection: Linking service and learning—linking students and communities. *Journal of Social Issues, 58,* 517–34.

Eyler, J., & Giles, D. (1999). *Where's the learning in service-learning?* San Francisco, CA: Jossey-Bass.

Eyler, J., Giles, D. E., Jr., & Braxton, J. (1997). The impact of service-learning on college students. *Michigan Journal of Community Service Learning, 4,* 5–15.

Eyler, J., Giles, D. E., & Schmeide, A. (1996). *A practitioner's guide to reflection in service-learning: Student voices and reflections.* Nashville, TN: Vanderbilt University Press.

Facts about the death penalty. (2010, August 30). Death Penalty Information Center. Retrieved August 31, 2010, from http://www.deathpenaltyinfo.org/documents/FactSheet.pdf

Facts & figures. (2010). National Coalition to Abolish the Death Penalty. Retrieved August 29, 2010, from http://www.ncadp.org/index.cfm?content=5

Fair Sentencing Act of 2010, S. 1789, 111th Congress (2010).

Fairhurst, G. T., & Putnam, L. (2004). Organizations as discursive constructions. *Communication Theory, 14,* 5–26.

Families Against Mandatory Minimums, 2009. *Alternatives to Incarceration Fact Sheet.* Washington, DC: July, 2009.

Fantham, E. (2007). *The Roman world of Cicero's De Oratore.* New York: Oxford University Press.

Federal Bureau of Prisons. (2012). Quick facts about the Bureau of Prisons. Retrieved March 23, 2012, from http://www.bop.gov/news/quick.jsp

Fellner, J., & Vinck, P. (2008). *Targeting Blacks: Drug law enforcement and race in the United States.* New York: Human Rights Watch.

Fenzel, L. M., & Peyrot, M. (2005). Comparing college community participation and future service behaviors and attitudes. *Michigan Journal of Community Service Learning, 12,* 23–31.

Ferber, A. (2007). The construction of black masculinity: White supremacy now and then. *Journal of Sport and Social Issues, 31*(11), 11–24.

Financial Times (2010, August 21). US private prisons, p. 16.

Flavin, J., & Rosenthal, D. (2003). *La bodega de la familia: Supporting parolees' reintegration within a family context.* Fordham Urban Law Journal, 30(5), 1603–20. Retrieved October 24, 2012, from http://www.caction.org/rrt_new/professionals/articles/FLAVIN-LA%20BODEGA.pdf

Fleming, P., & Spicer, A. (2008). Beyond power and resistance: New approaches to organizational politics. *Management Communication Quarterly, 21*, 301–9.

Fletcher, B., Rolison, G., & Moon, D. (1993). The woman prisoner. In B. Fletcher, L. Shaver, & D. Moon (Eds.), *Women prisoners: A forgotten population* (pp. 15–26). Westport, CO: Praeger.

Foucault, M. (1977). *Discipline and punish: The birth of the prison.* Translated by Alan Sheridan. New York: Vintage Books.

Foucault, M. (1988). Technologies of the self. In L. Martin, H. Gutman, & P. Hutton (Eds.), *Technologies of the self: A seminar with Michel Foucault* (pp. 12–25). Amherst: University of Massachusetts Press.

Foucault, M. (1993). About the beginning of the hermeneutics of the self. *Political Theory, 21*, 198–227. (Original lecture 1980).

Fredrickson, G. M. (1971). *The black image in the white mind: The debate on Afro-American character and destiny, 1817–1914.* New York: Harper Row.

Freudenberg, N. (2001). Jails, prisons, and the health of urban populations: A review of the impact of the correctional system on community health. *Journal of Urban Health Bulletin of the New York Academy of Medicine, 78*, 214–35.

Frey, L. R. (2009). What a difference more difference-making communication scholarship might make: Making a difference from and through communication research. *Journal of Applied Communication Research, 37*, 205–14.

Friedmann, P. D., Taxman, F. S., & Henderson, C. E. (2007). Evidence-based treatment practices for drug-involved adults in the criminal justice system. *Journal of Substance Abuse Treatment, 32*, 267–77.

Fulmer, J. L. (1995). A brief report on the direct and indirect cost of prison incarceration in the state of Alabama. *Journal of Correctional Education, 46*, 16–18.

Gandy, O. (2009). *Coming to terms with chance: Engaging rational discrimination and cumulative disadvantage.* Surrey, England: Ashgate Publishing.

Garbarino, J. (2000). *Lost boys: Why our sons turn to violence and how we can save them.* New York: Anchor Books.

Garland, D. (2001). *The culture of control: Crime and social order in contemporary society.* Chicago: University of Chicago Press.

Garland, D., & Sparks, R. (2000). Criminology, social theory and the challenge of our times. *British Journal of Criminology, 40*(2), 189–204.

Gartner, R. (1999). *Betrayed as boys.* New York: Guilford.

Garver, N., & Reitan, E. (1995). *Nonviolence and community: Reflections on the Alternatives to Violence Project.* Pendle Hill Pamphlet #322. Wallingford, PA: Pendle Hill.

Geidel, M. (2005). Supermaxes, stripmines, and hip-hop. *Journal of Popular Music Studies, 17*, 67–76.

Genty, P. M. (2003). Damage to family relationships as a collateral consequence of parental incarceration. *Fordham Urban Law Journal, 30*, 1671–84. Retrieved from http://law.fordham.edu/fordham-urban-law-journal/ulj.htm

Gerbner, G., & Gross, L. (1976). Living with television: The violence profile. *Journal of Communication, 26*(2), 173–99.

Gerbner, G., Gross, L., Morgan, M., & Signorielli, N. (1982). Charting the mainstream: Televison's contributions to political orientations. *Journal of Communication, 32*(2), 100–127.

Gerbner, G., Gross, L., Morgan, M., Signorielli, N., & Shanahan, J. (2002). Growing up with television: Cultivation processes. In J. Bryant and D. Zillman (Eds.),

Media effects: Advances in theory and research (2nd ed., pp. 43–67). Mahwah, NJ: Lawrence Erlbaum.

Gergen, K. J. (1999). *An invitation to social construction*. London: Sage.

Gilbert, P. (Producer & Director), & James, S. (Producer & Director). (2008). At the death house door [Motion picture]. USA: Independent Film Channel.

Gilliam, F., and Iyengar, S. (2000). Prime suspects: The impact of local television news on attitudes about crime and race. *American Journal of Political Science, 44*, 3, 560–73.

Gilligan, C. (1982). *In a different voice*. Cambridge, MA: Harvard University Press.

Gilligan, J. (2001). *Preventing violence*. New York: Thames and Hudson.

Giroux, H. (2009). *Youth in a suspect society: Democracy or disposability?* New York: Palgrave Macmillan.

Girshick, L. B. (1994). I leave in the dark of morning. *The Prison Journal, 74*(1), 93–97. doi: 10.177/0032855594074001007

Girshick, L. B. (1999). *No safe haven: Stories of women in prison*. Boston: Northeastern University Press.

Glaser, B. (1978). *Theoretical sensitivity*. Mill Valley, CA: Sociology Press.

Glaser, B. G., & Strauss, A. L. (1967). *The discovery of grounded theory: Strategies for qualitative research*. Chicago, IL: Aldine.

Glassner, B. (2010). *The culture of fear*. New York: Basic Books.

Glaze, L. E. (2010, December). Correctional populations in the United States, 2009. U.S. Department of Justice, Office of Justice Programs, Bureau of Justice Statistics. Retrieved January 29, 2011, from http://bjs.ojp.usdoj.gov/index.cfm?ty =pbdetail&iid=2316

Glaze, L. E. & Parks, E. (2012, November 29). Correctional populations in the United States, 2011. U.S. Department of Justice. Office of Justice Programs. Bureau of Justice Statistics. Retrieved January 14, 2013, from: http://bjs.gov/index.cfm?ty =pbdetail&iid=4537.

Goffman, E. (1959). *The presentation of self in everyday life*. New York: Doubleday Books.

Goffman, E. (1961). *Asylums: Essays on the social situation of mental patients and other inmates*. New York: Anchor.

Goffman, E. (1963). *Stigma: Notes on the management of spoiled identity*. Englewood Cliffs, NJ: Prentice-Hall.

Gottschalk, M. (2006). *The prison and the gallows: The politics of mass incarceration in America*. Cambridge, UK: Cambridge University Press.

Gough, R. (1998). *Character is destiny*. Roseville, CA: Prima Publishing.

Governor Bill Richardson signs repeal of the death penalty [Press release]. (2009, March 18). State of New Mexico: Governor Bill Richardson. Retrieved August 30, 2010, from www.deathpenaltyinfo.org/documents/richardsonstatement.pdf

Gray, J. (2001). *Why our drug laws have failed: A judicial indictment of war on drugs*. Philadelphia: Temple University Press.

Green, E., Staerklé, C., & Sears D. (2006). Symbolic racism and whites' attitudes towards punitive and preventive crime policies. *Law and Human Behavior, 30*, 435–54.

Green, K. M., Ensminger, M. E., Robertson, J. A., Juon, & H.-S. (2006). Impact of adult sons' incarceration on African American mothers' psychological distress. *Journal of Marriage and Family, 68*, 430–41. doi: 10.1111/j.1741-3737.2006.00262.x

Green, S., & Renzi, M. (Producers), & Sayles, J. (Director). (1991). *City of hope* [Motion Picture]. United States: Sony Pictures.

Greene, S., Haney, C., & Hurtado, A. (2000). Cycles of pain: Risk factors in the lives of incarcerated mothers and their children. *The Prison Journal, 80,* 3–23.

Griffith, A. (1995). Mothering, schooling and children's development. In M. Campbell & A. Manicom (Eds.), *Knowledge, experience, and ruling relations: Studies in the social organization of knowledge* (pp. 109–21). Toronto: University of Toronto Press.

Gross, L. (2001). *Up from invisibility: Lesbians, gay men, and the media in America.* New York: Columbia University Press.

Habermas, J. (1984). *The theory of communicative action: Vol. 1. Reason and the rationalization of society.* Boston: Beacon Press.

Hagan, J., & Dinovitzer, R. (1999). Collateral consequences of imprisonment for children, communities, and prisoners. In M. Tonry & J. Petersilia (Eds.), *Prisons (Crime and justice: A review of research)* (pp. 121–62). Chicago: University of Chicago Press.

Haines, H. H. (1996). *Against capital punishment: The anti–death penalty movement in America, 1972–1994.* New York: Oxford University Press.

Hairston, C. F. (1988). Family ties during imprisonment: Do they influence future criminal activity? *Federal Probation, 52,* 48–52. Retrieved August 31, 2012, from http://www.uscourts.gov/FederalCourts/ProbationPretrialServices/FederalProbation Journal.aspx

Hairston, C. F. (1991). Family ties during imprisonment: Important to whom and for what? *Journal of Sociology and Social Welfare, 18,* 87–104. Retrieved August 31, 2012, from http://www.wmich.edu/hhs/newsletters_journals/jssw/

Hall, S. (1995). The whites of their eyes: Racist ideologies and the media. In G. Dines and J. Humez (Eds.), *Gender, race and class in media, A text reader* (pp. 18–22). Thousand Oaks, CA: Sage.

Hall, S., Critcher, C., Jefferson, T., Clarke, J., & Roberts, B. (1978). *Policing the crisis: Mugging, the state, and law and order.* Hampshire, UK: Palgrave Macmillan.

Hallman, H. L. (2009). "Dear Tupac, you speak to me": Recruiting hip hop as curriculum at a school for pregnant and parenting teens. *Equity & Excellence in Education, 42,* 36–51.

Harer, M. (1994). *Recidivism among federal prison releasees in 1987: A preliminary report.* Washington DC: Federal Bureau of Prisons.

Harm, N. (1992). Social policy on women prisoners: A historical analysis. *Affilia, 7,* 90–108.

Hart, T. (2004). Opening the contemplative mind in the classroom. *Journal of Transformative Education, 2*(1), 28–46.

Hartnett, S. J. (1995). Imperial ideologies: Media hysteria, racism, and the addiction to the war on drugs. *Journal of Communication, 45,* 161–69.

Hartnett, S. J. (1998). Lincoln and Douglas meet the abolitionist David Walker as prisoners debate slavery: Empowering education, applied communication, and social justice. *Journal of Applied Communication Research, 26,* 232–53.

Hartnett, S. J. (2000). A rhetorical critique of the drug war, slavery, and the "nauseous pendulum" of reason and violence. *Journal of Contemporary Criminal Justice, 16,* 247–71.

Hartnett, S. J. (2000). Prisons, profit, crime and social control: A hermeneutic of the production of violence. In A. Light and M. Nagel (Eds.), *Race, class and community identity* (pp. 199–221). New York: Humanity Books.

Hartnett, S. J. (2004). *Incarceration nation: Investigative prison poems of hope and terror*. Walnut Creek, CA: AltaMira.

Hartnett, S. J. (Ed.) (2005–2012). *Captured words/free thoughts*, 1–10. Denver, CO.

Hartnett, S. J. (2009). The annihilating public policies of the prison-industrial complex: Crime, violence, and punishment in an age of neo-liberalism. *Rhetoric & Public Affairs*, 11(3), 491–533.

Hartnett, S. J. (Ed.) (2010). *Captured words/free thoughts: Writings from the poetry workshop at the Colorado Women's Correctional Facility, 8*. Retrieved January 21, 2011, from http://is.gd/odIglZ

Hartnett, S. J. (2010). Communication, social justice, and joyful commitment. *Western Journal of Communication*, 74(1), 68–93.

Hartnett, S. J. (2010). *Executing democracy: Capital punishment and the making of America, 1683–1807.* East Lansing: Michigan State University Press.

Hartnett, S. J. (Ed.) (2011a). *Challenging the prison-industrial complex: Activism, arts, and educational alternatives*. Champaign: University of Illinois Press.

Hartnett, S. J. (2011b). Introduction: Empowerment or incarceration? Reclaiming hope and justice from a punishing democracy. In S. J. Hartnett (Ed.), *Challenging the prison-industrial complex: Activism, arts, and educational alternatives* (pp 1–12). Champaign: University of Illinois Press.

Hartnett, S. J., & Larson, D. M. (2006). "Tonight another man will die": Crime, violence, and the master tropes of contemporary arguments about the death penalty. *Communication and Critical/Cultural Studies*, 3, 263–87.

Hartnett, S. J., Wood, J. K., & McCann, B. J. (2011). Turning silence into speech and action: Prison activism and the pedagogy of empowered citizenship. *Communication and Critical/Cultural Studies*, 8, 331–52.

Haskell, H. J. (1964). This was Cicero: Modern politics in a toga. New York: Alfred A. Knopf.

Hatcher, J. A., & Bringle, R. G. (1997). Reflection: Bridging the gap between service and learning. *College Teaching*, 45, 153–58.

Hausman, M. (Producer), & D. Mamet (Director). (1987). *House of games* [Motion Picture]. United States: Filmhaus.

Haynes, D. (2005). Contemplative practice and the education of the whole person. *ARTS: The Arts in Religious and Theological Studies*, 16(2).

Henderson, C. E., Taxman, F. S., & Young, D. W. (2008). A Rasch model analysis of evidence-based treatment practices used in the criminal justice system. *Drug and Alcohol Dependence*, 93, 163–75.

Herek, G. M. (1996). Why tell if you're not asked? Self-disclosure, inter-group contact, and heterosexuals' attitudes toward lesbians and gay men. In G. M. Herek, J. Jobe, & R. Carney (Eds.), *Out in force: Sexual orientation and the military* (pp. 197–225). Chicago: University of Chicago Press.

Herek, G. M. (2007). Confronting sexual stigma and prejudice: Theory and practice. *Journal of Social Issues*, 63, 905–925. doi: 10.1111/j.1540-4560.2007.00544.x

Herivel, T., & Wright, P. (Eds.) (2007). *Prison profiteers: Who makes money from mass incarceration*. New York: New Press.

Herman, E., & Chomsky, N. (1988). *Manufacturing consent: The political economy of the mass media*. New York: Pantheon.

Higgins, D. (2009). *Hip hop world: A groundwork guide*. Toronto: Groundwood Books.

Hinck, E. A., & Hinck, S. S. (1998). Service-learning and forensics. *National Forensic Journal*, *16*, 1–26.

Hollis, J. (1996). *Swamplands of the soul: New life in dismal places*. Toronto: Inner City Books.

Homer, E. L. (1979). Inmate-family ties: Desirable but difficult. *Federal Probation*, *43*, 47–52. Retrieved November 15, 2012, from http://www.uscourts.gov/FederalCourts/ ProbationPretrialServices/FederalProbationJournal.aspx

hooks, b. (1992). *Black looks: Race and representation*. Boston: South End Press.

Hopkins, E. D. (2005). *Life after life: A story of rage and redemption*. New York: Free Press.

Hoppe, D. (2010, January 20). Death penalty receives major blow. *Nuvo*. Retrieved August 21, 2010, from http://www.nuvo.net/indianapolis/death-penalty-receives -major blow/Content?oid=1329169

Hornbeck, M. (2009, June 6). Michigan to close 3 prisons, all 5 low-security camps. *The Detroit News*. Retrieved April 15, 2012, from www.lexisnexis.com

Horton, D., & Wohl, R. R. (1956). Mass communication and parasocial interaction: Observations on intimacy at a distance. *Psychiatry*, *19*, 215–29.

Huff, M., Phillips, P., & Project Censored (2010). *Censored 2011*. New York: Seven Stories Press.

Hughes, E. C. (1951). Work and the self. In J. H. Rohrer & M. Sherif (Eds.), *Social psychology at the crossroads* (pp. 313–23). New York: Harper and Brothers.

Irwin, J. (2005). *The warehouse prison: Disposal of the new dangerous class*. Los Angeles: Roxbury.

Jackson, G. (1998). Soledad brother. In Franklin, H. B. (Ed.), *Prison Writing in 20th Century America* (pp. 155–65). New York: Penguin. (Reprinted from *Soledad brother: The prison letters of George Jackson*, 1970. New York: Random House.)

Jacobi, T. (2008) *Can anyone hear me scream?* Fort Collins, CO: SpeakOut! Women's Writing Workshop.

Jacobson, C. (2008). Creative politics and women's criminalization in the United States. *Signs: Journal of Women & Culture in Society*, *33*(2), 462–70.

Jacoby, B. (1996). Service-learning in today's higher education. In B. Jacoby (Ed.), *Service-learning in higher education: Concepts and practices* (pp. 3–25). San Francisco, CA: Jossey-Bass.

Jailbirds [video documentary]. (1998). Dir. Jon Rutter and Stephen Hartnett. Muncie, IN: Jalapeño and Pineapple Productions.

Jay-Z (Performer). (2003). "99 Problems." On *The black album*. New York: Roc-a-Fella/Def Jam.

Jenson, G. (2000). *Storytelling in Alcoholics Anonymous: A rhetorical analysis*. Carbondale: Southern Illinois University Press.

Jhally, S., & Lewis, J. (1992). *Enlightened racism: The Cosby Show, audiences, and the myth of the American dream*. Boulder, CO: Westview.

Jhally, S., & Lewis, J. (1998). The struggle over media literacy. *Journal of Communication*, *48*(1), 109–20.

Jiang, S., & Winfree, L. T. (2006). Social support, gender, and inmate adjustment to prison life: Insights from a national sample. *The Prison Journal*, *86*(1), 32–55. doi: 10.1177/0032885505283876

John Howard Association of Illinois. *Cuts in prison education put Illinois at risk*. Retrieved April 22, 2012, from www.thejaha.org/education

Johnson, K. (2000, February 10). Unready, unrehabilitated and up for release. *USA Today*, p. 13A.

Johnson, P., Logan, J. A., & Davis, A. J. (2004). *Inner lives: Voices of African American women in prison*. Albany: New York University Press.

Johnson, R. A. (1986). *Inner work: Using dreams and active imagination for personal growth*. New York: HarperSanFrancisco.

Johnson, R. A. (1991). *Owning your own shadow: Understanding the dark side of the psyche*. New York: HarperSanFrancisco.

Johnson, R. B. (1999). Appendix A: Examining the validity structure of qualitative research. In A. K. Milinki (Ed.), *Cases in qualitative research: Research reports for discussion and evaluation* (pp. 160–65). Los Angeles, CA: Pyrczak Publishing.

Jones, N. T., Ji, P., Beck, M., & Beck, N. (2002). The reliability and validity of the revised conflict tactics scale (CTS2) in a female incarcerated population. *Journal of Family Issues, 23*, 441–57. doi: 10.1177/0192513X02023003006

Jovanovic, S., & Wood, R. (2004). Speaking from the bedrock of ethics. *Philosophy and Rhetoric, 37*(4), 317–34.

Juda, D. P. (1983). On the special problems in creating group cohesion within the prison setting. *Journal of Offender Counseling, Services, and Rehabilitation, 8*, 47–59.

Jung, C. G. (1959). *Aion: Researches into the phenomenology of the self (vol. 9 of the collected works of C.G. Jung)*. Princeton, NJ: Princeton University Press.

Jung, C. G. (1981). *The Archetypes and the collective unconscious (the collected works of C. G. Jung, vol. 9, part 1)*. Princeton, NJ: Princeton University Press.

Jung, C. G. (1982). *Aspects of the feminine*. Princeton, NJ: Princeton University Press.

Kabat-Zinn, J. (1994). *Wherever you go, there you are: Mindfulness meditation in everyday life*. New York: Hyperion.

Kahane, D. (2009). Learning about obligation, compassion, and global justice: The place of contemplative pedagogy. In C. Kreber (Ed.), *Internationalizing the curriculum in higher education: New directions for teaching and learning*, no. 118 (pp. 49–60). Hoboken, NJ: Wiley Periodicals.

Kahane, D. (2011). Mindfulness and presence in teaching and learning. In I. Hay (Ed.), *Inspiring academics: Learning with the world's great university teachers* (pp. 17–22). London: Open University Press.

Katz, J. (2011). Advertising and the construction of violent white masculinity: From BMWs to Bud Light. In G. Dines and J. M. Humez (Eds.), *Gender, race, and class in media: A critical reader* (pp. 261–69). Los Angeles: Sage.

Kellner, D. (2003). *Media spectacle*. London: Routledge.

Kenemore, T., & Roldan, D. (2006). Staying straight: Lessons from ex-offenders. *Clinical Social Work Journal, 34*(1), 5–21.

Kernochan, R. A., McCormick, D. W., & White, J. A. (2007). Spirituality and the management teacher. *Journal of Management Inquiry, 16*(1), 61–75.

Kilbourne, L. (1999). *Can't buy my love: How advertising changes the way we think and feel*. New York: Touchstone.

King, M. L. (1957). *The power of non-violence*. Speech June 4, 1957, University of California at Berkeley. Retrieved August 31, 2012, from http://teachingamericanhistory. org/library/index.asp?document=1131

King, M. L. (1963). *Strength to love*. New York: Harper and Row.

King, R. (2003). *Don't kill in our names: Families of murder victims speak out against the death penalty*. Piscataway, NJ: Rutgers University Press.

King, S. (1998). Transformative nonviolence: The social ethics of George Fox and Thich Nhat Hanh. *Buddhist-Christian Studies, 18*, 3–36.

Kitwana, B. (2002). *The hip hop generation: Young blacks and the crisis in African American culture*. New York: Basic Civitas Books.

Kitwana, B. (2004). The challenge of rap music from cultural movement to political power. In M. Forman & M. A. Neal (Eds.), *That's the joint!: The hip-hop studies reader* (pp. 391–402). New York Taylor and Francis.

Kitwana, B. (2005). *Why white kids love hip hop: Wangstas, wiggers, wannabes, and the new reality of race in America*. New York: Basic Civitas Books.

Kivel, P. (2002). *Uprooting racism: How white people can work for racial justice*. Revised ed. British Columbia: New Society Publishers.

Kohler-Hausmann, J. (2011). Militarizing the police: Officer Jon Burge, torture, and war in the "urban jungle." In S. J. Hartnett (Ed.), *Challenging the prison-industrial complex: Activism, arts, and educational alternatives* (pp. 43–71). Champaign: University of Illinois Press.

Kornfield, J. (1993). *A path with heart: A guide through the perils and promises of spiritual life*. New York: Bantam.

Kondo, D. K. (1990). *Crafting selves: Power, gender, and discourses of identity in a Japanese workplace*. Chicago: University of Chicago Press.

KRS-One (Performer). (1989). Who Protects Us from You? On *Ghetto music: The blueprint of hiphop* [CD]. New York: Jive Records.

Kundera, M. (1984, 1999). *The unbearable lightness of being*. New York: Harper Perennial.

Kunichoff, Y. (2012, February 22). Occupy for Prisoners comes out against mass incarceration. Retrieved October 18, 2012, from http://truth-out.org/news/item/6843:occupy-for-prisoners-comes-out-against-mass-incarceration

Kyckelhahn, T. (2012, May 30). Justice expenditure and employment extracts, 2007–revised. U.S. Department of Justice. Office of Justive Programs. Bureau of Justice Statistics. Retrieved January 14, 2013, from: http://bjs.ojp.usdoj.gov/index.cfm?ty=pbdetail&iid=4332.

Lamb, W. (2003). *Couldn't keep it to myself: Wally Lamb and the women of York Correctional Institution*. New York: ReganBooks/HarperCollins.

Lamb, W. (2007). *I'll fly away: Further testimonies from the women of York Prison*. New York: HarperCollins.

Lantos, R., Eberts, J., Héroux, D., & Moore, B. (Producers), & Beresford, B. (Director). (1991). *Black robe* [Motion Picture]. United States: Samuel Goldwyn Company.

Larson, D. M. (2011). Killing democracy; or, How the Drug War drives the prison-industrial complex. In S. J. Hartnett (Ed.), *Challenging the prison-industrial complex: Activism, arts, and educational alternatives* (pp. 72–104). Champaign: University of Illinois Press.

Lasn, K. (1999). *Culture jam: How to reverse America's suicidal consumer binge—and why we must*. New York: Harper Collins.

Lebel, T. (2012). Invisible stripes: Formerly incarcerated persons' perceptions of stigma. *Deviant Behavior, 33*, (2), 89–107.

Leder, D. (2000). *The soul knows no bars: Inmates reflect on life, death, and hope*. Lanham, MD: Rowman and Littlefield.

Lil' Kim: Countdown to lockdown. (Aired 2006). Retrieved October 22, 2012, from http://www.tvrage.com/shows/id-8993/episode_list

Lindlof, T. R., & Taylor, B. C. (2002). *Qualitative communication research methods* (2nd ed.). Thousand Oaks, CA: Sage.

Lindquist, C. (2011). *Multi-site adult drug court evaluation*. Research Triangle Park, NC: RTI International. Retrieved October 22, 2012, from http://www.urban.org/uploadedpdf/412354-MADCE-Study-Overview-and-Design.pdf

Lindquist, C. (2011). *Multi-site adult drug court evaluation*. Research Triangle Park, NC: RTI International. Retrieved January 22, 2011, from http://www.rti.org/brochures/adultdrugcourteval.pdf

Lindquist, C., Hardison, J., & Lattimore, P. K. (2003). *Reentry courts process evaluation (phase 1), final report*. Washington, DC: U.S. Department of Justice. Retrieved January 30, 2010, from http://www.ncjrs.gov/pdffiles1/nij/grants/202472.pdf

Link, B. G. (1987). Understanding labeling effects in the area of mental disorders: An assessment of the effects of expectations of rejection. *American Sociological Review*, 52, 96–112. Retrieved August 31, 2012, from http://www.asanet.org/journals/asr/

Link, B. G., Cullen, F. T., Struening, E. L., Shrout, P. E., & Dohrenwend, B. P. (1989). A modified labeling theory approach to mental disorders: An empirical assessment. *American Sociological Review*, 54, 400–423. Retrieved August 31, 2012, from http://www.asanet.org/journals/asr/

Link, B. G., Mirotznik, J., & Cullen, F. T. (1991). The effectiveness of stigma coping orientations: Can negative consequences of mental illness labeling be avoided? *Journal of Health and Social Behavior*, 32, 302–20. Retrieved August 31, 2012, from http://hsb.sagepub.com/

Liptak, A. (2010, January 5). Shapers of death penalty give up on their work. *The New York Times*. Retrieved August 21, 2010, from LexisNexis Academic.

Liptak, A. (2010, May 17). Justices limit life sentences for juveniles. *The New York Times*. Retrieved August 31, 2010, from http://www.nytimes.com/2010/05/18/us/politics/18court.html

Lipton, D. S. (November, 1995). The effectiveness of treatment for drug abusers under criminal justice supervision. Presentation at the Conference on Criminal Justice Research and Evaluation, National Institute of Justice. Retrieved February 1, 2010, from http://www.ncjrs.gov/pdffiles/drugsupr.pdf

Loewen, J. W. (1995). *Lies my teachers told me: Everything your American history textbook got wrong*. New York: Simon and Schuster.

Lopoo, L. M., & Western, B. (2005). Incarceration and the formation and stability of marital unions. *Journal of Marriage and Family*, 67, 721–34. doi: 10.1111/j.1741-3737.2005.00165.x

Lowenstein, A. (1984). Coping with stress: The case of prisoners' wives. *Journal of Marriage and Family*, 46, 699–708. Retrieved August 31, 2012, from http://www.wiley.com/bw/journal.asp?ref=0022-2445

Lowenstein, A. (1986). Temporary single parenthood—The case of prisoners' families. *Family Relations*, 35(1), 79–85. Retrieved August 31, 2012, from http://www.ncfr.org/journals/family_relations/home.asp

Loya, J. (2005). *The man who outgrew his prison cell: Confessions of a bank robber*. New York: HarperCollins.

Lozoff, B. (1985). *We're all doing time: A guide to getting free*. Durham, NC: Human Kindness Foundation.

Lyons, W., & Drew, J. (2006). *Punishing schools: Fear and citizenship in American public education*. Ann Arbor: University of Michigan Press.

Magnani, L., & Wray, H. L. (2006). *Beyond prisons. A new interfaith paradigm for our failed prison system*. American Friends Service Committee. Minneapolis, MN: Fortress Press.

Makau, J. M. (1996). Notes on communication education and social justice. *Communication Studies, 47*, 135–41.

Malone, C. (2008). *Razor-wire dharma: A Buddhist life in prison*. Boston: Wisdom Publications.

Mandela, N. (1994). *Long walk to freedom: The autobiography of Nelson Mandela*. Boston: Back Bay Books.

Manza, J., & Uggen, C. (2006). *Locked out: Felon disenfranchisement and American democracy*. New York: Oxford University Press.

Markus, P. (2010, March 12). JBC debate over prison funding is today. *Denver Daily News*. Retrieved April 22, 2012, from www.statebillnews.com/2010/03/jbc-debate-over

Marsh, K., Fox, C., & Hedderman, C. (2009). Do you get what you pay for? Assessing the use of prison from an economic perspective. *Howard Journal of Criminal Justice, 48*, 144–57.

Martin, B., & Varney, W. (2003). Nonviolence and communication. *Journal of Peace Research, 40*(2), 213–32.

Martin, D., & Sussman, P. (1993). *Committing journalism: The prison writings of Red Hog*. New York: Norton.

Martinson, R. (1974). What works? Questions and answers about prison reform. *Public Interest, 35*, 22–54.

Maruna, S., & King, A. (2009). Once a criminal, always a criminal? 'Redeemability' and the psychology of punitive public attitudes. *European Journal of Criminal Policy Research, 15*, 7–24.

Mason, P. (2007). Misinformation, myth and distortion. *Journalism Studies, 8*(3), 481–96.

Massey, D. (2009). Racial formation in theory and practice: The case of Mexicans in the United States. *Race and Social Problems, 1*(1), 12–26.

Master class with Jay-Z. (2011, January 9). Oprah Winfrey Network.

Masters, J. J. (1997). *Finding freedom: Writings from death row*. Junction City, CA: Padma Publishing.

Mauer, M. (1994). Americans behind bars. Retrieved August 31, 2012, from http://www.druglibrary.org/schaffer/other/sp/abb.htm

Mauer, M. (1999). *Race to incarcerate*. The Sentencing Project. New York: The New Press.

Mauer, M., & Coyle, M. (2004). The social cost of America's race to incarcerate. *Journal of Religion and Spirituality in Social Work, 23*, 7–25.

Maull, F. (2005). *Dharma in hell: The prison writings of Fleet Maull*. Boulder, CO: Prison Dharma Network.

May, J. M. (1988). *Trials of character: The eloquence of Ciceronian ethos*. Chapel Hill: University of North Carolina Press.

McCann, B. J. (2007). Therapeutic and material <victim>hood: Ideology and the struggle for meaning in the Illinois death penalty controversy. *Communication and Critical/Cultural Studies, 4*, 382–401.

McChesney, R. W. (1999). *Rich media, poor democracy*. Urbana: University of Illinois Press.

McChesney, R. W. (2004). *The problem of the media: U.S. communication politics in the 21st century*. New York: Monthly Review Press.

McChesney, R. W. (2008). *Communication revolution: Critical junctures and the future of media*. New York: The New Press.

McCombs, M. E., and Shaw, D. L. (1972). The agenda-setting function of mass media. *Public Opinion Quarterly, 36*, 176–87.

McCracken, G. (1988). The long interview. *Qualitative Research Methods Series 13*. Thousand Oaks, CA: Sage.

McDaniels-Wilson, C. (1998). The relation of sexual abuse history to the MMPI-2 profiles and criminal involvement of incarcerated women. *Dissertation Abstracts International: Section B: The Sciences and Engineering, 59*(5-B), 2472.

McQuillar, T. L. (2003). *Rootwork: Using the folk magick of black America for love, money and success*. New York: Simon and Schuster.

McQuillar, T. L. (2007). *When rap music had a conscience: The artists, organizations and historic events that inspired and influenced the Golden Age of Hip-Hop*. Cambridge, MA: Da Capo Press.

McQuillar, T. L. (2010). *Tupac Shakur: The life and times of an American icon*. Cambridge, MA: Da Capo Press.

McWhorter, J. (2008). *All about the beat: Why hip-hop can't save black America*. New York: Gotham Books.

Meehan, E. (2005). *Why TV is not our fault: Television programming, viewers, and who's really in control*. Lanham, MD: Rowman and Littlefield.

Meiners, E. (2011). Building an abolition democracy: The fight against public fears, private benefits, and prison expansion. In S. J. Hartnett (Ed.), *Challenging the prison-industrial complex* (pp. 15–40). Champaign: University of Illinois Press.

Meiners, E. R. (2007). *Right to be hostile: Schools, prisons, and the making of public enemies*. New York, NY: Routledge.

Mendleson, R. (2010, January 25). Hip hop helps young offenders. *Maclean's*. Retrieved August 31, 2012, from http://www2.macleans.ca/2010/01/21/hip-hop-helps-young-offenders/

Meranze, M. (1996). *Laboratories of virtue: Punishment, revolution, and authority in Philadelphia, 1760–1835*. Chapel Hill: University of North Carolina Press.

Mettee, D. L. (1983, November). *Report of a therapeutic drama program in a federal prison: Implications for applied communication*. Paper presented at the annual meeting of the Speech Communication Association, Washington, DC.

Metzl, J. (2010). *The protest psychosis: How schizophrenia became a black disease*. Boston: Beacon Press.

Michigan shutting 3 prisons, 5 camps to save money. (2009, June 5). *Eagle Tribune*. Retrieved October 10, 2012, from http://www.eagletribune.com/business/x1650958318/Michigan-shutting-3-prisons-5-camps-to-save-money

Micken, R. A. (1986). Introduction. In J. S. Watson (Ed.), *Cicero on oratory and orators* (pp. xiii–xlix). Carbondale: Southern Illinois University Press.

Miller, C. (2007). What can automation tell us about agency? *Rhetoric Society Quarterly, 37*(2), 137–57.

Miller, C. T., & Major, B. (2000). Coping with stigma and prejudice. In T. F. Heatherton, R. E. Kleck, M. R. Hebl, & J. G. Hull (Eds.), *The social psychology of stigma* (pp. 243–72). New York: Guilford Press.

Miller, J. (1994). Linking traditional and service-learning courses: Outcome evaluations utilizing two pedagogically distinct models. *Michigan Journal of Community Service Learning, 1*, 29–36.

Miller, J., & Johnson, D. C. (2009). *Problem solving courts: New approaches to criminal justice in the United States.* New York: Rowman and Littlefield.

Miller, J. G. (1996). *Search and destroy: African-American males in the criminal justice system.* Cambridge, UK: Cambridge University Press.

Miller, W. R. (2000). Rediscovering fire: Small interventions, large effects. *Psychology of Addictive Behaviors, 14*, 6–18.

Mipham, S. (2003). *Turning the mind into an ally.* New York: Riverhead Books.

Moffitt, J., & Decker, R. (2000) Service-learning reflection for engineering: A faculty guide. In E. Tsang (Ed.), *Concepts and models for service-learning in engineering* (pp. 31–40). Washington, DC: American Association for Higher Education.

Moore, B. (1985, 1997). *Black robe: A novel.* New York: Plume.

Moore, R., & Gillette, D. (1990). *King, warrior, magician, lover: Rediscovering the archetypes of the mature masculine.* San Francisco, CA: HarperSanFrancisco.

Moore, R., & Gillette, D. (1992a). *The king within: Accessing the king in the male psyche.* New York: William Morrow.

Moore, R., & Gillette, D. (1992b). *The warrior within: Accessing the knight in the male psyche.* New York: William Morrow.

Moore, R., & Gillette, D. (1993a). *The lover within: Accessing the lover in the male psyche.* New York: William Morrow.

Moore, R., & Gillette, D. (1993b). *The magician within: Accessing the shaman in the male psyche.* New York: William Morrow.

Moore, S. (2009, February 10). Court orders California to cut prison population. *The New York Times.* Retrieved August 31, 2010, from http://www.nytimes.com/2009/02/10/us/10prison.html

Moreno, I. (2009, March 2). Report: 1 in 29 in Colo. in criminal justice system. *DenverPost.Com.* Retrieved March 3, 2009, from www.denverpost.com

Morgan, M., Shanahan, J., & Signorielli, N. (2009). Growing up with television: Cultivation processes. In J. Bryant and M. B. Oliver (Eds.), *Media effects: Advances in theory and research* (pp. 34–49). New York: Routledge.

Moser, D. J., Arndt, S., Kanz, J. E., Benjamin, M. L., Bayless, J. D., Reese, R. L., Paulsen, J. S., & Flaum, M. A. (2004). Coercion and informed consent in research involving prisoners. *Comprehensive Psychiatry, 45*, 1–9.

Mumby, D. K. (2001). Power and politics. In F. M. Jablin & L. L. Putnam (Eds.), *The new handbook of organizational communication: Advances in theory, research, and methods* (pp. 585–623). Thousand Oaks, CA: Sage.

Mumby, D. K. (2005). Theorizing resistance in organization studies: A dialectical approach. *Management Communication Quarterly, 19*, 19–44.

Mumby, D. K., & Deetz, S. A. (1990). Power, discourse, and the workplace: Reclaiming the critical tradition. *Communication Yearbook, 13*, 18–47.

Mumola, C. (2000). *Incarcerated parents and their children.* Washington, DC: U.S. Department of Justice, Bureau of Justice Statistics.

Murray, J. (2005). The effects of imprisonment on families and children of prisoners. In A. Liebling & S. Maruna (Eds.), *The effects of imprisonment* (pp. 442–62). Portland, OR: Willan Publishing.

Musca, T. (Producer), & Menéndez, T. (Director). (1988). *Stand and deliver* [Motion Picture]. United States: Warner Brothers.

Nandi, M. (2002). Re/Constructing black masculinity in prison. *Journal of Men's Studies, 11*(1), 91–107.

Nas (Performer). (1994). "One love" and "represent." On *Illmatic* [CD]. New York: Sony.

Nas (Performer). (1999a). "Ghetto prisoners." On *I am* [CD]. New York: Columbia.

Nas (Performer). (1999b). "Last words." On *Nastradamus* [CD]. New York: Columbia.

Natapoff, A. (2009). *Snitching: Criminal informants and the erosion of American justice.* New York: New York University Press.

Nellis, A., & King, R. S. (2009, July). *No exit: The expanding use of life sentences in America.* Washington, DC: The Sentencing Project.

Neruda, P. (1967). *Fully empowered.* New York: New Directions.

New Mexico Gov. Bill Richardson bans death penalty. (2009, March 18). Reuters. Retrieved August 21, 2010, from http://www.reuters.com/article/idUSTRE52I01820090319

Newman, R., & Scott, B. (2005). *The future of media: Resistance and reform in the 21st century.* New York: Seven Stories Press.

Newport, F. (2009, October 13). In U.S., two-thirds continue to support death penalty. Gallup. Retrieved August 21, 2010, from http://www.gallup.com/poll/123638/in-u.s.-two-thirds continue-support-death-penalty.aspx

Nhat Hanh, T. (1975, 1976). *The miracle of mindfulness: An introduction to the practice of meditation.* Boston: Beacon Press.

Nixon, R. M. (1968, August 8). Nixon's acceptance of the Republican Party nomination for President. Retrieved August 29, 2010, from http://watergate.info/1968/08/08/nixon-accepts-republican-nomination-for-president.html

Norris, P. (2000). *Digital divide: Civic engagement, information poverty, and the internet worldwide.* New York: Cambridge University Press.

Novek, E. (2005). "Heaven, Hell, and Here": Understanding the impact of incarceration through a prison newspaper. *Critical Studies in Media Communication, 22*(4), October 2005, 281–301.

O'Brien, P. (2001). *Making it in the free world.* New York: State University of New York Press.

Oh, J. H. (2005). Social disorganizations and crime rates in US central cities: Toward an explanation of urban economic change. *Social Science Journal, 42*, 569–82.

Owen, B. (1998). *"In the mix": Struggle and survival in a women's prison.* New York: State University of New York Press.

Pager, D. (2007). *Marked: Race, crime, and finding work in an era of mass incarceration.* Chicago: University Of Chicago Press.

Parenti, C. (2000). Crime as social control. *Social Justice, 27*(3), 43–49.

Parenti, C. (2008). *Lockdown America: Police and prisons in the age of crisis.* London: Verso.

Parenti, M. (1992). *Make-believe media: The politics of entertainment.* New York: St. Martin's Press.

Parenti, M. (1993). *Inventing reality: The politics of news media.* New York: St. Martin's Press.

Payne, W. D. (1973). Negative labels: Passageways and prisons. *Crime and Delinquency, 19*, 33–40.

PCAP (Prison Creative Arts Project). University of Michigan. Web site retrieved April 1, 2012, from http://www.lsa.umich.edu/pcap

PCARE (2007). Fighting the prison-industrial complex: A call to communication and cultural studies scholars to change the world. *Communication and Critical/Cultural Studies, 4*, 402–20.

Pennebaker, J. W. (1990). *Opening up: The healing power of confiding in others.* New York: Morrow.

Petchauer, E. (2011). *Hip-hop culture in college students' lives: Elements, embodiment, and higher edutainment.* New York: Routledge.

Pew Center on the States. (2008). *One in 100: Behind bars in America, 2008.* New York: Pew Center on the States. Retrieved August 31, 2012, from http://www.pewstates.org/uploadedFiles/PCS_Assets/2008/one%20in%20100.pdf

Pew Center on the States (2009). *One in 31: The long reach of American corrections.* Washington, DC: The Pew Charitable Trusts.

Pew Center on the States. (2010, April). *Prison count 2010: State population declines for the first time in 38 years.* Philadelphia: Pew Center on the States. Retrieved August 31, 2012, from http://www.pewtrusts.org/uploadedFiles/wwwpewtrustsorg/Reports/sentencing_and_corrections/Prison_Count_2010.pdf

Pew Charitable Trusts, The. (2010). *Collateral costs: Incarceration's effect on economic mobility.* Washington, DC: The Pew Charitable Trusts.

Peters, K. F., Apse, K. A., Blackford, A., McHugh, B., Michalic, D., & Biesecker, B. B. (2005). Social and behavioral research in clinical genetics. Living with Marfan syndrome: coping with stigma. *Clinical Genetics, 68*, 6–14. doi: 10.1111/j.1399-0004.2005.00446.x

Phelps, M. (2011). Rehabilitation in the punitive era: The gap between rhetoric and reality in U.S. prison programs. *Law & Society Review, 45*(1), 33–68.

Phillips, J. (2008). *Letters from the dhamma brothers: Meditation behind bars.* Onalaska, WA: Pariyatti Press.

Pipher, M. (1994). *Reviving Ophelia: Saving the selves of adolescent girls.* New York: Riverhead Books.

Poehlmann, J. (2005). Children's family environments and intellectual outcomes during maternal incarceration. *Journal of Marriage and Family, 67*, 1275–1285. doi: 10.1111/j.1741-3737.2005.00216.x

Pompa, L. (2004). Disturbing where we are comfortable: Notes from behind the walls. *Reflections, 4*(1), 24–34.

Pompa, L. (2011). Breaking down the walls: Inside-out learning and the pedagogy of transformation. In S. J. Hartnett (Ed.), *Challenging the prison-industrial complex: Activism, arts, and education alternatives* (pp. 149–78). Champaign: University of Illinois Press.

Porter, N. D. (2011, February). *The state of sentencing 2010: Developments in policy and practice.* Washington, DC: The Sentencing Project. Retrieved August 31, 2012, from http://sentencingproject.org/doc/publications/publications/Final%20State%20of%20the%20Sentencing%202010.pdf

Porter, N., & Wright, V. (2011). *Cracked justice.* Washington, DC: Sentencing Project. Retrieved August 31, 2012, from http://www.sentencingproject.org/detail/publication.cfm?publication_id=343&id=106

Postman, N. (1985). *Amusing ourselves to death: Public discourse in the age of show business.* New York: Penguin.

Pratt, C. (Producer), & Carlino, L. G. (Director). (1979). *The great Santini* [Motion Picture]. United States: Warner Brothers.

Prejean, H. (1993). *Dead man walking*. New York: Vintage Books.

Press, J. E., & Townsley, E. (1998). Wives' and husbands' housework reporting: Gender, class, and social desirability. *Gender and Society, 12*, 188–218. doi: 10.1177/089124398012002005

Prison Policy Initiative. (1997). Complete illiteracy in the prisoner and general populations (graph). Retrieved October 24, 2010, from www.prisonpolicy.org/graphs/illiteracy.html

PrisonTalk Online (2010). Homepage. Retrieved January 29, 2011, from http://www.prisontalk.com/

PrisonTalk Online. (2010b). Introduction and stories forum. Retrieved September 4, 2010, from http://www.prisontalk.com/forums/forumdisplay.php?f=38

Provine, D. (2006). Creating racial disadvantage: The case of crack cocaine. In R. D. Peterson, L. J. Krivo, and J. Hagan, *The many colors of crime: Inequalities of race, ethnicity, and crime in America* (pp. 277–94). New York: New York University Press.

Pryor, M. (2010). The unintended effects of prisoner reentry policy and the marginalization of urban communities. *Dialectical Anthropology, 34*, 513–17.

Pulido, I. (2009). "Music fit for us minorities": Latinas/os' use of hip hop as pedagogy and interpretive framework to negotiate and challenge racism. *Equity and Excellence in Education, 42*, 67–85.

Radelet, M. L., Vandiver, M., & Berardo, F. M. (1983). Families, prisons, and men with death sentences: The human impact of structured uncertainty. *Journal of Family Issues, 4*(4), 593–612. doi: 10.1177/019251383004004005

Rapping, E. (2003). *Law and justice as seen on TV*. New York: New York University Press.

Raptivist Capital-"X" gives a voice to the voiceless. (n.d.). Retrieved August 31, 2012, from http://www.hiphoppress.com/2010/01/raptivist-capitalx-gives-a-voice-to-the-voiceless-with-his-may-19-2010-debut-release-305375-the-voic.html

Reed, I. (1990, May). Antihero: Opinion. *Spin*, 59–62.

Reese, R. (2006). *Prison race*. Durham, NC: Carolina Academic Press.

Reeves, J. L., & Campbell, R. (1994). *Cracked coverage: Television news, the anti-cocaine crusade, and the Reagan legacy*. Durham, NC: Duke University Press.

Reiman, J. (2004). *The rich get richer and the poor get prison: Ideology, class, and criminal justice* (7th ed.). Boston, MA: Allyn and Bacon.

Reitz, K. R. (1998). Sentencing. In M. Tonry (Ed.), *The handbook of crime and punishment* (pp. 542–62). New York: Oxford University Press.

RIAA launches new gold and platinum award for ringtones. (2006, June 14). Recording Industry Association of America. Retrieved August 31, 2012, from http://tinyurl.com/4dclcbn

Richburg, K. B. (2007, December 14). N.J. approves abolition of death penalty: Corzine to sign. *The Washington Post*. Retrieved August 21, 2010, from LexisNexis Academic.

Rideau, W., & Wikberg, R. (Eds.). (1992). *Life sentences: Rage and survival behind bars*. New York: Times Books.

Roberts, D. (2008). Constructing a criminal justice system free of racial bias: An abolitionist framework. *Columbia Human Rights Law Review, 39*, 261–85.

Roberts, J., & Hough, M. (2005). The state of the prisons: Exploring public knowledge and opinion. *The Howard Journal of Criminal Justice, 44*(3), 286–306.

Rockwell, I. N. (2002). *The five wisdom energies: A Buddhist way of understanding personalities, emotions and relationships*. Boston: Shambhala.

Rodríguez, D. (2006). *Forced passages: Imprisoned radical intellectuals and the U.S. prison regime*. Minneapolis: University of Minnesota Press.

Rodriguez, R. (1982). *Hunger of memory*. New York: Bantam.

Room, R. (2005). Stigma, social inequality and alcohol and drug use. *Drug and Alcohol Review, 24*, 143–55.

Rose, W. (2002). Crimes of color: Risk, profiling, and the contemporary racialization of social control. *International Journal of Politics, Culture and Society, 16*(2), 179–205.

Rottman, D. B., & Kimberly, J. R. (1975). The social context of jails. *Sociology and Social Research, 59*, 344–61.

Rough Justice. (2010, July 24). *The Economist*. Retrieved August 31, 2010, from Lexis-Nexis Academic database.

Ryan, G. (2003, November 1). Gov. George Ryan's commutation announcement. *Northwestern Law*. Retrieved. October 10, 2012, from http://www.sfgate.com/nation/article/Text-of-Gov-George-Ryan-s-speech announcing-his-2680319.php

Ryan, K. J., & Natalle, E. J. (2001). Fusing horizons: Standpoint hermeneutics and invitational rhetoric. *Rhetoric Society Quarterly, 31*, 69–90.

Sabo, D., Kupers, T.A., & London, W. (2001). Gender and the politics of punishment. In D. Sabo, T. A. Kupers, & W. London (Eds.), *Prison masculinities*. Philadelphia: Temple University Press.

Sabol, W., West, H., & Cooper, M. (2009). *Prisoners in 2008*. U.S. Department of Justice, Office of Justice Programs, Bureau of Justice Statistics, March 2009, NCJ 228417.

Sabol, W. J., & Couture, H. (2008). Prison inmates at midyear 2007. Washington, DC: U.S. Department of Justice.

Said, E. (1978). *Orientalism*. New York: Vintage Books.

Sarat, A. (2002). *When the state kills: Capital punishment and the American condition*. Princeton, NJ: Princeton University Press.

Scaife, J. (Ed.) (2008). *Open line*. San Quentin, CA: Prison University Project.

Schiller, H. I. (1989). *Culture, Inc.: The corporate takeover of public expression*. Oxford, UK: Oxford University Press.

Schiller, H. I. (1996). *Information inequality: The deepening social crisis in America*. London: Routledge.

Schlenker, B. R. (2003). Self-presentation. In M. R. Leary and J. P. Tangney (Eds.), *Handbook of self and identity* (pp. 492–518). New York: Guilford.

Schor, J. (2004). *Born to buy: The commercialized child and the new consumer culture*. New York: Scribner.

Schram, P., Koons-Witt, B., Williams, F., III, & McShane, M. (2006). Supervision strategies and approaches for female parolees: Examining the link between unmet needs and parolee outcome. *Crime and Delinquency, 52*, 450–71.

Schultz, P. (2005). *Not monsters: Analyzing the stories of child molesters*. New York: Rowman and Littlefield.

Schwartz, J. (2010, March 17). Report finds states holding fewer prisoners. *The New York Times*. Retrieved April 22, 2012, from www.nytimes.com/2010/03/17/us/17prison.html

Scott, B. (2008, July 4). Gov. pulls switch on death cell. *New York Post*. Retrieved March 14, 2012, from http://is.gd/Qjf1aX

Scott, J. C. (1985). *Weapons of the weak: Everyday forms of peasant resistance*. New Haven, CT: Yale University Press.

Scott, J. C. (1990). *Domination and the arts of resistance: Hidden transcripts*. New Haven, CT: Yale University Press.

Scraton, P., & McCulloch, J. (Eds.) (2008). *The violence of incarceration*. New York: Routledge.

Segrin, C., & Flora, J. (2001). Perceptions of relational histories, marital quality, and loneliness when communication is limited: An examination of married prison inmates. *Journal of Family Communication, 1*(3), 151–73. doi: 10.1207/S15327698JFC0103_01

Selfa, L. (2008). *The Democrats: A critical history*. Chicago: Haymarket Books.

Sentencing Project, The (2009). *Racial disparities in the criminal justice system*. Testimony of Marc Mauer, Executive Director, the Sentencing Project. Prepared for the House Judiciary Subcommittee on Crime, Terrorism, and Homeland Security, October 29, 2009. Washington, DC: The Sentencing Project; http://www.sentencingproject.org

Sentencing Project, The (2010). *Reducing racial disparity in the criminal justice system: A manual for practitioners and policymakers*. Washington, DC: The Sentencing Project; http://www.sentencingproject.org

Shailor, J. (2008, May). When muddy flowers bloom: The Shakespeare Project at Racine Correctional Institution. In *Publications of the Modern Language Association (PMLA), 123*, pp. 632–41.

Shailor, J. (2011a). Humanizing education behind bars: Shakespeare and the theater of empowerment. In S. J. Hartnett (Ed.), *Challenging the prison-industrial complex: Activism, arts, and educational alternatives* (pp. 229–51). Champaign: University of Illinois Press.

Shailor, J. (2011b). Prison theatre and the promise of reintegration. In J. Shailor (Ed.), *Performing New Lives: Prison Theatre* (pp. 180–96). London: Jessica Kingsley.

Shakespeare, W. (2006). *Hamlet*. London: Arden Shakespeare (Third Series).

Shambhala International (Vajradhatu) (2009). Shambhala: Vision, lineage, meditation, community. Retrieved April 1, 2012, from www.shambhala.org

Shanahan, J., & Morgan, M. (1999). *Television and its viewers: Cultivation theory and research*. Cambridge, UK: Cambridge University Press.

Sharp, G. (1959). The meanings of non-violence: A typology. *The Journal of Conflict Resolution, 3*(1), 41–66.

Sholle, D., & Denski, S. (1995). Critical media literacy: Reading, remapping, rewriting. In P. McLaren, R. Hammer, D. Sholle, & S. Reilly (Eds.), *Rethinking media literacy: A critical pedagogy of representation* (pp. 7–31). New York: Peter Lang.

Silvergate, H. A. (2009). *Three felonies a day*. Jackson, TN: Encounter Books.

Simon, J. (2007). *Governing through crime: How the war on crime transformed American democracy and created a culture of fear*. (Oxford, UK: Oxford University Press).

Sloop, J. (1996). *The cultural prison: Discourse, prisoners, and punishment*. Tuscaloosa: University of Alabama Press.

Smith, D. E. (1987). *The everyday world as problematic: A feminist sociology*. Toronto: University of Toronto Press.

Smith, D. E. (2002). Institutional ethnography: An introduction. In T. May (Ed.), *Qualitative research in action* (pp. 17–53). London: Sage.

Smith, R. A. (2007). Language of the lost: An explication of stigma communication. *Communication Theory, 17*, 462–85. doi: 10.1111/j.1468–2885.2007.00307.x

Smith, S., & Watson, J. (1996). Introduction. In S. Smith & J. Watson (Eds.). *Getting a life: Everyday uses of autobiography* (pp. 1–26). Minneapolis: University of Minnesota Press.

Snell, T. (1994). *Women in prison* (NCJ 145321). Washington, DC: Bureau of Justice Statistics. United States Department of Justice, Bureau of Justice Statistics. (2009). Prison Statistics. Retrieved May 19, 2011, from http://bjs.ojp.usdoj.gov/content/pub/pdf/ppus06.pdf

Sprecher, S., & Fehr, B. (2005). Compassionate love for close others and humanity. *Journal of Social and Personal Relationships*, 22(5), 629–51.

Stabile, C. A. (2006). *White victims, black villains: Gender, race and crime news in U.S. culture.* New York: Routledge.

Starosta, W., & Shi, L. (2007). Alternate perspectives on Gandhian communication ethics. *China Media Research*, 3(4), 7–14.

Steinhauer, J. (2009, March 25). To cut costs, states relax prison policies. *The New York Times.* Retrieved April 22, 2012, from www.nytimes.com/2009/03/25/us/25prisons.html

Stern, A. (2011, March 9). Illinois gov. Quinn signs bill banning death penalty. Reuters. Retrieved March 14, 2012, from http://is.gd/1l6nph

Steurer, S. J. (1996). Correctional education: A worthwhile investment. *Linkages*, 3(2). Washington, DC: National Adult Literacy and Learning Disabilities Center.

Steurer, S. J., Linton, J., Nally, J., & Lockwood, S. (August 2010). The top-nine reasons to increase correctional education programs. *Corrections Today*, pp. 43–44.

Steurer, S. J., Smith, L., & Tracy, L. (2001). *Three state recidivism study.* Study sponsored by the Correctional Education Association and submitted to the U.S. Department of Education (Office of Correctional Education).

Stewart, C. J., Smith, C. A., & Denton, R. E., Jr. (2001). *Persuasion and social movements* (4th ed.). Prospect Heights, IL: Waveland Press.

Strauss, A. (1987). *Qualitative analysis.* New York: Cambridge University Press.

Strauss, A., & Corbin, J. (1990). Grounded theory methodology: An overview. In N. Denzin & Y. Lincoln (Eds.), *Handbook of qualitative research* (pp. 273–85). Thousand Oaks, CA: Sage.

Strauss, A., & Corbin, J. (1998). *Basics of qualitative research: Techniques and procedures for developing grounded theory* (2nd ed.). Thousand Oaks, CA: Sage.

Strover, S. (2003). Remapping the digital divide. *The Information Society*, 19, 275–77. Doi: 10.1080/01972240309481

Sturges, J. E., & Al-Khattar, A. M. (2009). Survey of jail visitors about visitation policies. *The Prison Journal*, 89, 482–96. doi: 10.1177/0032885509351009

Sudbury, J. (2005). *Global lockdown: Race, gender, and the prison-industrial complex.* London: Routledge.

Sullivan, L. E. (1990). *The prison reform movement: Forlorn hope.* Boston, MA: Twayne.

Suzuki, S. (1970, 2011). *Zen mind, beginner's mind.* Boston: Shambhala Publications.

Swisher, R. R., & Waller, M. R. (2008). Confining fatherhood: Incarceration and paternal involvement among nonresident white, African American, and Latino fathers. *Journal of Family Issues*, 29, 1067–88. doi: 10.1177/0192513X08316273

Switching off the death penalty. (2010, January 8). *The Christian Science Monitor.* Retrieved August 21, 2010, from LexisNexis Academic.

Tannenbaum, J. (2000). *Disguised as a poem: My years teaching poetry at San Quentin.* Boston: Northeastern University Press.

Tannenbaum, J., & Jackson, S. (2010). *By heart: Poetry, prison, and two lives.* Oakland, CA: New Village Press.

Tewksbury, R., & Dabney, D. (2004). Prison volunteers: Profiles, motivations, satisfaction. *Journal of Offender Rehabilitation, 40*(1/2), 173–83.

Tonry, M. (2011). *Punishing race: A continuing American dilemma.* New York: Oxford University Press.

Tracy, S. J., & Scott, C. (2006). Sexuality, masculinity, and taint management among firefighters and correctional officers: Getting down and dirty with "America's heroes" and the "scum of law enforcement." *Management Communication Quarterly, 20*(1), 6–38. doi: 10.1177/0893318906287898

Travis, J. (2007). Reflections on the reentry court movement. *Federal Sentencing Reporter, 20,* 84–87.

Travis, J., Solomon, A. L., & Waul, M. (2001). *From prison to home: The dimensions and consequences of prisoner reentry.* Washington, DC: The Urban Institute.

Trebach, A. S. (2005). *The great drug war, and rational proposals to turn the tide.* Bloomington, IN: Unlimited.

Trethewey, A. (1999). Disciplined bodies. *Organization Studies, 20,* 423–50.

Tretheway, A. (2000). Cultured bodies: Communication as constitutive of culture and embodied identity. *Electronic Journal of Communication, 10.* Retrieved January 30, 2010, from http://shadow.cios.org:7979/journals/EJC/010/1/01016.html

Trungpa, T. (2007). *Shambhala: The sacred path of the warrior.* Boston: Shambhala Publications.

Truthout. (2012, February 22). Occupy for Prisoners comes out against mass incarceration. Retrieved October 10, 2012, from http://truth-out.org/news/item/6843:occupy -for-prisoners-comes-out-against-mass-incarceration

Tupac (Performer). (1991). Trapped. On *2pacalypse now* [CD]. New York: Jive Records.

U.S. Department of Justice, Office of Justice Programs. (2010). *Reentry.* Retrieved on August 24, 2010, from http://www.reentry.gov

Vacca, J. S. (2004). Educated prisoners are less likely to return to prison. *Journal of Correctional Education, 55,* 297–305.

Valentine, K. (1998). "If the guards only knew": Communication education for women in prison. *Women's Studies in Communication, 21*(2), 238–43.

Van den Bulck, J., & Vandebosch, H. (2003). When the viewer goes to prison: Learning fact from watching fiction. A qualitative cultivation study. *Poetics 31,* 103–16.

Vanden Heuvel, K. (2007, December 17). New Jersey leads on capital punishment [blog entry]. Retrieved October 10, 2012, from http://www.thenation.com/blog/ newjersey-leads-capital-punishment

Victims/survivors. (2010). New Yorkers for Alternatives to the Death Penalty. Retrieved August 30, 2010, from http://www.nyadp.org/content/victims-survivors

Vock, D. C. (2003, September 17). Justices consider legality of death row commutations. *Chicago Daily Law Bulletin,* 1.

Wacquant, L. (2001). Deadly symbiosis: When ghetto and prison meet and mesh. *Punishment and Society, 3,* 95–134.

Wacquant, L. (2002). From slavery to mass incarceration. Rethinking the "race question" in the U.S. *New Left Review, 13*(1), 41–60.

Wacquant, L. (2009). *Punishing the poor: the neoliberal government of social insecurity.* Durham, NC: Duke University Press.

Wagenheim, K. (Ed.) (2000). *Inside/out: Voices from the New Jersey State Prison,* Livermore, CA: WingSpan.

Wallace, B. A. (1999). *The four immeasurables: Cultivating a boundless heart*. Ithaca, NY: Snow Lion.

Walmsley, R. (Ed.). (2009). World prison population list. (8th ed.). London: International Centre for Prison Studies, School of Law, King's College.

Walters, G. (1998). *Changing lives of crime and drugs: Intervening with substance-abusing offenders*. New York: Wiley.

Warhol, R. R., & Michie, H. (1996). Twelve-step teleology: Narratives of recovery/recovery as narrative. In S. Smith & J. Watson (Eds.), *Getting a life: Everyday uses of autobiography* (pp. 327–50). Minneapolis: University of Minnesota Press.

Warriner, A. A. (1998). Forensics in a correctional facility. *National Forensic Journal*, 16, 27–42.

Wasko, J. (2001). *Understanding Disney*. Cambridge, UK: Polity.

Waxler, R., & Trounstine, J. (2005). *Finding a voice: The practice of changing lives through literature*. Ann Arbor: University of Michigan Press.

Weber, M. (1978). *Economy and society*. Berkeley: University of California Press.

Wehrenfenning, D. (2008). Conflict management and communicative action: Second track diplomacy from a Habermasian perspective. *Communication Theory*, 18(3), 356–75.

Wenzel, S. L., Longshore, D., Turner, S., & Ridgely, M. S. (2001). Drug courts—A bridge between criminal justice and health services. *Journal of Criminal Justice*, 29, 241–53.

West, C. (1994). *Race matters*. New York: Vintage.

West, H. C. (2010). U.S. Department of Justice, Office of Justice Programs, Bureau of Justice Statistics. *Prison inmates at midyear 2009-Statistical tables* (NCJ Publication No. 230113). Retrieved from http://bjs.ojp.usdoj.gov/index.cfm?ty=pbsc&sid=38

West, H. C., Sabol, W. J., & Greenman, S. J. (2010). *Prisoners in 2009*. Washington, DC: Bureau of Justice Statistics. Retrieved May 28, 2011, from http://bjs.ojp.usdoj.gov/content/pub/pdf/p09.pdf

Western, B. (2007). *Punishment and inequality in America*. New York: Russell Sage Foundation.

Wheeler, S. (1961). Socialization in correctional communities. *American Sociological Review*, 34, 492–504.

Whitney, K. S. (2003). *Sitting inside: Buddhist practice in America's prisons*. Boulder, CO: Prison Dharma Network.

Wideman, J. E. (1995). Doing time, marking race. *The Nation*, 261(14), 503–5.

Wilczynski, A. (1991). Images of women who kill their infants: The mad and the bad. *Women and Criminal Justice*, 2(2), 71–88.

Wilkinson, R. A., Bucholtz, G. A., & Siegfried, J. D. (2004). Reform through offender reentry: A partnership between courts and corrections. *Pace Law Review*, 24, 609–29.

Williams, J. (2007). *Enough: The phony leaders, dead-end movements, and culture of failure that are undermining black America*. New York: Broadway.

Willie Horton [Video file]. (1988). Retrieved June 9, 2009, from http://www.livingroomcandidate.org/commercials/1988/willie-horton

Wilson, C. C., Gutierrez, F., & Chao, L. M. (2003). *Racism, sexism, and the media: The rise of class communication in multicultural America*. Thousand Oaks, CA: Sage.

Wilson, W. J. (2009). Toward a framework for understanding forces that contribute to or reinforce racial inequality. *Race and Social Problems*, 1(1), 3–11.

Winant, H. (2000). The theoretical status of the concept of race. In L. Back & J. Solomos (Eds.), *Theories of race and racism* (pp. 181–94). New York: Routledge.

Winterfield, L., Coggeshall, M., Burke-Storer, M., Correa, V., & Tidd, S. (2009, May). *The effects of postsecondary correctional education: Final report.* Washington, DC: The Urban Institute, Justice Policy Center.

Withers, L., Hinck, S. S., & Hinck, E. A. (2007, November). *Reflections on tensions arising out of teaching in prison contexts.* Paper presented at the annual meeting of the National Communication Association, Chicago, IL.

Wittenberg, P. M. (1996). Language and communication in prison. *Federal Probation, 60*, 45–50.

Wolf, N. (1991). *The beauty myth: How images of beauty are used against women.* New York: Morrow.

Wolff, N., & Draine, J. (2004). Dynamics of social capital of prisoners and community reentry: Ties that bind? *Journal of Correctional Health Care, 10*, 457–90.

Wood, B. (1999). Understanding rap as rhetorical folk-poetry. *Mosaic: A Journal for the Interdisciplinary Study of Literature, 32*, 129–47.

Wood, J. K. (2003). Justice as therapy: The Victim Rights Clarification Act. *Communication Quarterly, 51*, 296–311.

Wood, J. K. (2005). In whose name? Crime victim policy and the punishing power of protection. *National Women's Studies Association Journal, 17*(3), 1–17.

Wu-Tang Clan (Performer). (2000). "I can't go to sleep." On *The W.* [CD] New York: Sony.

X, M. & Haley, A. (1964). *The autobiography of Malcolm X.* New York: Ballantine.

Yochelson, S., & Samenow, S. (1976). *The criminal personality, volume 1: A profile for change.* New York: Jason Aronson.

Yousman, B. (2008). Media literacy: Creating better citizens or better consumers? In J. Gray and R. Andersen (Eds.). *Battleground: The media* (pp. 238–47.) Santa Barbara, CA: Greenwood.

Yousman, B. (2009). *Prime time prisons on U.S. TV: Representation of incarceration.* New York: Peter Lang.

Zaentz, S. (Producer), & Kaufman, P. (Director). (1988). *The unbearable lightness of being* [Motion Picture]. United States: The Saul Zaentz Company.

Zajonc, A. (2009). *Meditation as contemplative inquiry: When knowing becomes love.* Great Barrington, MA: Lindisfarne Books.

Contributors

Beth M. Cohen worked as a research assistant in the department of Communication Arts and Sciences at Pennsylvania State University. She has studied a variety of communication issues in the hope of generating effective interventions that might lead toward social justice. She presented parts of her chapter at PSU's undergraduate research exhibition and earned the first place award for her research.

David Coogan is an associate professor of English at Virginia Commonwealth University and the founder and co-director of *Open Minds: Shared Inquiries, Shared Hope*, which enables college students and prisoners at the Richmond City Jail to take courses in the liberal arts together. Coogan is the co-editor with John Ackerman of *The Public Work of Rhetoric: Citizen Scholars and Civic Engagement* (2010). His essays have appeared in the journals *College Composition and Communication, College English*, and *Community Literacy*, and in the books *Active Voices* and *Texts of Consequence*.

Craig Lee Engstrom is assistant professor in the Department of Communication Arts and Sciences at Elmhurst College, where he teaches business and organizational communication from interpretive and rhetorical perspectives. His research has appeared in *Peace Education, TransFormations, Journal of Critical Organizational Inquiry*, and *Communication Quarterly*. He volunteers as a business-plan advisor for the Prison Entrepreneurship Program (www.pep.org), which provides a transformative educational experience for Texas prisoners nearing parole.

Jeralyn Faris is a continuing lecturer in the Brian Lamb School of Communication at Purdue University in West Lafayette, Indiana, where she is the director of the interviewing courses in the department. Her 2011 dissertation was a qualitative study of a reentry Problem Solving Court. She continues to serve as a volunteer for the reentry court in the capacity of court coordinator and as a member of the reentry-court team. Faris is also a member of the chaplain's team for a large county jail. Her essays have been published in *Prison Journal* and in the book *Problem Solving Courts: New Approaches to Criminal Justice*.

Stephen John Hartnett is professor and chair of the Department of Communication at the University of Colorado Denver, where he is the editor of *Captured Words / Free Thoughts*, a magazine crafted by imprisoned writers. His previous books include *Executing Democracy, Volume Two: Capital Punishment and the Making of America, 1835–1845* (2012); the edited *Challenging the Prison-Industrial Complex: Arts, Education, and Activist Alternatives* (2011), which received the PASS Award from the National Council on Crime and Delinquency; *Executing Democracy, Volume One: Capital Punishment and the Making of America, 1683–1800* (2010); *Globalization and Empire* (2006); *Incarceration Nation* (2004); *Sweet Freedom's Song* (2002, co-authored with the late Robert James Branham); and *Democratic Dissent and The Cultural Fictions of Antebellum America* (2002), which won the Winans and Wichelns Memorial Award for Distinguished Scholarship in Rhetoric and Public Address. For the past twenty-three years, Hartnett has been teaching in, writing about, and protesting at America's prisons. In recognition of this work, he has received numerous awards, including the University of Colorado's 2010 Thomas Jefferson Award and the Western States Communication Association's 2012 Distinguished Teacher Award.

Edward A. Hinck is professor of communication and director of forensics at Central Michigan University. He teaches undergraduate courses in introduction to debate, communication in social influence, and communication in leadership, and graduate courses in rhetorical criticism and communication theory. His research interests concern the study of political debates and argumentation about policy issues. He is the author of *Enacting the Presidency* (1993) and a co-author of *Politeness in Presidential Debates* (2007). He has been recognized by the Michigan Campus Compact award for service-learning in 1998, the Pi Kappa Delta E. R. Nichols Award for forensics education in 2002, and the National Forensics Association Eddie Myers Award for service in 2006, and was a co-recipient (with William Dailey and Shelly Hinck) of the American Forensic Association's Dan Rohrer Research Award in 2006, was a co-finalist (with Shelly Hinck and Lesley Withers) for a Carter Award for community service in 2008, and received the Pi Kappa Delta John Shields Award for service in 2010.

Shelly Schaefer Hinck is the associate dean of the College of Communication and Fine Arts at Central Michigan University. As a professor in the Department of Communication and Dramatic Arts, she taught courses in interpersonal, gender, and instructional communication, often incorporating service-learning activities into her classes. Her research on political debates, service-learning, and rape myths has been published in *Argumentation and Advocacy, Sex Roles, American Behavioral Scientist*, and *Teaching and Learning:*

Journal of Natural Inquiry; she co-authored the book *Politeness and Presidential Debates* (2007). She was the service-learning coordinator for Central Michigan University (1996–2000), was recognized by Michigan Campus Compact as a service-learning educator (2002), and was a national finalist (top ten) for the Thomas Erhlich Service-Learning Award (2001) offered by Campus Compact. Hinck and her classes have worked with prisons in the Central Michigan area providing communication programming for over fifteen years. In 2008, Ed Hinck, Lesley Withers, and Shelly Hinck were recognized as finalists for the Carter Partnership Award given by Michigan Campus Compact for their work with Michigan prisons.

Bryan J. McCann is assistant professor of communication studies at Wayne State University. His work engages the intersection of rhetoric and cultural studies, and focuses on social movements, discourses of race and violence, and the prison-industrial complex. His work has appeared in *Communication and Critical/Cultural Studies*, *Critical Studies in Media Communication*, *Social Epistemology*, the *Western Journal of Communication*, and in the edited volume *Communication Activism*. Working as a community activist, he has been involved in the anti–death penalty movement for several years. In addition to appearing on local newscasts and the national program *Democracy Now!*, he has written articles about the death penalty for the online periodicals *AlterNet* and *Jurist*.

Nikki H. Nichols is academic advisor and adjunct communication instructor at the University of Louisiana at Monroe. Her work with women ex-prisoners stems from research conducted at transitional programs in Ohio. Along with conducting research in these programs, Nikki volunteered in a transitional program for women where she taught interpersonal-communication seminars, assisted with job-readiness skills, and worked on the day-to-day operations of the program.

Eleanor Novek is associate professor in the Department of Communication at Monmouth University in West Long Branch, New Jersey, where she teaches courses in journalism, media studies, and communication ethics. A former journalist, she now conducts research on journalism produced by marginalized groups, service-learning, and communication in prison. Her essays have been published in *Critical Studies in Media Communication*; *Journalism*; *The Atlantic Journal of Communication*; *Discourse & Society*; *Media, Culture & Society*; *The Howard Journal of Communications*; *Communication Studies*; *Women's Studies in Communication*; *Education, Citizenship and Social Justice*; *Peace Review*; *The Journal of Children and Poverty*; and a number of edited books. Novek is the New Jersey chapter coordinator and a workshop facilitator of the Alternatives to Violence Project, an international volunteer organization that teaches nonviolent conflict transformation in prisons and community settings. She has taught writing classes and workshops in prisons since 2001.

Brittany L. Peterson is assistant professor in the School of Communication Studies at Ohio University, where she teaches courses in organizational communication. Her research focuses on challenging traditional constructions of membership in organizations and exploring how these matters of membership are tied to the processes of socialization, assimilation, identification, and dis-identification. Peterson works with the Girl Scouts Beyond Bars program, and conducts her research by interviewing incarcerated individuals, correctional officers, wardens, and prison teachers in U.S. and Norwegian prisons.

Jonathan Shailor is the founder and lead facilitator of the Theater of Empowerment and the Shakespeare Prison Project (shakespeareprisonproject. blogspot.com), programs that provide opportunities for community groups to use performance and dialogue for personal and social development. Shailor is also the founder and director of the Certificate Program in Conflict Analysis and Resolution (CP-CARE) at the University of Wisconsin–Parkside, where he serves as an associate professor of communication. His directing credits include *King Lear, Othello, The Tempest,* and *Julius Caesar.* His published work includes *Performing New Lives: Prison Theater* (2011), *Empowerment in Dispute Mediation* (1994), and various essays.

Rachel A. Smith is associate professor in the Department of Communication Arts & Sciences at the Pennsylvania State University, where she is an affiliate of the Huck Institute for Life Sciences and the Center for Infectious Disease Dynamics and Methodology Center. Her research focusses on social influence in health communication and has appeared in the *Journal of Health Psychology, Health Communication, Human Communication Research, Communication Monographs, Communication Theory,* and other journals in the health sciences.

Derrick L. Williams is a specialist in antiviolence, gender-justice, and prison-advocacy work. He serves as the violence prevention coordinator at Southern Illinois University Carbondale. As the founder of Progressive Masculinities Mentors, a grassroots social-change men's group, he works with young college men through a multitiered mentoring strategy designed to support local community boys who lack male guidance. Williams also teaches in the Departments of Africana Studies and Speech Communication at Southern Illinois University.

Lesley A. Withers is professor of communication and dramatic arts at Central Michigan University, where she teaches courses in interpersonal, nonverbal, and gender communication, the dark side of communication, and communication in virtual worlds. Her research focuses on presentation of self and teaching and collaborating in virtual environments. Along with Drs. Edward and Shelly Hinck, Withers has served as instructor for a longitudinal service-learning project that brings students into midwestern correctional facilities to develop citizenship concerns and address stigma. She received (with C. Arthur VanLear, Megan Sheehan, and Robert Walker) the 2005 B. Aubrey Fisher Outstanding Article Award and was a co-finalist (with Ed and Shelly Hinck) for a Carter Award for community service in 2008.

Jennifer K. Wood is associate professor of communication arts and sciences at Penn State New Kensington, where she teaches courses in conflict resolution, rhetoric, and effective speech. Her research focuses on crime-victim policy, the prison-industrial complex, and restorative justice, and has appeared in *Communication and Critical/Cultural Studies, The National Women's Studies Association Journal*, the *Western Journal of Communication, Communication Research, Qualitative Research Reports in Communication*, and *College Literature*. Wood has taught several college communication courses at the Pennsylvania State Correctional Institution in Pittsburgh. She is a trained volunteer mediator for the Victim/Offender Dialogue Program for Crimes of Violence, which is run by the Office of Victim Advocate in the Pennsylvania Department of Corrections. Wood has also served as a mediator for the Pittsburgh Mediation Center's Victim/Offender Mediation program and has volunteered as a medical advocate for Pittsburgh Action Against Rape.

Bill Yousman is an assistant professor of communication at Eastern Connecticut State University, where he teaches courses in communication and media studies. His research focuses on media and race, ideology in popular culture, and the representation of incarceration on television. His *Prime Time Prisons on U.S. TV: Representations of Incarceration* was published in 2009. His essays have appeared in *Communication and Critical/Cultural Studies; Communication Theory;* the *Journal of Communication; Communication Quarterly; Race, Gender, and Class; Communication Research Reports; Tikkun;* and a number of edited books. A longtime member of PCARE, Yousman was the program coordinator for a shelter for abused, neglected, and runaway teenagers for many years and is the former managing director of the Media Education Foundation in Northampton, Massachusetts.

Index